Scotch and Holy Water
Tales from Turkey 1958-68

Scotch and Holy Water
Tales from Turkey 1958-68

John D. Tumpane

TESL-EJ Publications
Berkeley, California & Kyoto, Japan

Front cover: This Hittite sun disc, with a sacred deer in the center, was discovered at Hattusas, the capital of the Hittite Kingdom, about 175 miles east of Ankara. The Hittites were a powerful race of Indo-Europeans who ruled Anatolia from 2000 to 1200 B.C. This sun disc, approximately 12 inches in diameter and made of bronze, was mounted on a standard and carried in ceremonial processions. The original can be seen in the Hittite Museum in Ankara.

All rights reserved. Except for brief passages quoted in an internet, newspaper, magazine, radio, or television review, no part of this book may be reproduced in any form or by any means, electronic or mechanical, including photocopying and recording, or by any information storage and retrieval system, without permission in writing. Previously published in 1981 by St. Giles Press, Lafayette, CA.

TESL-EJ edition © 2019 by Scott Alkire. All rights reserved.

Managing Editor: Dr. Maggie Sokolik

Map drawings: Mary Jean Lachowicz
Production editing: Hunter Greer
Proofreading: Mark Handy

Library of Congress Cataloging-in-Publication Data
Tumpane, John D., 1922–1997
Scotch and Holy Water: Tales from Turkey 1958–68 (TESL-EJ edition)

Library of Congress Control Number: [forthcoming]
ISBN 978-0-578-48588-1

I. Tumpane, John D. II. Title.

Appendix documents and photographs courtesy of Keith Lachowicz.

TESL-EJ Publications
Berkeley, California & Kyoto, Japan

10 9 8 7 6 5 4 3 2 1

Contents

Editor's Preface	11
Acknowledgments	19

Part 1 Diyarbakir

The Mouse	23
The Fortune Teller	27
The Driver's License	36
The Camel	48
The Landlord	49
Hiring and Firing Turks	54
The Van Adventure	61
The Icon	83
Thirty Below Zero	90
Christmas in Chaldea	98
That Rascal Ibrahim	103
Making Babies—Turkish Style	122
Mr. Isn't-It	129
Selma	134
Genghis Khan Rides Again	156
Smitty and the Sergeant	163
Theresa's Mountain	179

Part 2 Izmir

Jimmy	197
"May I Have Your Eyes?"	210
Nuri	212
Scotch and Holy Water	222
The City Under the Sea	232
Honeymoon in Didyma	240
Crash MacKenzie	260
The Russians	274

Part 3 Ankara

The Circumcision Party	289
Bert Organizing the Olive-Pickers of Nicea	296
That Midnight Ride	306
Trauma in Termessos	321
The Amphora	334
The Curse of Troy	347
My Favorite Ruin	374

Appendix

A Letter to Readers	384
Sand and Siddiqqi, chapter 1	386
Dear John, You Send Me Plenty Of (poem)	389
The Baby Bottle	391
About the Author	395

To Anne

Editor's Preface

≈

WHISKEY and lustral water are two things you might not associate with Turkey, but you can't miss them in John D. Tumpane's 1960s memoir of the country—particularly the whiskey. *Scotch and Holy Water*—Tumpane's account of ten years in Diyarbakir, Izmir, and Ankara—describes plenty of drinking. It also describes expeditions to ruins, hijinks in nightclubs, and wacky interactions with Turks, Kurds, and expats. Although entertaining and well written, the book was never picked up by a publisher. Tumpane self-published *Scotch* in 1981 but, without national distribution and marketing, the book was doomed to a cult following. The casual reader today, when perusing the 1981 edition, might assume that the book was little more than a vanity project.

The assumption would be false. Tumpane's memoir is a collection of deftly constructed anecdotes that are as hilarious and astute as anything ever written about living in (as opposed to passing through) a foreign country. It is a rollicking throwback to pre-1980s expat writing, when writers brazenly reported what they felt, said, and did. It is an unabashedly extravagant book.

Tumpane's intrepid exploring establishes *Scotch*'s ethos early. After moving to Diyarbakir in 1958 to work for a U.S. military contractor (The Tumpane Company—founded by John's older brother Jim and their uncle), John is soon zooming off to remote regions of the country in the company Plymouth (later an Oldsmobile). With his basic Turkish (soon to improve appreciably), he engages with natives everywhere to locate famous and not-so-famous ancient sites. He evocatively evokes the places he visits. Here is his impression of Miletus, the greatest Greek city in the east prior to 500 B.C.:

> We arrived at Miletus at two o'clock. Miletus was once on the sea, at the mouth of the Meander River, but the river had silted up. Now there was only a stagnant inlet in front of the magnificent marble stairs leading up out of the green slime. It was easy to imagine the Emperor Hadrian arriving in his burnished barges, or St. Paul in a rowboat with Timothy pulling the oars.
>
> Everything at Miletus was in shambles except for the theater. Unlike most ancient theaters which were built on the side of a hill, this one was free-standing, next to the sea, with its own special harbor where you could anchor your barge to see a play by Euripides or Aristophanes. For a theater that had had no reconstruction, it was in marvelous condition. There was a huge vaulted semi-circular tunnel underneath with inside stairways leading up to the highest tiers. The theater held 25,000 spectators.

Tumpane throws himself into his adopted country and renders hilariously the inevitable cultural conflicts—and pleasures. He jousts with Turkish civil servants over absurd regulations, slyly rescues and restores neglected artifacts, and parties like there is no tomorrow in Turkish nightclubs. Occasionally he makes politically incorrect statements, but their veracity (at least figuratively) redeems him. Early in the book he takes on *Inshallah*:

> I wasn't the only one who learned to loathe the word *Inshallah*. I've seen many Americans grab a Turk by the throat and say, "Don't give me that *Inshallah* shit!" But to the Turk it was quite logical. You make an appointment for a Turk to come to your house for an important meeting at five o'clock sharp, and he says, *"Inshallah"* knowing full well he has an airline ticket in his pocket to take his dying grandmother to a hospital in Ankara that very same afternoon. But maybe the weather would be bad, and the plane wouldn't fly; then he would cheerfully come to your house on time.
>
> While reading the Koran one night, I was humbled by a foot-

note. It seems that Mohammed was asked a sly question by some of his skeptical followers, and he said, "I'll have the answer for you tomorrow." That night he got no revelations from Allah. Nor the next night, nor the following night. Mohammed was very embarrassed and confused. Finally Allah spoke to him and gave him the answer, then said: "But the next time you promise to give an answer 'tomorrow,' say 'Inshallah.'"

Unlike many expat memoirs, *Scotch* is free of the annoying "gone-native" attitude. Tumpane aims to entertain us, not impress us. Yet impress us he does, through unselfconscious enthusiasm, irony, and just the right amount of cultural and linguistic explanation to serve his stories, not his ego.

Some readers may find Tumpane's stories lacking in depth. To be fair, Tumpane is more interested in describing his adventures than in "finding himself" or in ruminating on the lives of others (a wise move: most of his fellow expats spend their time partying or whining. Score another point for veracity). At times he treats the locals differently from Westerners (a sad expat truth). But with a few Turks and one Greek (members of a submerged population, to use Frank O'Connor's term), Tumpane shows uncommon sensitivity.

Though a sophisticate with a degree from Yale (George H. W. Bush was a classmate) and a former lecturer at Notre Dame (Phil Donahue was a student), Tumpane understands—perhaps because he was a closeted gay man—what it means to live a stifled life. His chapters on his handyman Nuri, his Greek housemaid Jemileh (Jimmy), and the nightclub manager Selma are haunting; hope for the future is a concept alien to these wage-laborers. Tumpane's portraits of Nuri, Jimmy, and Selma show us the great divide between these quietly desperate natives and the happy-go-lucky, devil-may-care international workers they serve. His chapter on Selma is especially nuanced and poignant.

The strongest stories in *Scotch* appear in Parts 1 and 2, where Tumpane has his most memorable experiences in Diyarbakir and Izmir. Part 3 is dominated by Tumpane's relationships with expats. The expats, prone to boorishness out of boredom, begin to wear on the reader. For this edition four stories featuring them have been excised. In their place are the previously unpublished pieces "A Letter to Readers"; chapter 1 of John's unfinished book about Saudi Arabia; "Dear John, You Send Me Plenty Of" (poem by Mary Jean Lachowicz, John's "Beloved Baby Sister"); and "The Baby Bottle." The selections appear in the Appendix.

As frank a writer as he is, Tumpane remains something of an enigma. One suspects that his decision to move to Turkey and to explore its ruins, collect artifacts, and enjoy a robust nightlife is rooted in something deeper than mere curiosity. But his descriptions of his exploits are so colorful that we don't mind his keeping something to himself. And happily, Tumpane's personal reticence is not a factor in his larky interactions with co-workers, friends, and strangers. His exchange with a businessman in Van, in eastern Turkey, is a delightful duet.

> While I was waiting for my room, a well-dressed, darkly handsome man of 30 sat down in the chair beside me and struck up a conversation in Turkish.
> "Welcome," he said.
> "Thank you."
> "Are you German?"
> I laughed because I had been asked this many times. Apparently the Germans were the first tourists in these out-of-the-way places. They have a reputation of being at least two years ahead of any other tourists.
> "No, I am an American."
> "Where are you from?"
> "From Diyarbakir. I came today."
> "No, no, no. *I* am from Diyarbakir. I was born there. I came on Tuesday. I am a hat salesman. But *you*, do you come from New York? Chee-cago? Texas?"
> "Well, I'm originally from Massachusetts."
> "Oh, a Red Indian," he said matter-of-factly.
> "No, there are no more Red Indians in Massachusetts."
> "Why did you come to Van?"

"To see it."
"Are you looking for oil?"
"No."
"Gold?"
"No."
"The Americans never come here unless they are looking for oil, or gold. Are you a spy?"

"No, no," I laughed. "I just came to *see* Van. To take pictures." I displayed the Polaroid camera hanging around my neck. "I'm just a tourist." It was obvious that he didn't believe me, but he bowed politely and welcomed me again.

"By the way," I said, "I've been sitting here 20 minutes waiting for a room, and I'm getting slightly tired of it. That boy there asked me to wait only one minute, but it's been almost half an hour. Are there any other hotels in Van?"

"Oh yes, there are many. Now let's see—." And he started to count them off on his fingers. "There's the Chichek Palas (Flower Hotel), Temiz Palas (Clean), Bacheh Palas (Garden), Gul Palas (Rose), and the Emperiyal Palas (Imperial). But this is the only one without bugs."

I decided to wait.

This duet is but one of many pitch-perfect exchanges in *Scotch*. By turns deadpan, outrageous, comic, and melancholic, they reflect Tumpane's finest skill as a writer.

As for the alcohol in Tumpane's memoir—well, Johnnie Walker *is* practically a minor character. But *Scotch and Holy Water* is not an undisciplined work; it is artfully constructed and deceptively astute. Tumpane's experiences feel deeply authentic: impossible to fake, impossible to invent.

And the holy water? It makes its appearance halfway through the book. History, Christianity, and Johnnie Walker all come together in hilarious fashion.

~

John Tumpane left Turkey in 1968 to work in Saudi Arabia and Iran. In 1976 he returned to the U.S. and began writing *Scotch*. His sister Mary Jean, an accomplished artist, drew pen-and-ink maps for the frontispiece and for each of the book's three parts.

Tumpane pitched his memoir to publishers without success. In a letter to *San Francisco Chronicle* Book Editor Patricia Holt he wrote that he had received "201 rejection slips—one more than Ernest Hemingway before he got his first acceptance—and why I named my press after St. Giles [patron saint of beggars]."

St. Giles Press published *Scotch and Holy Water* in November 1981. Tumpane promoted the book through the Turkish American Association of California and by writing autobiographical essays for newspapers. A few regional newspapers gave *Scotch* good reviews. On August 8, 1982 the *San Francisco Chronicle* published a glowing endorsement. Reviewer Joe Cottonwood wrote, "This book is a delight, a surprise, a rare find...I recommend it."

Readers who had spent time in Turkey wrote to Tumpane to tell him how much they enjoyed his book and how well he captured 1960s expat life. Tumpane personally responded to many of his correspondents and included a form letter in which he explained how he wrote *Scotch*:

> Many people have asked me if I kept a diary while I was in Turkey. No. But when I returned to the States 20 years later, the Polaroid pictures brought back total recall. I had written my parents at least once a week while I was gone, and they saved all the pictures I had sent them. I was glad I had included on the backs of the pictures the dates, names, and historical information which was fresh in my mind at the time, like "This is where Caesar stood when he said, 'Veni, vidi, vici' after he defeated the king of Pontus in 47 B.C.—on this very same hill 240 miles east of Ankara" or "This is the first known Christian church built in a cave near Antakya (Antioch), just after a visit by St. Peter in 42 A.D. Antioch was the largest city in the world in those days."

Tumpane began work on a second set of memoirs about Turkey as well as a book about his tenure in Saudi Arabia (1968–1974). When not working on these projects, he continued to write articles, short stories, and reviews of books. He sent packets of his writings to family and friends. Always the extrovert, Tumpane was the life of parties. His nephew Keith Lachowicz observed, "John loved storytelling, performing. He thrived on holding court and being funny, outrageous, off-color. His being a speech and drama professor was a big contributor to his storytelling acumen. His storytelling sessions were like mini performances."

In the mid-1990s, John developed Parkinson's disease. His friend Ahmet Toprak, who visited or telephoned him at least once a month, remembers John's being unwell but did not know to what extent. One day in October 1997 Ahmet dialed John's number, and Mary Jean answered. John had died. She and Keith were cleaning out his apartment.

It is our good fortune that TESL-EJ Publications, in conjunction with the Tumpane family, is bringing John Tumpane's memoir back into print. In an era where many expat books seem like watered-down Tiki drinks, *Scotch and Holy Water* is 100-proof liquid gold. It is genuine and extravagant, a work to be treasured.

Scott Alkire
The California State University
July 2019

Acknowledgments

≈

I wish to thank Denise della Santina, Keith Lachowicz, and Kathleen Tumpane for their kindness and generosity in helping me prepare this new edition of *Scotch and Holy Water*. Without their help, this book would not be possible.

Thanks also to Elizabeth Collison, Zerrin Erkal, Hunter Greer, Mark Handy, and Ciaran Mac Gowan for their meticulous work at every stage of the publication process.

Finally, I am grateful to Dr. Maggie Sokolik of TESL-EJ Publications for her steadfast support.

S.A.

The Mouse

≈

THE FIRST full sentence I constructed in Turkish was: "There's a mouse in my bedroom." This wasn't just an idle exercise; it was a dire emergency! And it wasn't really a mouse—it was a rat! A foot long!

I had just got back to the hotel after work when I opened the door to my room and noticed something big and black scurrying across the rug. I moved warily down the passageway into the room and Zoom! the lightning flash of a rat! I had been promising myself to learn Turkish—the time had come! I grabbed my dictionary, flipped madly through it, picked up the phone and shouted to the desk clerk: *"Fahre oda var!!!"* (Rat, bedroom, there is.) I flipped again and added, *"Imdat! Imdat!"* (Help, help!) I considered it a triumph of communication, a breakthrough in Turkish-American relations. I hung up and waited, owl-eyed.

When I first arrived in Diyarbakir, I was told I could live on the American air base, rent-free. I was shown to my room: two iron army cots, two iron chairs, two steel desks, two steel wall lockers, and one roommate. The next day I moved to town. I had won the war in the Pacific *only* to get out of the Army, and I wasn't about to put up with that lifestyle again.

I moved into the Turistik Palas Otel, just outside the great wall of the old city of Diyarbakir. It was considered by the local Turks to be *choke luks* (very deluxe). I had a walnut bed with a lumpy mattress, a walnut table with a case of rickets, a walnut wardrobe whose doors refused to stay shut (they would open eerily at unexpected times as if to see what was going on in the room), and a walnut rocking chair that squeaked and made me feel like Whistler's mother. The carpet was a flamboyant red, the chintz curtains were black with orange-and-blue mythical flowers, but still, I considered all this a step up from the base accommodations. That is, until I got a Turkish roommate: the *fahre!*

I waited five minutes, rigid, listening to my heartbeat, then lifted up the phone again and started shouting, *"Imdat! Imdat!"* loud enough for them to hear me without Alexander Graham Bell's invention. Eventually there was a tap-tap-tap on my door, hardly the proper signal that emergency help had arrived—I was expecting the fire department. I rushed to the door, ripped it open, and there stood the smallest bellboy I had ever seen in my life, except for the Phillip Morris midget. He was actually an adult and had a fierce mustache, but he was hardly a match for *this* adversary. He also had a weapon in his hand: one of those sawed-off brooms that look like a bunch of weeds tied together. Was this to be my savior???

I pushed him into the middle of the arena. He started poking around the corners of the room, behind the drapes, behind the wardrobe, and out shot the enemy! I jumped onto the bed while the bellboy swatted the monster as it went tearing around the room. I had never seen a rat so big, and I realized I was holding my breath all the while—I must have been turning purple. Suddenly all became quiet.

"Tamam," said the bellboy, bowing to me in triumph.

Well! I knew that *tamam* had a variety of meanings in Turkish: "finished" or "all gone" or "complete" or "enough" or even "okay," but *none* of them applied in this situation.

"What do you mean *tamam???* It is like hell *tamam!!!* That *damn fahre* is still in this *oda!* Now, look behind those curtains."

He poked gingerly around the bottom of the drapes and stirred the animal into action. The rat ran up the draperies and poised on the top of the curtain rod, 12 feet off the floor. The bellboy jumped up and down swinging ineffectually. Then the rat took a flying swan dive over his head and ran out the door. The bellboy followed, hot on his tail. I, too, took a spectacular leap off the bed (it was like a trampoline) and ran toward the door just as the rat came running back in. Apparently the damn bellboy had headed it off at the pass instead of letting it escape into the upper reaches or lower depths of the hotel. I let out a blood-curdling howl which caused the creature to leap straight up, do a 180° turn in mid-air, plop down and streak out again. I grabbed the doorknob and swung the door hard enough to break it off its hinges. But the rat had run into the bellboy again and turned back into my room. It saw the door zooming toward it, turned again, and the door slammed shut on it, catching it right in the middle! Its head was on the outside, its rump and tail were on my side.

"Kill it!" I screamed in English. "Kill it!" Oh God, I thought, do I have to get my dictionary?

I could hear the bellboy swatting it with the broom.

"Not the broom! Step on it! Take off your shoe and beat it to death!"

I doubt if he understood me, but I began to hear more substantial thumping. I had my shoulder against the door, pushing it with such strength that I began to worry that the doorjamb might give way. The wiggling, squirming rump and tail began subsiding, and finally fell limp.

"*Tamam,*" said the bellboy cheerily, but I wasn't about to open the door until rigor mortis had set in.

After about five minutes, I poked the rump with the tip of my shoe, and it didn't do anything. Was it shamming? Warily, I opened the door. It didn't move. Then I saw the head, quite properly mashed. The bellboy was beaming triumphantly, holding his shoe in the air like a gladiator.

"Remove the carcass."

He picked it up by the tail.

"And clean up the blood."

He held out his hand.

"I'll give you your reward tomorrow."

I locked the door, slid the bolt, and took to my bed and

bottle.

This was my charming introduction to Turkey. I had been apprehensive about accepting a job overseas—especially in the land of the "Terrible Turks"—but I survived.

I even thrived!

The Fortune Teller

≈

WE ENTERED the old walled city of Diyarbakir through the Urfa Gate. We were on foot because the cobblestone streets were too narrow for a car. Dr. Tosun led the way, and I followed, peering at the high mud walls surrounding the houses on both sides of the street. I knew they enclosed courtyards, some of which were charming with a small pool and a large fig or mulberry tree, but on this sunny Sunday morning in September, we saw only the unbroken sun-baked walls with an occasional unpainted wooden balcony projecting over the street.

Shortly we stopped, and the doctor knocked loudly on a wooden door. A voice on the inside, far away, answered after repeated knockings by the doctor. The doctor carried on a loud exchange in Turkish, none of which I could understand, but I could tell that the voice on the inside was irritated and wished we would go away. The doctor, leaning with his ear to the door, looking at the ground, shouted away, unfazed. I started to say we were unwelcome, we had come at the wrong time, but the doctor shushed me confidently with his right hand, smiling, and shouted some more to the ground. Then silence.

"Maybe we should come back some other day. Maybe we have to make an appointment—"

Again the hand movement, the smile, the wink. "Don't worry, she's coming."

The door opened a crack, and Dr. Tosun carried on a bullying exchange with the voice behind it. Finally the door opened just wide enough to let us slip through. We were in a yard, an empty lot. It was square, flat, without flowers or trees, just gravel. Three sides were blank mud walls; the fourth was a two-story unpainted wooden house with an outside staircase to an upstairs balcony. The whole thing looked impoverished, almost deserted.

I turned to see who had let us in. She was a woman about 50, dressed in the old Turkish style with blue-flowered baggy trousers, a pink-flowered long-sleeved blouse, and a white shawl wrapped around her head. Her clothes were old and faded, but certainly colorful. She was very thin and surprisingly tall for a Turkish woman. Without a word, holding the shawl across her mouth, she climbed the stairs.

"That's the sister," said the doctor. "She's gone to get Gerdji Badji."

This is only an approximate spelling of her name, but she was a fortune teller, fabulously famous throughout Turkey, and her name meant something like "The Blind Aunt." The doctor had told me that ministers and government officials from Ankara had flown to Diyarbakir to consult her—even the Prime Minister, Adnan Menderes. She would never leave Diyarbakir—they had to come to her. Soccer coaches from the wildly popular teams all around the country would come to see her before an important game and ask her if they were going to win. If they were, she would say yes. If not, she would always give some ambiguous answer like, "The best team will win."

I was newly arrived in Diyarbakir. In July of 1958, our company had won a contract with the U.S. Air Force to maintain nine American air bases in Turkey. I had spent a month in Ankara working under my older (and only) brother who was the General Manager. I was first put in charge of accommodations—finding hotel rooms for newcomers and meeting them at the airport. Since I was a bachelor, he felt I could stay up half the night meeting airplanes that were always late. It would also keep me out of the bars and nightclubs, an activity of which he wholeheartedly disapproved. After a few days I had trained our Turkish drivers to hold up signs at the airport with the names of the newcomers, and soon they were perfectly capable of handling that job. I was then put in charge of registration. Every newcomer had to have his passport stamped to show that he was associated with the American military and as such was authorized to work in Turkey. I trained a pretty little secretary to do that. Then I was put in charge of security—every person had to have a "secret" security clearance to get on any base in Turkey. Every other day I was given a new job: to untangle a bottleneck or stick my finger in a dike. I knew this would go on and on as long as I was under my brother's thumb, so I started looking for an out.

I studied the manning charts at each of the bases and learned that Diyarbakir was the most difficult site to fill positions. Nobody wanted to go there! Diyarbakir was in eastern Turkey, a part of Kurdistan, near the Syrian, Iraqi, and Iranian borders. The stories that filtered back to us in Ankara were hair-raising (primitive, barbaric, brigands, highway robberies, murders), but I suspected they were concocted or embroidered by the Americans stationed there to get sympathy and a possible transfer. The job of Administrative Supervisor was open and had been for a month, and I knew the Air Force was bugging us to fill slots in remote locations. I went to my brother one evening after everyone had left the office.

"I want the job of Administrative Supervisor at Diyarbakir."

"What???"

"You heard me."

"Diyarbakir! Are you mad?"

"No. I want to get out of this rat race here at the Central Office, and I know I can fill the job."

"But—but—Diyarbakir! From what I've heard it's a terrible place. You don't want to go there. You, a bachelor. No night life, no cocktail parties, no duplicate bridge, no girls!"

"I'll survive."

I knew he was secretly pleased that I wanted to go because it would show the reluctant newcomers that even the

General Manager's brother had agreed to go to Diyarbakir. He gave me his blessing although, I later heard, he made a bet that I wouldn't last a month.

I flew to Diyarbakir early in August 1958. After we landed, I was the first one at the door of the airplane. When the hostess opened the door, I fell backward from the blast of heat that rushed in. It was 120°. The other passengers pushed me out the door. An Air Force vehicle was waiting to pick up the new chaplain, Father Bloch, and I hitched a ride to the base with them. It was a 12-mile ride over a flat plain, strewn with lava boulders covered in red dust. We drove in stony silence. As we approached the base, a structure began looming in the distance and got larger and larger. It reminded me of the picture one gets driving across the green fields of France, which I had visited on my way to Turkey, and Chartres Cathedral looms up on the horizon until it overwhelms you. But this was the radar antenna, a gridwork of steel and wires the size of a football field, turned on end and aimed at Russia.

"The American Chartres, eh, Father?"

He glared at me and moved a little away.

At the base the name of Gerdji Badji came up many times, especially at the bar at the Officers Club after work. Most of our new employees, American and Germans, had been to see her and had their fortunes told. She told each of them how long they would be in Diyarbakir. She would say, "I see the number two." This was taken to mean two weeks or two months or two years. She told Lino, a gentle German, "As long as you want." He resigned five months later in a dispute with our Site Manager. But the stories they told about her predictions were priceless, so I arranged with Dr. Tosun, the first Turkish friend I made in Diyarbakir, to take me to her.

A door on the upstairs porch opened, and Gerdji Badji came out. She came down the steps very slowly, preceded and helped by her sister. She was much shorter and fat—certainly more typically Turkish than her sister, but similarly dressed. She came across the courtyard to us, holding her shawl across her mouth, and shook hands with the doctor and me. One eye appeared to be closed, but I wasn't sure. The other eye was frightening—milky and greenish like a boiled pearl you find in oyster stew. She spoke to the doctor and then turned abruptly and walked to the other end of the courtyard.

"Well, you have two questions, Mister John. What do you want to ask?" I was a bit shook up; I didn't know that I would have to ask the questions. If I had known that, I would have stayed up all night thinking up good ones. I also wondered why the sister remained with us (this was too easy), but I was afraid of offending the sister or the doctor, so I said, "Will I go to jail while I'm in Turkey?"

This question just popped out of my mouth and it probably surprised me more than the doctor. But coming back from the base the night before, I almost ran over a Turkish soldier. The driver of an oncoming truck maddeningly refused to dim his lights, and when it passed, there was a soldier in his olive drab suit, right in the middle of my lane, walking blithely with his back to me. I swerved the car madly to the left, off the road into a wide ditch, then wrenched the steering wheel violently to the right so that the car swerved over the highway and into another ditch, then back on the highway. I had my brakes on the whole time and allowed the car to come to a stop. When I stopped shaking, I eased the car into gear and crawled into town, cursing Turkish soldiers and truck drivers and myself for having had a little too much to drink at the Officers Club.

"Okay, what else?" asked the doctor.

"Well, how long will I be in Diyarbakir?"

"Good."

Then the three of us walked to the corner of the courtyard, where Gerdji Badji was standing with her back to us like someone who was "It" in a game of hide-and-seek. She turned around and faced us. The sister stood opposite her; I stood between them and the doctor opposite me—like a cross. The sister had been carrying a small tea glass, urn-shaped with gold bands around it, and full of water. She held the glass up with her left hand at eye level, precisely in the middle of all of us. Then she put her right index finger into the water, paused momentarily, and flipped a small spray into the air.

Gerdji Badji let her head fall back and began spouting my fortune. The doctor translated so fast and furiously that I caught my breath.

"You want to know if you will go to jail while you're in Turkey—no! You will be in Diyarbakir three weeks or three months or three years. You will marry and have two children, a boy and a girl. You do not work with your hands, you work with your head. You have many enemies all around you, many insects, many bugs, you know, the ones with many legs, what do you call them in English?" The doctor could hardly keep up with her.

"Centipedes," I shouted.

"Yes, many centipedes, but you needn't worry, you have a clean heart! You will take a trip across water. You will be near death in the sky. You will be arrested but released. Someone close to you, not exactly Turkish, will die. You will be rich and successful."

And suddenly she stopped. She had almost fallen over backward. Slowly she relaxed and bowed her head, as if saying, "Your humble servant." The sister lowered the glass and threw the water out on the dirt. I watched it as my fortune seeped into the earth and made dark spots. The doctor and the sister were amiably working out the monetary end of our visit. Gerdji Badji had turned and was walking slowly toward the staircase, as if exhausted. The sister followed. They climbed the stairs and disappeared.

"Come on, Mister John, let's go."

I let out my breath and followed the doctor to the gate.

"Isn't she good? Didn't I tell you? Come on, we go now to my house and sit in my garden and drink *raki*.[1] My wife will be so interested in hearing about it. Come along,

---

1. A strong alcoholic spirit, typically made of different fruits (grapes, figs, or plums, depending on the region) and aniseed.

Mister John. Why are you so white? It was a good fortune. Wonderful! She is always right. You are a lucky boy! Rich and successful! Oh, wait until you see my dahlias!"

The doctor chattered happily all the way back to his house, which was outside the wall in the New City. It was very modest but new, painted white with blue trim. His garden was four times the size of his house and a riot of dahlias: big ones, little ones, formal, informal, football, pompoms, cactus, dwarf. Nothing but dahlias!

"You see!" he said, stretching out his hands as if raining blessings down on them. "We call them *yildiz*—star flowers. Don't they look like stars? Every color of the rainbow except blue, but I'm working on a blue. Ah! There's my wife."

And there she was, as much a shock as the dahlias and twice as beautiful: golden hair in an upswept feather cut, a white sheath dress which revealed everything (and she had a lot to reveal), silk stockings on her firm, classical legs, and high-heeled shoes. She was leaning back against the jamb of the open doorway in profile, her arms behind her back, her neck arched and one leg lifted on a toe. I think she was trying to make a good first impression.

"This is my wife, Humeyra." He introduced me to her in Turkish as "John Bey."

She dropped her pose and laughed gaily with flashes of gorgeous white teeth as she shook my arm out of its socket. I was enchanted with her lack of guile after that ridiculous pose.

"Humeyra welcomes you to our home and says lunch is ready, but first we must sit in the garden and have *raki* and *mezeh* (hors d'oeuvres) while we tell her your fortune."

She brought out tray after tray of meats, pastries, and assorted Turkish mysteries that would have been enough for 10 soldiers coming back from the war, then poured us all *raki* over ice. I loved watching the clear liquid turn milky white as it splashed over the ice.

"You like Turkish *raki?*" she asked through her husband, her brown eyes sparkling with pleasure.

"Oh yes, very much." I told them I had just come from

France where I had gotten used to Pernod. "But this is much better. It's not so sweet, and I like the color."

"We call it lion's milk," said the doctor raising his glass.

"*Sherefinize!*" said the wife.

"To your honor!" translated the doctor.

"And to yours," I said. "*Sherry-fizzy!*"

We all laughed and dug into the hors d'oeuvres.

The doctor told Humeyra my fortune in Turkish, and she clapped and laughed and bubbled over.

"She hopes you stay in Diyarbakir 33 years."

I almost choked on my lion's milk.

"Are you married?" she poked her husband to ask me.

"No."

"Wonderful," she said. "We'll find you a Turkish girl so you can make Turkish-American babies."

"But I'm 36 years old!"

"The perfect age! Ekrem was 38 when I married him; I was 18. Turkish girls love older men!" she said, shaking the loose flap of skin under her husband's chin. He purred. "And your hair is too beautiful. Turkish girls love a little snow on the mountain."

"And a fire in the furnace?" I asked playfully. But my joke was a dud.

"Now we need a Turkish name for John Bey," said Humeyra. "Let me think—"

"Oh, I've already got one! It's Mehmet Ali. I chose it myself. John is the most common name in English, so I chose the most common name in Turkish."

They both congratulated me as if I had just been baptized. Humeyra clapped her hands and then took a deep breath. She gently poked a lacquered fingernail into my chest and said, in labored English, "You Toorkish name—Mehmet Ali!" Then she poked the same fingernail deep into her bosom and said, "I Amerikan name—Cadillac!" And dissolved into giggles, covering her face.

The doctor hastily explained. Everyone in Diyarbakir called her "Cadillac," he said, especially all the young bucks who called her on the telephone every day to talk sweet nothings to her. She pretended she had no idea why, but I think she knew she was sleek and stacked and loaded with extras. The Turks, being dark and swarthy, adored blonde hair. Hers, I noticed, came out of a hydrogen peroxide bottle. Being a doctor's wife, she knew it had other uses than disinfecting wounds.

About three o'clock in the afternoon I staggered back to my hotel, my stomach bulging with shish kebab, chicken, veal balls, liver, kidney, pressed red caviar, potato balls, rice pilaf, cheese, fruits, and Turkish Delight—and my head reeling with *raki*. I stretched out on my bed, shoes pointed straight at the ceiling, and tried to sort out in my mind the predictions of Gerdji Badji.

It turned out that she got everything wrong:

—The number three had nothing to do with my stay in Diyarbakir. I stayed exactly two years there (my favorite brother lost his bet) but I actually spent a total of 10 years in Turkey. By that time I was half-Turk!

—I didn't make any babies, but I did everything else I could think of to cement Turkish-American relations and steered clear of centipedes.

But Gerdji Badji was right on one thing: although I got into every delicious kind of trouble possible, I didn't go to jail!!!

The Driver's License

≈

"ABDUL, take me to the traffic bureau tomorrow morning. I want to get a Turkish driver's license."

"Oh, sir, you don't need to go. Just give me your American driver's license and a carton of Salem cigarettes, and I'll get it for you."

I glared at him, incensed. Abdul was my Turkish right-hand man—Personnel & Payroll Supervisor—impassive, impeccable in dress, and infallible with advice on "when in Turkey,..."

"Did I hear you say a carton of Salems?"

"Or Camels."

"You mean a bribe?"

"A little present. I got all the driver's licenses for the other company before you came."

"And maybe that's why the other company lost the contract and we got it! There will be no bribes paid by our company, do you understand??? What's the word for bribe in Turkish?"

"*Rushvet,*" he said wearily.

"No *rushvets!*"

"Yes, sir."

Our company was new in Turkey—it was our first overseas contract—and we wanted to do everything right from the very beginning. We decided to learn all the labor laws, customs regulations, traffic rules, tax laws—even the mores of the people—and to abide by them. I knew we would all have to have Turkish driver's licenses, so I decided to be the guinea pig.

"Tomorrow morning! Eight o'clock sharp! Traffic bureau!" I said.

"Oh no, sir. They only handle driver's licenses on Saturday morning, and the office doesn't open until nine."

We were sitting on the stoop when the sergeant arrived to open up. It was a barren office with a bench for applicants (or traffic violators) to sit on, an L-shaped counter, and behind it pigeonholes from floor to ceiling bulging with file folders.

Abdul spoke quietly to the policeman as to our purpose, and we were told to sit down—the Captain was not there. (Probably hadn't gotten out of bed yet, I thought.) We sat. After 15 minutes I said to Abdul, "Why wait for the Captain? We can start filling out the forms now. Here's my U.S. driver's license."

Abdul gave me an old-worldly look: "Oh, you Americans, you're so impatient." After 30 minutes a street-seller burst into the station hawking lettuce. *"Marul! Marul!"* he shouted in the tiny office. The policeman bought several bunches and offered one of them to us, with a little packet of salt wadded up in a piece of newspaper. Naturally Abdul offered it first to me, while the policeman watched. I hesitated since the American medics had told us to soak all vegetables in Clorox for 30 minutes, but all eyes were on me. I took a deep breath and a stalk of lettuce—it was romaine—and surreptitiously tried to wipe it off on my pants. Abdul explained that we got lettuce only twice a year, in April and September, the cool months, so I'd better enjoy it. I did. We sat there happily sprinkling *tuz* (salt) on our *marul* and munching away till the Captain arrived.

He was very polite and gentle, and he shook my hand limply, bowing his head and saying how glad he was that I had come to him for a driver's license. (Americans never get used to those cold-fish handshakes—"They're all a bunch of fairies," said one of our engineers—but I later learned that a bone-crushing handshake was offensive to the Turks—and all Moslems—since the Koran says to be modest and lower your eyes when you are introduced to someone to show that you are peaceful. "Turks won't even look you in the eye," said the engineer.)

The Captain gave us a sheaf of forms and told us to come back next Saturday.

"But I want my license now!" I said. "We'll fill them out right here. Look! Here's my American driver's license." The Captain was bewildered by my outburst, and Abdul didn't bother to translate but dragged me out of the police station saying to me, "Please, sir, a carton of Salems?"

"Never!"

The following weekend we returned with all the forms filled out (in Turkish, by Abdul). The Captain was late again and this time we munched cucumbers—a once-a-year delicacy available only in September. I wasn't really learning patience, but I took the opportunity to learn Turkish.

Abdul taught me car words: *fren* (brake), *debreyaj* (clutch), *buji* (spark plug), *lastik* (tire), *akumulateur* (battery), and *direksiyon* (steering wheel). Suddenly I realized that they were all French and I knew them all! Then I remembered that in 1928 when Ataturk decided to switch from Arabic writing to the Roman alphabet, he hired the most famous phonetician of the time, a Frenchman, to design a new Turkish alphabet. When the Frenchman came across a situation where the Turks had no word, he simply gave them the French word spelled phonetically. It was a great help to me in learning Turkish to come across a French word: *aparteman, enternasyonal, garaj* and *baraj, radyo, otel, shatobriyan,* and even *otomobil*. Each word was like an oasis, and I blessed the Frenchman. He made the spelling so phonetic that I learned to read the newspaper in one hour! Couldn't understand a word, but I could read it, by God!

The Captain arrived. We bowed and exchanged limp handshakes. He scanned through our forms, pleased, and gave us another one. Abdul dragged me out and ordered me to drive us into the center of the old walled city. We parked the station wagon and took a narrow, twisting alley by foot. We stopped at a weatherbeaten wooden gate in a stone wall.

Abdul pulled a chain-bell. After a few moments, the gate opened a crack and Abdul conversed with a female voice. We then started roaming the streets looking into every coffee and teahouse until we finally sat down in one of them and Abdul said, "Let's have some tea."

"What's going on?!!" I asked.

"We're looking for the head of the district where you live, so that he can certify that you're a respectable member of his district."

"But he won't even know me! And besides, I'm not."

"*Bosh ver!*" It literally means "you give it empty" but can be translated as "So what? Never mind! It doesn't matter, forget it!" It's one of the few Turkish words that have come into English unchanged in our expression "Oh, bosh!"

At noon, after three teas, we went back to the burgomeister's house. He still wasn't home, so we camped on the curb. He arrived half an hour later, invited us into his courtyard, gave us tea, signed my papers as if I were one of the pillars of society, and clapped me on the back urging me to come back anytime—his door was always open.

The following Saturday we went back to the police station. The Captain was charmed to see that I was such a respected member of the community in Diyarbakir. He gave us another sheaf of papers and wished us well as we left.

"Now what?" I said despondently.

"To the hospital."

"What for?"

"Tests. Examinations."

"Oh, God," I said, as I put the Plymouth in gear.

"Sah-lem?" said Abdul, pronouncing as the Turks do.

"Never!"

On the way Abdul filled out each form with my name, age, etc., and pinned a passport photo to each form. (When we told newcomers to bring 40 passport photos with them, they thought we were mad. Mine were already gone. Every form you fill out in Turkey requires a photo.)

At the hospital we got into the end of a line in front of the eye doctor's office—I understood the drawing of an eye. I started pulling myself together to take an eye test, blinking and lubricating my orbs. Each time the doctor's door opened, there was a mad surge forward. Three or four people were projected into his office while one poor patient was struggling to get out. There was pandemonium as the nurses ejected all but one of the new patients.

"This will never do," said Abdul. And suavely and smoothly he elbowed everyone out of the way and got me to the door, the first in line. I was very embarrassed and vainly tried to console myself with Biblical expressions. But all these people had serious eye problems. I saw several with that milky eye of trachoma. I distinctly remember one old woman, on the back of what must have been her grandson, with an eyeball hanging out of its socket by a thick viscous thread. I tried to reproach Abdul, but he pushed my nose into the door. No one objected; they seemed to know that I was a foreigner.

When the door opened, I was blasted into the room like a human cannonball, right up against the eyechart. The doctor and the nurses herded the excess out, beating and pummeling them like sheep. One nurse threw me into a chair and held me down, while the other slapped a card over my left eye.

"What's this?" shouted the doctor, smacking the top letter of the chart with a pointer.

"E," I said. "I mean 'Eh.'"

"This?" he said, whacking a letter on the fourth row down.

I froze. It was also an "E" but it was facing backward. I flashed my eyes over the whole chart. They were all "E's"! Up, down, left, right—no other letters. The doctor was screaming at me and beating the chart. I took a deep breath and pointed left with my index finger. This went on and on with each eye and I kept pointing like an idiot, but apparently I passed.

The nurse then thrust a sewing basket in my lap, full of little balls of colored yarn.

"*Kirmizi!*" barked the doctor. I was as pleased as a first-grader who knew his colors, and I fished out a red one.

"*Yeshil!*" I grabbed a green one and held it up.

"*Sari!*" There were several shades of yellow. I was trying to choose between a canary, a lemon, and a banana when he barked again. I grabbed all three and threw them at him.

"*Tamam!*"

He signed my form and gave it to me. I tried to shake his hand, but he shook me off, spun me around, and aimed me toward the door. With his hands on my hams, he gave the signal to the nurses to open the door. It was a mad scramble, bodies coming at me like a stampede. I even got whacked once by the doctor with his pointer. I was a wreck.

"Did you pass?" said Abdul.

"I think so."

"Good! Follow me."

"How many more?"

"Only eight."

"Allah! Allah!"

There were only three people in front of the ear doctor's door. Abdul made quick work of them, maneuvering me right to the head of the line. Inside, the doctor put me in a booth and positioned himself on the other side of a wooden screen with a cloth over it. Just like confession, I thought.

"*Merhaba*" (greetings) he whispered.

"*Merhaba*" I whispered back automatically.

"*Nasilsiniz?*" (How are you?)

"*Iyiyim, teshekkur ederim.*" (I'm good, thank you.)

"*Yavash, yavash,*" he whispered.

"Slowly, slowly," I translated softly.

"*Yavash!*" he yelled.

I decided I'd better say "*Yavash.*"

"*Dur!*" (Stop)

"*Dur!*"

"Okay," he said in English.

He was very cordial as he signed my form. "*Siz Alman?*" (Are you German?)

"No, no, *Amerikali!*"

"Good, good. Happy Birthday." It must have been the

only expression he knew in English.

The next door we came to was marked *Jinokolojist*.

"In here," said Abdul. I couldn't believe it: the word obviously meant "gynecologist." There was one striking young lady waiting in front of the door. She smiled and nodded to me in greeting. I blushed. When the door opened, she gestured me to go first. I tried to protest, but she insisted. I was beet red as I went past her. The doctor took my sheaf of papers and flipped through them until he found his form. He glanced at me distastefully up and down, then signed my form. I slunk out.

"Did you pass?" said Abdul, with a sly smile.

"What's the word for bastard in Turkish?"

"*Pich,*" he said airily. (He pronounced it "peach.") "At the market, make sure you ask for *sheftali,* not peach. The best ones come from Bursa."

We started climbing stairs. Second floor, third... "Where are we going?"

"To the laboratory."

"What for?" I was running out of breath.

"For tests. Blood, urine, stool..."

"Oh, God!" I stopped him on the stairway. "Abdul, I have something to say."

"Salems?"

"*Olur,*" I said miserably. "So be it."

"Good, I've got them with me in my briefcase. Let's go down to the Administration Office."

"Where did you get them?"

"All good interpreters carry a carton of Salems—*and* a dictionary, of course. But you must pay me back, in kind."

"God forgive me."

The hospital administration office was small, with three clerks at desks piled high with file folders. Abdul went to the most impressive personage in the far corner. He spoke to him so quietly he couldn't be heard a foot away. The clerk smiled and nodded to me. I smiled back, but I felt sick. Abdul put his briefcase under the desk, and the clerk deftly removed the Salems, slipping them into his desk drawer. The other clerks didn't even notice, but I knew they could smell what was going on.

The clerk pasted some official stamps on all my forms, rubber stamped them loudly, and scribbled a signature across each. (No one can read any Turkish signature. The kids are taught in school to make their signature distinctive and unreproducible. Most of them look like exploding stars.) Abdul slipped the forms into his empty briefcase, and the clerk shook my hand as if congratulating me on having passed all my tests—good blood, fine urine, and all that.

We went back to the police station, but it was closed. On Monday after lunch, I went to the PX (air base store).

"A carton of Salems, please."

"Oh, Mister John," said Orhan, "you've switched to Salems! Very good!" Was he leering at me? Did everybody know?

In a quiet moment during the afternoon, I called Abdul into my office. "And bring your briefcase." I slipped him the cigarettes behind my desk. "So it's all finished now, eh?"

"Oh no, sir. I'll arrange your road test on Saturday."

We arrived at the driving area about 9 a.m. It was just inside the wall—an open gravelled spot between the asphalt road and the wall. There were about five other cars there, each with a learner and a friend who had driven him there. There were quite a few people milling about: urchins, old men, black-veiled ladies lingering on their way to market, and vendors hawking *marul,* cucumbers, fruits, pumpkin seeds, sherbet (a drink of water and syrup), *gazoz* (soda pop), and cigarettes. Beasties were sitting on top of the wall and in all the openings, which were originally designed for military uses. It was a festive occasion—apparently a regular Saturday entertainment.

I noticed a curving trail, outlined by rocks, about six feet in width and 100 yards long. This was obviously an obstacle course which didn't look very difficult to me, but I was hoping I wouldn't be first.

Two policemen roared up in an open jeep and screeched to a halt in a cloud of dust. A fine example, I thought. The beasties cheered. One policeman, fierce in dark glasses, was obviously in charge. He shouted something, and people started scrambling in all directions. Abdul pushed me into a line with the other applicants. The policeman walked up and down in front of us, looking us over and sizing us up. All our knees were knocking.

"You!" he pointed to a frightened farm boy. The kid stepped forward. The policeman pointed out the rocky obstacle course and, I assumed, told him to drive through it without hitting any of the rocks. The policeman got into the right front seat of the boy's battered Chevrolet, the other policeman in the back, and then the young man got into the driver's seat. Everyone ran for the walls and hid in nooks and crannies, like bedbugs with their eyes peeping out.

"Mister John! Mister John!" yelled Abdul. "Come quick! *Chabuk!*"

Just then the young man threw the car into gear and went zooming backward. I leapt out of the way and the car crashed into the wall. Neither the car nor the wall were damaged, but the wall could ill afford it. The beasties on top of the wall howled with laughter and clapped for more. The policemen jumped out of the car, dragged the driver out, and gave him a cuff on the ear. Everybody cheered. The young man tried to kiss the policeman's hand, but the cop shook him off and his friend drove him away in disgrace.

Both policemen brushed themselves off, slicked back their hair with a comb, and replaced their caps. The big one pointed to me. "You next." They got into the Plymouth and everyone ran for the walls. I tried to get them to let Abdul come along.

"*Yasak!*" (forbidden), he said. "*Dogru!*" (straight ahead) he barked, pointing to the rocky road. I was still a little shook up from my brush with death, and my eyes weren't focusing too well, but I managed to get through the obstacle course successfully. The beasties cheered wildly, and I wanted to acknowledge their applause, but didn't dare.

"*Sag!*" (right) barked the policeman. I turned right. "*Sol!*" I turned left. By that time we were on the asphalt road heading into the city. I drove unnaturally slowly to avoid the chickens, the goats, the sheep, the toddlers, the lame, the halt, and the blind. At the Mardin Gate, I was ordered to turn right, and we left the city and drove down to the Roman bridge. I began to relax and rested my left elbow out the window with my fingers lightly on the steering wheel, driving mainly with my right hand. The policemen were jibber-jabbering constantly, hardly paying any attention to my driving. The only thing I understood was: "Look at how cold-blooded these Americans are!" said by the one in the front seat. "He has only one hand on the *direksiyon* (steering wheel)." I wasn't quite sure if it was a compliment, but I slipped my elbow inside and drove more intently. We went about 10 miles—I thought we might even end up in Syria—when they told me to turn around.

The beasties on top of the wall sighted us as we came back to the driving area, and a great cheer went up. When we got out, the policeman signed my form and handed it to Abdul. The other applicants shook my hand and clapped me on my back. The beasties wanted my autograph.

When we left, I said to Abdul, "What next?"

"*Tamam!*"

"Allah be praised!"

At the police station, the Captain congratulated me (for my endurance, presumably) and gave me my license. It was a tiny red booklet with my name, photo, and the word "*Profesiyonel.*" I was terribly proud of that rating until Abdul told me it simply meant I was licensed to drive a station wagon or a pickup, as well as a passenger car.

I displayed it to all our American employees at the base.

"What was it like?" they all asked. "Was it difficult? When can I get mine?"

"Abdul will arrange it. I expect each of you to cooperate with him in *every* way." I told Abdul that I didn't care to hear *any* of the details of getting driver's licenses for the others. Many people switched to Salems during the following weeks.

My little red booklet had 16 blank pages in it to record traffic violations. I drove for 10 years in Turkey and never had an accident, although I was nearer my God many more times than I cared to be. Every country likes to brag that they have the worst traffic and the maddest drivers in the world, but the Turks win hands down. The American Embassy puts out a booklet called "Traffic Rules and Regulations in Turkey." I studied it carefully the night before I took my driver's test and was disappointed that I couldn't see any real difference between their rules and ours. But after leading a charmed life of dodging donkeys, sheep, buses, bikes, taxis, carts, cows, chickens and even camels, I feel eminently qualified to publish my own rules for driving in Turkey.

MISTER JOHN'S TRAFFIC RULES IN TURKEY

CITY DRIVING

1. The first shall be first, and the last shall be guilty. If you are entering a main artery from a side street, simply step on the gas and get there first. After the accident, the police will survey your car. If the damage is anywhere behind the headlights, you are innocent.

2. Always use your horn, not the brakes. Horns rarely wear out. Blow your horn with or without provocation—it wards off evil spirits.

3. Always aim right at a pedestrian crossing the street. If you slow down or swerve right or left, you will ruin his timing.

4. If the street is blocked, use the sidewalks—pedestrians never do.

5. Ignore stop signs. If you stop, you will be rammed from the rear.

6. When you go through an intersection, don't look to the right or left—otherwise you may be expected to give testimony later.

7. U-turns are permitted on any street—they save time and gas.

8. A one-way street simply means a narrow street. Use it in either direction. If you encounter a car coming at you, hold your ground or you will lose face. Turning off the ignition and reading a newspaper is very effective.

9. Always drive down the middle of the street so that you can attempt to avoid hitting anything. Dogs and cats are dispensible, but the Turks get a little sticky about chickens and children.

10. If you approach a traffic light that is red, stop *only* if there is a policeman hanging around. If you are the second car to approach, pull in front of the

first. If you are the third car, pull in front of both. If you are the fourth car, pass on the right and pull in front of all of them. If you are driving a horsecart, pass the whole damn bunch and go right through the light. The policeman will only box your ears.

COUNTRY DRIVING

11. If you see a tractor approaching the highway, even a mile away, jam on your brakes and stop. He won't.

12. When approaching a down-grade, push in the clutch and turn off the ignition to save gas. This is particularly effective if you have others in the car, like visitors newly arrived in Turkey.

13. If you sense something is going wrong with your engine, keep going until smoke starts pouring out of the hood and the car breaks down in the middle of the road. It is not necessary to pull off the highway since there are no shoulders. Get out, open the hood, pull some wires, and then abandon it. Be sure to put a circle of rocks around your car to protect it.

14. If you are driving a truck and have a flat tire, come to a stop on the highway and unload the cargo in either lane. Jack up the truck, remove the wheel, and hitch a ride on a bus, since you won't have a spare tire.

NIGHT DRIVING

15. When approaching an oncoming car at night, dim your lights at the last endurable moment. This is a form of "chicken." Then, seconds before you pass, flip on your high beams so that you can see the road ahead. Spotlights may also be used in conjunction with this maneuver.

16. If you see an eerie green light, like a laser beam stretching across the highway, about three feet off the ground, jam on your brakes! Stop dead! It's a flock of sheep coming toward you. The green light is a reflection of your headlights in their eyes.

17. If you have to abandon your car or truck at night (breakdown or out of gas), don't leave your parking lights on as this will only run down the battery. Don't forget, however, to put the circle of rocks around the vehicle.

18. Finally, if you have an accident in Turkey, Allah forbid, you have just changed your career in life.

Welcome to Turkey. Happy Motoring!

The Camel

≈

ONE SUNDAY AFTERNOON Alvin, our accountant, and I were out for a ride and saw our first camel. "We must have a picture of that!" I said. We stopped, got out, and moved cautiously toward it. It was standing on the side of the road, munching grass. It had a rope around its neck but wasn't tethered. "Alvin, get a little closer to the camel."

Just then we heard a shouting and a hollering. I turned and saw a young boy racing toward me, his feet flying higher than his head. He grabbed my arm and said, breathlessly, "My camel doesn't like to have his picture taken." Neither Alvin nor I could speak very much Turkish, but we got his drift.

"I think he just wants a *bakshish*," said Alvin.

The boy immediately picked up the word and started rubbing his fingers together, smiling beguilingly.

"Here's five lira," I said. "Now, bring your camel over here so we can get our money's worth."

The boy pocketed the money happily and raced over to his camel. The animal leapt into the air and took off into the fields. The boy took off after him, leaping over huge black volcanic boulders almost bigger than himself, but losing ground all the time. Finally both disappeared over the crest of a hill. Alvin and I looked at each other like dumb bunnies.

"I guess he's right; his camel sure doesn't like having his picture taken."

The Landlord

≈

I WAS LUCKY to find a nice two-bedroom apartment in Diyarbakir in a brand-new five-story building, not yet occupied. I had the choice of any apartment I wanted. I chose one on the third floor with a view of the city. The color scheme wasn't exactly what I wanted—the living room was orchid, one bedroom aquamarine, the other Polish pink, and the kitchen was sunflower. (Oh, those Turks!) But that could be easily altered. The real selling point was that it had *kalorifer*—central heating. It was the first building in Diyarbakir to install this modern invention.

Abdul went with me to see the landlord and sign the lease. The rent was $90 a month, which Abdul thought was outrageous (oh, you Americans!) but I thought was very reasonable. He didn't even know what *kalorifer* was and, when I explained it to him, didn't see the necessity for it. Cold, damp winters were a way of life in Diyarbakir, and tuberculosis was rampant. Dr. Tosun told me about a peasant woman who brought her sickly babe to him; he diagnosed it as having *verem* (tuberculosis). She wrapped up her baby and said, "Oh, Allah be praised, I thought it was something serious!" and left.

The landlord, Muharrem Bey, ran a plumbing shop in the Old City. His shop was more like an open warehouse with dusty plumbing fixtures all over the floor and a small enclosed office at the far end of the building. Muharrem Bey was very urbane with silver hair and a blue pinstriped suit, and we concluded our negotiations without a hitch. I paid him the rent, he gave me the key, we bowed and shook hands. "Now, *that's* the way to do business," I said to Abdul as we left and headed for a furniture store.

Actually, there were no furniture stores in Diyarbakir, only carpenter shops where they made furniture, usually right on the sidewalk. All I wanted to begin with was a bed. I had prepared my own design: seven feet square, very low, no head board, no foot board, and no springs—just hard slats like Trappist Monks use. I handed him the drawing which he kept turning upside down.

"And paint it black," I said.

"Black?!!"

"Flat black!"

"But sir, this wood is *jeviz* (walnut), the finest!"

I didn't have the heart to tell him it looked like rejected railroad ties.

I decided I'd better buy the paint myself since Abdul didn't know what I meant by "flat." The owner of the paint store spoke surprisingly good English. He was a young man, about 25, clean shaven and modest, named Kerim. He didn't know the word "flat" either, except as it applied to the earth, but as we were searching his shelves I saw the word "matte" on a can of French paint. "That's it!" I shouted. "What do you call it in Turkish?"

"*Mat*," said Kerim, giving it the French broad "a."[2]

I sent Abdul to the carpenter with a liter of *mat* black while I questioned Kerim as to where he learned his English.

"From the dictionary," he said casually, as if everyone learned another language that way. He showed me a well-thumbed Oxford English-Turkish Dictionary. "I read a chapter every night, if I am not too exhausted after work."

I glanced through it (he was on Chapter "G"), and it was excellent—the pronunciation was in the Turkish alphabet, and the explanations included a lot of idioms. I sent off to Brentano's for one the very next day.

---

2. A characteristic French sound, halfway between the *a*'s in "ah" and "at" in American pronunciation; not the usual sound of *a* in Turkish.

When Abdul returned, we went next to the mattress shop.

"I want a mattress two meters square, half a meter thick, and fill it with *new* cotton," I said, giving him a beady eye. "I'll bring you the material to cover the mattress with."

At the yardgoods shop I selected a red-and-black plaid, and enough material for the bedroom draperies as well. (I had no intention of making my bed every morning—I'd just throw the bed clothes into the closet, and the bedroom would always be ready for inspection, or whatever.)

I bought a refrigerator and a case of beer from the PX and had them all delivered to the new apartment the following Friday evening.

The bed barely made it up the narrow winding staircase. The refrigerator was put on the back of one old Turk by three helpers, and he carried it up alone! He survived, but I almost didn't—I couldn't watch. I'd tell the landlord later that I'd pay for repainting the scarred walls. I plugged in the refrigerator, put in the beer, and went back to the hotel for the last night, smug and content, thinking, "A bed, a refrigerator, and a case of beer—now *that's* the way to start a new life!"

The next morning I paid my bill, tipped the maids and bellboys, and loaded up a *fayton* (horse and buggy) with all my worldly possessions: a suitcase, a portable phonograph, and 20 LPs. I felt like Wells Fargo as we clomped through the streets to my new apartment.

The front door of the building was locked! I was surprised because I had been there many times and it had never been locked before. I shouted for the *kapiji* (the building's resident janitor)—none! Then I had a bright idea: was it possible that this very modern *aparteman* with the *kalorifer* also had a front door with a master lock that could be opened by all of the individual apartment keys? It didn't. Damn!

I took over the reins, and we went galloping to Muharrem Bey's shop. I stumbled over sinks and toilets to the office and demanded to know where Muharrem Bey was.

"He's gone to Adana," his accountant said.

"I rented an apartment from him, paid my rent, moved all my furniture in, and now I find the front door is locked! Do you have the key?"

The accountant shrugged. Maybe he didn't speak English. I played the record over again in my wild Turkish: "*Anahtar!* Key? *Anahtar!*"

He shrugged.

I calmed myself and said icily. "When will Muharrem Bey be back?"

"Monday, *Inshallah*" (God willing).

I went back to the Diyarbakir "Hilton" and sulked all weekend. On Monday after work I went straight to the plumbing shop. "Is Muharrem Bey back?"

"No."

"Will he be back tomorrow?"

"*Inshallah*."

Every evening when I came home from the base, I would make my rounds: 1) the THY (Turkish Air Lines) office to make reservations or purchase tickets, 2) the PTT (post office) to check our mailbox, and 3) Muharrem Bey's shop, where I was always told: "Tomorrow, *Inshallah*."

Six weeks later, I routinely went to Muharrem Bey's shop, and there he was! You could see that silver head of hair a mile away. I leaped over the plumbing fixtures and stormed into his office.

"Before you say *one* word, Mister John," he said, holding up his hand to fend me off, "I've sold the apartment! The whole building! To the Health Insurance Department! They're turning it into a hospital! You must move all your furniture by Monday! Here is your rent money back!" And he counted out nine crisp, newly minted 100-lira notes.

I sputtered for a while, but what could I do?

I went back to my *palas* (hotel), took to my bed and bottle, and said to myself, "Allah doesn't love me anymore."

The next day I found another apartment, brand-new, but still under construction. It was much more modern than Muharrem Bey's, but it didn't have any central heating.

Still, it had a parquet floor in the living room, floor-to-ceiling windows, and a charming design—you entered a foyer which led to the dining room, to the living room, to a large balcony, to the kitchen, and back to the foyer—a circular rotation which I immediately recognized would be perfect for parties. The top three floors were finished; only the ground floor was a mess and there was no water and no electricity yet.

"When will it be finished?" I asked the *kapiji*.

"Three weeks."

"Good."

"*Inshallah*."

"Oh, God!"

It actually turned out to be three months, during which time I was driven to distraction by the word *Inshallah*. The absentee landlord lived in Ankara and was rich. He didn't care when the building was finished; as long as he had started construction, he didn't have to pay taxes until the building was occupied.

I wasn't the only one who learned to loathe the word *Inshallah*. I've seen many Americans grab a Turk by the throat and say, "Don't give me that '*Inshallah*' shit!" But to the Turk it was quite logical. You make an appointment for a Turk to come to your house for an important meeting at five o'clock sharp, and he says, "*Inshallah*" knowing full well he has an airline ticket in his pocket to take his dying grandmother to a hospital in Ankara that very same afternoon. But maybe the weather would be bad, and the plane wouldn't fly; then he would cheerfully come to your house on time.

While reading the Koran one night, I was humbled by a footnote. It seems that Mohammed was asked a sly question by some of his skeptical followers, and he said, "I'll have the answer for you tomorrow." That night he got no revelations from Allah. Nor the next night, nor the following night. Mohammed was very embarrassed and confused. Finally Allah spoke to him and gave him the answer, then said: "But the next time you promise to give an answer tomorrow, say '*Inshallah*.'"

Hiring and Firing Turks

≈

IN DIYARBAKIR we hired mostly Turks, many Kurds, a Chaldean[3] or two, and one Armenian. I couldn't distinguish one from another because they all looked alike to me—black hair, black eyes, black mustache, and olive skin.

One day a young man showed up looking for a job—blond hair, blue eyes, clean-shaven, slim, tan jacket, white shirt, blue tie, blue trousers. I couldn't believe my eyes. What kind of Turk was this?

He was sent to me by Dr. Tosun, who begged me to give him a job because his father was dead, his mother was sick, he had to support all his brothers and sisters, he had just gotten out of the army, etc., etc., etc. The only job we had open was firefighter. Our firefighters were all burly creatures with wild hair, bushy eyebrows, handlebar mustaches, and black baggy trousers—but our Fire Chief said he'd give the boy a chance for one month.

The day before his probation period was up, Abdul asked me if he should prepare a permanent contract for him. I decided to call the chief for his opinion.

"Well—we've been having a little trouble with him."

"What kind of trouble?"

"Well, you know the Turks and the Kurds—they never get along very well together—"

"Look, you tell that little prima donna that we have all

---

3. Chaldeans are Eastern Rite Catholics indigenous to Iraq, Turkey, Syria, and Iran. They are descendants of the ancient Assyrians.

kinds working for us—Kurds and Armenians and Chaldeans and Zazas and Hittites and Mongolians—and we're not going to have anyone making fun of the Kurds just because they're scruffy and wear baggy trousers and pray all the time—"

"But *he's* the Kurd!"

"Oh."

"The Turks are giving *him* a hard time."

"Oh."

"But I think we have everything smoothed out now. Let's put him on contract. He's the smartest one I've got!"

Within a year he was the Assistant Fire Chief.

Firing Turks is like firing any employee anywhere in the world—a very painful process. However, with the Turks, their own laws made it a nightmare.

Emile, our very nervous French Supply Supervisor, came running to me one day, distraught. "I can't find Refik!"

"Who's Refik?"

"You know, ze Tourk with ze beeg black moustache!"

"Emile, calm down. They all have big black mustaches."

"Refik! Ze Tourk we gave notice to last week! He came to work zis morning at ten o'clock, as usual, and now he is gone! *Disparru! Mon Dieu!*"

"Emile, please sit down."

"Oh, Monsieur Jean, zis is terreeble!!! I don't understand zis Tourkish law. I am sure zat he is hiding somewhere."

"Well, by God, I'll find him! I know every nook and cranny on this base. You're sure he's not in Supply, behind one of those bins of yours?"

"No, no, Monsieur Jean! I swear by my muzzer's grave!"

"You go back to work. I'll find him."

According to Turkish Labor Law, Refik had to work out his two-week notice period after he had received his written termination. He was allowed two hours off every day to look for another job, but he had to come back to work to complete his eight hours. *Or,* he could elect to save up all his off-time and use it at the end of his notice period. Refik had sullenly decided to take two hours off every day. Since he was our very first test of the Turkish Labor Law, I was determined to implement the law.

As I searched the Carpenter Shop, behind stacks of lumber, I was preparing my angry speech to Refik: "Look, we Americans didn't make this law, you did! This is Turkish law! Now, you have come to work two hours late every day—which is okay—but you must *work* the other six hours! I don't necessarily agree with this regulation, but..."

I looked in the Laundry behind bundles of sheets and shirts. I looked behind GMC trucks in the Motor Pool and even in their beds. I felt like a fool looking in a cement mixer, but I did. I was just about to give up when I remembered the boiler room behind the Engineering Building. Aha!

I raced over and ripped open the door, knowing there was no escape route, and there he was! Stretched out on the floor with his hands under his head—black hair, black mustache, black shirt, black baggy trousers, no socks, black pointy shoes—fast asleep.

"Get up! Get up!" I screamed. "Follow me!"

I could hear him padding behind me as I skirted the building, mounted the stairs, plopped in my chair behind my desk like an angry judge, and looked up—into the face of a total stranger.

"Oh my God! You're the wrong one. Go back to sleep." He was our boiler operator who could stretch out anytime he wanted to, as long as he kept the home fires burning. Oh God, forgive me, these Turks all look alike!

I went to Supply to admit defeat to Emile, but Refik had reappeared. He was still sullen and refused to tell us where he had been. I offered to pay him off—his full two-weeks pay—and he readily accepted. From then on we just paid off people we had terminated and told them they could leave the base immediately. It was humiliating for a terminated Turk to have to come to work every day and face his fellow workers.

Another incident occurred two weeks later. There was a knock on my door at the hotel. I opened it and there stood a dark gaunt unshaven Turk in a heavy black overcoat with one hand inside his bosom like Napoleon.

"Yes?"

"Mister John, I want my job back."

I finally recognized him as another one of our employees whom we had terminated that morning with two weeks of pay.

"Oh! Yes, it's you—er—what's your name?"

"Musa."

"Ah, yes, Musa. Well, I'm afraid it's not possible for us to take you back because you've been terminated with good cause according to Turkish—"

He pulled a long thin dagger out of his bosom. "*This* is the only way I can make my living now! I must have my job back."

The dagger was very rusty, but I wasn't about to test its efficacy. "Oh—er—yes, I see what you mean. I understand completely—heh, heh! Suppose you come to the base tomorrow and speak to Abdul. We'll see what we can do." Thank God he put the knife back in his coat and left.

The next morning I got to the office early to warn Abdul. He wasn't the least bit ruffled. "Don't worry, Mister John, I'll take care of him." Apparently he did, because I never saw the desperado again.

One day Fehmi, our intrepid interpreter, came into my office with a brand-new employee and said, "This one wants to quit."

"But why? We just hired him two days ago as a janitor, and I've had good reports of him from our Custodial Supervisor."

"He doesn't want to clean the shit house, sir."

"Fehmi, *please* say 'latrine.'"

"Yes, sir, but he doesn't want to work in the—those places, sir."

"All right, all right. See if Abdul has any other job this man could do."

"Thank you, sir."

Another time Fehmi was all excited because one of our Americans had sworn at a Turk. "Sir, we are a very proud race, and whenever anyone swears at us, we get pissed off."

I decided to bring up the subject of swearing at our next staff meeting. I made a speech to all our Americans and foreign nationals:

"In Turkish you can't say, 'This goddamned hammer is no good.' It comes out, 'God damn you, this hammer is no good.' Now, you realize that's pretty strong language. I don't believe I've ever said, 'God damn you' to anyone in my life. In Turkish you can't even say 'God damn it.' They only ask God to damn a person. They consider it irreverent, if not meaningless, to ask God to damn an inanimate object. And the same is true of the word 'f--king.' If you say, 'This f--king machine doesn't work,' they think you're saying, 'F--k you, this machine doesn't work.' Actually, the Turks only use this word as an insult as to what they will do to your sister or your mother. I know it's everybody's favorite adjective, but *please* don't use it around the Turks. That's especially true if you're angry. I always say, 'If you love God, bring me a decent hammer.'"

"Bravo!" said Smitty, our Site Manager.

Tom Curington said, "John, you never used a hammer in your whole life, come on now, confess."

Things went better after that, and we didn't have an incident until Mr. Crandell, our Food Service Accountant, came in looking as flustered and as red as his toupee, which was slightly askew. He was followed by a screaming Turk, Ismet, and a calm Fehmi.

"Oh, dear me!" said Mr. Crandell, wiping his face.

"What happened?"

"That's the worst of it, I don't know. Oh dear, this is so distressing."

"Fehmi! Tell Ismet to calm down. Now, what's the problem?"

"Sir, Ismet says that Mr. Crandell said to him, 'Shit on you.'"

"Oh, dear me, I never said that. I've never used that vulgar word in my life. And I certainly wouldn't think of saying anything like that to my good friend Ismet. Why, he's one of our best clerks down at the Dining Hall."

Mr. Crandell was a prissy old gentleman, hardly likely to use that kind of language. He was a former schoolteacher.

"Fehmi, tell Ismet there must be some misunderstanding, and let's get to the bottom of this."

After about 15 minutes, I finally pieced the puzzle together. It seems Mr. Crandell and Ismet were having a cup of coffee together, and Ismet was telling him of his prowess with the women. Mr. Crandell's Turkish was surprisingly good, and he had no trouble carrying on a conversation in Turkish. Apparently at the end of Ismet's recital of his conquests, Mr. Crandell said jokingly, "Oh, you *sheytan*, you." *Sheytan* means "satan" or merely "devil," but it's pronounced "shey-tahn," and Ismet thought Mr. Crandell had said, "Shit on you."

Finally everyone kissed and made up, and Mr. Crandell and Ismet went back to the dining hall arm in arm.

One Saturday morning four burly Turks marched into my office, lined up in front of my desk, crossed their arms, and said, "We quit!" With their fierce black mustaches they looked like executioners out of the bloody past. I sent for Fehmi, and when they all stopped talking at once, it turned out to be nothing—just that one of our Germans, Udo, had sworn at them.

I sent for Udo, who gave his side of the story. It seems Udo was down in a hole repairing a water pipe. When he finished the repair, he called for a bucket of hot tar to be lowered to him. The Turks spilled the tar, which didn't hurt Udo at all, but got all over his shoes. "Look at them!" shouted Udo, holding up one shoe, then the other. Udo admitted that he may possibly have used a strong word or two.

"In German?" I asked.

"Oh no, swearing iss much better in English, Mister Chon."

I asked Udo to apologize—he refused. I asked the Turks

to forgive—they refused. I asked them all to go back to work—Udo did, but the Turks insisted on quitting. There was nothing to do but pay them their wages and let them go.

The following Monday Udo received a summons to court. That afternoon the lead article in the *Diyarbakir Gazette* was about the incident. "GERMAN AT RADAR STATION INSULTS TURKISH NATION" screamed the headline. The article was three columns long, and I couldn't understand most of it, but four words stood out clearly in the article. They were in capitals and quotation marks:

"SANABICH"
"KOTEMIT"
"MADIRFAKIR"
"BALSHIT"

Suddenly I realized that they were English words. The Turks had told the reporter exactly the swear words Udo had used. I looked them over and came to the conclusion that Udo may have used the first three words, but I seriously doubted if anyone who is down in a hole and has hot tar poured over him has ever said, "Bullshit!"

Udo was fined 400 lira, 100 for each insultee. Poor Udo. He felt the company should pay the fine since it was in the line of duty, he said.

The Van Adventure

≈

Van, population 12,000, city in eastern Turkey on the shores of Lake Van, ancient capital of Armenia, and birthplace of Semiramis, first Queen of Mesopotamia.
—Hachette Blue Guide

I HAD to see it!

Turkish Air Lines flew from Diyarbakir to Van three days a week—Tuesday, Friday, and Sunday. Van was the end of the line, very near the Russian and Iranian borders, so the airplane returned the same days. I left on a Friday with reservations to return on Sunday, thus not having to ask for time off. None of my friends would come with me. They thought I was mad, or at least rash, at most stupid. They preferred to stay on the base, playing poker, feeding the slot machines, and getting drunk all weekend.

When I was taking off for Van (pronounced "Vahn" according to Mustafa, the airlines manager), he told me to be sure to stay at the Semiramis Palas as it was very new and modern. The one-hour trip through the mountains was hairy and scary. The DC-3 couldn't go over the 13,000-foot mountains, so it flew through the valleys, following the Tigris and Euphrates Rivers, both of which originate near Lake Van. We arrived without incident on a vast salt flat beside Lake Van, a gorgeous blue lake surrounded by snow-capped mountains. It was about the same size as Utah's Great Salt Lake and twice as salty. I boarded a battered blue bus (there were no taxis) along with the other two passengers from the plane, both Turkish. At that point about 20 villagers scrambled on, carrying great huge bundles and assorted animals. I counted five live chickens, two geese upside down with their feet tied, and two frisky goats, tethered. The bus bumped along the salt flats and then pushed up into the hills to the city of Van, overlooking the lake.

At the airlines office in the city, I asked for the Semiramis Palas.

"Up the hill, on the right."

It was not a difficult climb; I had a light suitcase. The hotel was a white, square, two-story frame building, unadorned except for the sign over the door, and looking like a pleasant country schoolhouse.

"Do you have a room? A single, please."

The clerk spoke no English. My Turkish was limited, but by holding up one finger and stabbing my chest, I think he got the point. After all, there was hardly any other reason why I had come to his hotel. He looked in his register and rustled a few pages, then studied the mailboxes behind him, then back to the register again. I really didn't see the problem—I could see by the boxes that there were only 12 rooms in the entire hotel.

"Do you mind waiting a minute, sir? Please sit down in the lobby."

The lobby was nothing more than one leather couch and one leather chair just opposite his desk-counter. I chose the couch and opened my *Blue Guide*. While I was waiting for my room, a well dressed, darkly handsome man of 30 sat down in the chair beside me and struck up a conversation in Turkish.

"Welcome," he said.

"Thank you."

"Are you German?"

I laughed because I had been asked this many times. Apparently the Germans were the first tourists in these out-of-the-way places. They have a reputation of being at least two years ahead of any other tourists.

"No, I am an American."

"Where are you from?"

"From Diyarbakir. I came today."

"No, no, no. *I* am from Diyarbakir. I was born there. I came on Tuesday. I am a hat salesman. But *you,* do you come from New York? Chee-cago? Texas?"

"Well, I'm originally from Massachusetts."

"Oh, a Red Indian," he said matter-of-factly.

"No, there are no more Red Indians in Massachusetts."

"Why did you come to Van?"

"To see it."

"Are you looking for oil?"

"No."

"Gold?"

"No."

"The Americans never come here unless they are looking for oil, or gold. Are you a spy?"

"No, no." I laughed. "I just came to *see* Van. To take pictures." I displayed the Polaroid camera hanging around my neck. "I'm just a tourist." It was obvious that he didn't believe me, but he bowed politely and welcomed me again.

"By the way," I said, "I've been sitting here 20 minutes waiting for a room, and I'm getting slightly tired of it. That boy there asked me to wait only one minute, but it's been almost half an hour. Are there any other hotels in Van?"

"Oh yes, there are many. Now let's see—." And he started to count them off on his fingers. "There's the Chichek Palas (Flower Hotel), Temiz Palas (Clean), Bacheh Palas (Garden), Gul Palas (Rose), and the Emperiyal Palas (Imperial). But this is the only one without bugs."

I decided to wait.

I had vaguely noticed a number of people rushing in and out of the hotel as I was talking to the hat salesman. I swear I saw a piece of 4' x 8' plywood go by, with a scruffy Turk at either end. I heard a lot of hammering, and everyone bowed to me as they streaked by.

Finally the desk clerk bowed, smiled, and said, "Your room is ready, sir."

A bellboy led me to the room and politely gestured me

to enter. The room was small: only a bed, a straight chair, a nightstand, a lamp, and a clothes tree. One whole wall was raw, unpainted plywood—the others were a vivid floral wallpaper. Suddenly, it struck me—they had literally *built* me a room while I waited. I learned later that each room in the hotel was large, with twin beds, and had *two* doors leading from the hallway. The carpenters had simply put a plywood partition down the middle. I even had a window.

I was delighted with the room, especially since there were no bugs. But I felt sorry for the poor guy who had left that morning happy, and would come home that night to find that his private world had been cut in half.

That evening I went down into the bustling nightlife of the city. It consisted of one main street, one long block. I passed the Flower Hotel and the Clean Hotel and came to a restaurant. It had six tables, each big enough to seat one, and only one was empty. I sat down, and a waiter rushed up to me, beaming and bowing.

"Welcome, welcome, welcome!" I was so obviously a foreigner honoring his establishment. He turned out to be, in addition to the waiter, the cook, the busboy, the dishwasher, the cashier, the manager, and the owner. And he managed to keep everyone well-attended to. He started reeling off a flood of Turkish, counting on his fingers and gazing at the ceiling from time to time. It must have been the menu. Since I couldn't understand a word of his machine-gun Turkish, I stood up and indicated I wanted to go to the kitchen.

"*Buyurun!*" (Please! After you!), he said.

The stove had two rows of identical pots on it, about 12 in all, boiling away madly. He lifted the lid of the first pot. It was a stew. Chunks of meat and potatoes kept bobbing to the surface, and every once in a while a carrot would erupt. The second pot was also a stew, as indeed were all twelve of them, although the cook carried on a running commentary on the presumably different delights of each. Finally I turned to the cook and asked plaintively, "Shish kebab?"

"Of course, of course!"

"And *raki?*"

"*Hi, hi!*"[4]

The lamb was delicious, succulent and tender, and the *raki* put me in a very mellow mood. It should have; it was 90 proof, and I drank a whole bottle. I had expected to drink only a glass or two, but the waiter brought me an unopened bottle, a small bottle to be sure. I noticed all the other diners had a bottle in front of them, so to preserve the American image, I downed the whole bottle, slo-o-owly. I paid my bill—it was less than a dollar—and wove my way up to my little room at the inn.

The next morning I went down the hill for breakfast and noticed a bowl of eggs in the window of my favorite restaurant. The manager welcomed me as a long-lost friend. I ordered two eggs, sunnyside up, toast, and coffee.

"*Hi, hi!*" he said, and brought me tea, goat cheese, black olives, cherry-flavored honey, bread, and two cold hard-boiled eggs, which he had taken out of the bowl in the window. I didn't mind. It was all good.

I next turned my mind to the problem of getting to Semiramis's castle on the shores of Lake Van—a problem since there were no taxis in Van. As I was walking along Main Street, I considered and dismissed the idea of taking a water buffalo, the most prominent means of transportation in view. Just then I noticed a bicycle leaning up against a coffeehouse. I walked in and said in a loud, clear voice in my best Turkish: "*Bisiklet, kim?*" (Bicycle, who?)

The coffeehouse was full of old men, middle-aged men, young men, and boys, all sipping tea and playing backgammon. Everyone was startled, and I had to repeat my demand three times, each time more imperiously. Finally, one 15-year-old raised his hand tentatively like a schoolboy, and I ordered him outside. I opened my wallet, took out a 50-lira note ($5), pressed it into his palm, and told him in a very authoritative voice (with gestures) that I was taking his bicycle

---

4. An Ottoman utterance meaning, "Yes, sure, certainly, of course." The expression is properly spelled *Hayhay!*, but Tumpane transcribes it "Hi, hi!" for comedic effect.

and would return it that afternoon at five o'clock.

"Right here!" I said, jabbing my finger downward. "Five o'clock!"

I pointed to the numeral on my watch and took off before he had a chance to protest.

On the way I bought apples, tangerines, and nuts and put them in my ditty bag with my camera and candy bars. I bicycled to the lake, leaned the bike against a boulder, then climbed the mountain to the castle. I met the local schoolmaster, who was also climbing on his day off. He was about 25 and wearing a 10-gallon hat (God knows where he got it), a double-breasted suit that was formerly white, a black shirt, and a blue string tie. Because I spoke a few words of Turkish, he assumed I understood the language perfectly, so he would stand on walls and parapets giving me lectures on the glorious beginnings of civilization which had taken place here. He looked and sounded exactly like a Texas senator from Mesopotamia.

He became obsessed with the stunning Polaroid pictures I took of him and got belligerent, even menacing, when I tried to get them back from him. I finally had to resort to subterfuge—snapping the picture, then disappearing behind a rock before I pulled it out of the camera. He surprised me once by following me, but I warded him off by unzipping my pants and making water.

It was a glorious day. My *Blue Guide* supplied all the information my schoolmaster failed to communicate:

> —The cuneiform inscriptions on the mud castle go back to the 11th century B.C. The inscriptions record the founding of the city of Urartu (Ararat), a civilization which preceded the Hittites and the Sumerians.
> —In the 6th century B.C. the Persian King Xerxes conquered this stronghold and said so in trilingual inscriptions in Babylonian, Persian, and Mede on the walls.
> —In the 3rd century B.C. Alexander the Great declined to conquer this province. He said it wasn't worth it, but historians of this impregnable fortress think he made a wise decision.

—In the 1st century A.D. Tigranes the Great founded the capital of Armenia here. He graciously lent his name to the Tigris River which originates just over the mountains, west of Lake Van. One hundred years later, his followers were the first people to embrace Christianity as a national religion.

I arrived back at the coffeehouse exactly at five o'clock. The frightened child was waiting, sure that he had made a bad bargain. When he realized he had not, I couldn't get rid of him. He kept pressing his bicycle on me, bugging me all the way back to the Semiramis Palas. He had probably never had so much money in his hot little palm his whole life.

The hat salesman was sitting in the lobby and invited me to have tea with him. We got better acquainted than we had the day before. His name was Nerghiz, which I recognized immediately as our word "narcissus." It was very appropriate. He had enviable unblemished olive skin, bright white teeth, slick blue-black hair, and a thick neat mustache, bristling with vitality. He held his head high and turned it from side to side as he talked, as if to display its beauty from all angles. Yes, a perfect name. He was gorgeous.

I told him about my day at the castle, and when I showed him the pictures I had taken, he finally believed that I was not looking for oil or gold. He got terribly excited about the Polaroid camera and inspected it intensely, looking for the little man inside who developed the pictures. This spurred him to tell me about other ruins in the vicinity, "*much* better than Semiramis's castle." He had a friend, the manager of the waterworks, who had a jeep, the only one in town. He would surely take us to see some of them tomorrow because Sunday was his day off. I knew Narcissus was simply enamored of the camera, but I readily agreed.

That evening we walked down into the town and up another hill to the house of the waterworks manager. Sure enough, there was a jeep outside the house. After only five minutes of welcoming, hugging, kissing, introducing, explaining, and planning, we left, agreeing to meet the next morning at ten o'clock.

As we were going down the hill, Nerghiz said to me, "Do you have an *igneh?*"

I thought—*igneh, igneh, igneh*. I know that word: what is it???

"Oh, never mind," he said, and began fingering under the lapels of his black pinstriped suit. "Ah!" he said, and extracted a pin. I remembered immediately that *igneh* meant pin, and that all Turks carry them under their lapels to attach papers and documents since paper clips were rare and staplers non-existent.

"Give me your finger," he said. He took my third finger, left hand, and stabbed it with the pin. The blood spurted out and he stuck my finger in his mouth and sucked it. "Now we are blood brothers," he said casually, replacing the pin under his lapel.

I was in a state of semi-shock. It had all happened so fast. I *liked* the Turks and all but—blood brothers? When I recovered, I resolved then and there that I'd better write my mother a letter and tell her she had another son, named Narcissus!

He then led me into a Turkish bath, a marvelous edifice of yellow brick with labyrinthine passageways, Romanesque arches, and alcoves with marble basins. Steaming hot water spurted out of the walls. We left our valuables at the desk, disrobed, and put on a thin white wraparound. Narcissus found an empty alcove and sat down beside one of the basins. He ordered me to sit on my clogs with my back to him. With a copper bowl he dipped into the marble basin and poured tons of water over me. The water was shockingly hot, but I had time for a quick breath between each dip and splash. He then proceeded to give me a shampoo. Rub-a-dub-dub with fingers and knuckles—an absolute drubbing. I gave up worrying about my hair coming out by the roots and began being concerned about saving my scalp. Then cascades of water came without letup so that I became concerned about drowning. My past passed before my eyes. Then abruptly he stopped.

"*Choke guzel?*" he asked. (Very good?)

"*Choke, choke,*" I said.

I felt I should reciprocate, but Narcissus brushed me aside and did his own hair, probably knowing that I was a neophyte in the Turkish bath business.

I felt marvelously refreshed and relaxed and slept like a baby that night, aided, of course, by the bottle of *raki* each of us drank at dinner.

The next morning everything went as planned—unbelievable in Turkey. The jeep arrived at 10. I had already checked out of the hotel and brought my suitcase with me, at Nerghiz's suggestion. We piled into the jeep and roared through town and up into the mountains.

I had told Narcissus that I *had* to be at the airport by three o'clock. He said, "Yeah, yeah," in such a casual manner that I decided *I'd* better keep track of the time. It was 10:15. We would have to start back by noon—12:30 at the latest.

Narcissus was right. The castles, fortresses, and bridges were architectural marvels and a photographer's delight. Each one was different: Persian, Greek, Roman, Ottoman. Anywhere else in the world there would have been busloads of tourists and Coca-Cola stands. I took pictures of Narcissus and Mr. Waterworks in arches, on parapets, under bridges, and against mysterious ancient inscriptions—pictures which they immediately confiscated with airy thanks. I managed to stash away a few for myself.

I looked at my watch: it was 12:05.

"It's time to turn back," I said.

"No, no, no!" said Mr. Waterworks, "there are more castles over this way!" and he made a sharp right turn that almost catapulted me out of the jeep. He was so excited by the instant pictures that he raced recklessly from ruin to ruin.

I have a good sense of direction, and I realized that we had driven north from Van, then turned east, and now we were turning south. After more castles and ruins, I was relieved when we came out of the mountains onto the salt flats and started turning north. We had made a complete circle. It was 2:58.

"What's that airplane I see flying over the lake toward

Diyarbakir?" I shouted.

"Calm down," said Narcissus. "That's not your plane. It's not even three o'clock."

"But what plane could it be?"

"That's a military plane," said Mr. Waterworks smugly.

We arrived at the airport at 3:10. I jumped out of the jeep, ran in, and thrust my ticket at the clerk.

"Oh, that plane left 10 minutes ago," he said cheerily.

"But it's not supposed to leave until 3:30!" I screamed. "It's only 10 minutes after three!"

"Well, the pilot didn't like the looks of the weather over the lake, so he took off early." Then he smiled sweetly at me like an indulgent truant officer and said, "You know you're supposed to be here 30 minutes before takeoff. It says so right here on the back of the ticket." I could have wrung his neck.

I was discombobulated and disoriented, but what could I do?

"When is the next plane back to Diyarbakir?" I asked, knowing full well.

"Tuesday, at 3:30, sir."

"Or whatever time the pilot feels like it, eh?" I said in English, baring my teeth.

"*Efendim?*"

"Never mind. Book me on Tuesday's plane, if you please."

So we went back to the Semiramis Palas. The clerk welcomed me back with a flood of greetings, but alas, my own special room had already been taken. Narcissus offered to share his room and I gladly accepted. It was as I suspected—exactly twice the size of my old room, with a bed on each side and two windows.

Secretly I was delighted to have such a good excuse to stay two more days. I broke out the Johnnie Walker, and we toasted Turkish Air Lines and Semiramis and Tigranes the Great. I could have gone on and on, but Nerghiz pulled himself together, saying he had to go to work. He asked if I would like to accompany him to a little village on the south shore of the lake.

"It's only an hour by bus," he said. "I go there every three months to sell caps. Suleyman is a very good customer of mine."

It didn't sound very interesting.

"They have lots of old ruins there. A Christian church, very ancient. The villagers are always finding old things around there: statues, gold coins, silver pots—"

"Is there a bus back tonight?"

"Naturally."

"Let's go!"

It was a bumpy but lovely ride. The lake was a deep blue, the snow on the mountains was turning gold, the poplar and birch trees glistened in the afternoon sun.

"Be sure to ask what time the last bus goes back to Van—as soon as we get there!"

"Don't worry."

The village was tiny, perhaps 10 houses, a small mosque, and Suleyman's shop: a miniature supermarket crowded into a space 10′ x 10′ stacked to the ceiling with fruits, vegetables, sacks of flour, dried beans, lentils, canned goods, loaves of bread, yard goods, notebooks, pencils, olive oil, motor oil, and farm implements. I didn't see any caps. Nerghiz had a carpetbag full.

Nerghiz and Suleyman gave each other bear hugs, kisses on both cheeks, and slaps on the back. I tugged at Nerghiz's sleeve. "The bus, remember?"

"Yes, yes." He asked Suleyman.

"Oh, there are no more buses back to Van tonight," he said. "The next one is tomorrow morning." I wasn't the least bit surprised. "But it's all right. You can stay at my house tonight. I will be honored."

"You see?" said Narcissus, triumphantly.

I gave myself entirely into their hands, and Allah's for good measure.

Narcissus didn't forget my interest in archeological ruins. In a flash Suleyman had rounded up an expeditionary force of five or six little beasties, who bounded up the hill like billy goats, waving me to follow.

On a promontory overlooking the village and the lake, we came upon the ruins of the church. The roof had fallen in, but the walls were still reasonably intact. It was quite modest—more like a chapel than a church. The interior was being used as a stable for donkeys. One of them was munching hay in the sanctuary.

The outside walls still had some nice decorative pieces on them: a cornice or a frieze. I began turning over stones at the base of the church. The beasties immediately followed suit, and each of them would rush over to me and show me what he had found. Rocks were flying in all directions.

I found a rock the size of my fist with lovely, delicate scrollwork on it, Roman or Corinthian. It was love at first sight.

"Is it all right if I take this?" I asked the beasties.

"What for??"

"For a souvenir," I said, so proud that I knew the word in Turkish. "*Hatira!*"

"Aaaugh! That's nothing!" said a beastie. "Last year Ihsan, the shepherd, found a big cup—gold—like this." He held his hands in such a way that I imagined it must have been a chalice. "We need a shovel," he said, "I'll go back and get one."

"No, no, no! I only want this. As a souvenir. It's enough." They shook their heads in disgust.

We stayed about half an hour. There was a cemetery right beside the church. The tombstone inscriptions were in Armenian, all those circles with curlicues. Fascinating, but indecipherable.

I posed the beasties in interesting positions in front of the church and took a picture. They naturally got hysterical when they saw the picture and tried to grab it away from me. I held it high over my head, and soon I had beasties climbing up me like a flagpole. One of them, on my back, grabbed it and they all went running down the mountain, whooping like Indians.

When I got back to the village, Suleyman asked me what

I had found. I showed him my scrollwork rock. "Oh, that's nothing," he said, and went on and on about all the fabulous things he and the other villagers had found. He never offered to show me any of them. Undoubtedly he had sold them.

"Take a picture of me and my store," he said as he struck a pose. Narcissus got into the picture, and then the beasties, and then the villagers who had gathered around us, having heard about the stranger in town with the magic camera. They were dumbstruck when they saw the picture. One woman was terrified—covered her mouth and ran.

Then they all started tugging at me, wanting their pictures taken. Unfortunately, I had run out of film. I opened the camera and removed the empty cartridge to show them.

Nerghiz suggested we walk down to the lake, since Suleyman wasn't closing up his shop until six o'clock. The lake looked so inviting that I took off my clothes and plunged in. It was ice cold, but I considered it a necessary bath. After a few minutes I got used to it and began to enjoy it. I took a drink to see how salty it was. It was salty. According to my *Blue Guide*, the lake has no outlet and therefore is very caustic. The streams that flow into Lake Van abound in fish, but only one type of fish has managed to survive in the lake.

I watched Narcissus standing on the small dock with his jacket tossed carelessly over his shoulders, his arms crossed, one leg crooked, and basking in the setting sun.

"Time to go," he said finally. I dressed, and we went to Suleyman's house in the woods not more than 50 yards from the lake.

The house was mud, one story, long and low with a peaked, thatched roof. In the middle was an open passageway that led from the front yard to the back orchard. Suleyman was waiting for us in the passageway, beckoning us to enter the living room, which was to the left. I noticed shoes on the doorstep, so while I was removing mine I sneaked a glance into the other part of the house, which was the kitchen and sleeping quarters. Entering the living room was a pleasant shock after the drab exterior. It was bright, cheerful, and comfortable. The walls were white-washed, with pictures and photographs, flowered chintz curtains on the windows, and potted plants in tin cans. Benches were built into the walls all the way around and were covered with colored pads and cushions. In the middle of the room was an open copper brazier with hot coals in it. I was introduced to Baba (Papa), who was sitting like royalty in the middle of the bench at the far end of the room. He gestured for me to sit beside him and introduced me to his five sons, each of whom came forward as Baba called out his name: Suleyman, 35; Ahmed, 30; Burhan, 26; Muharrem, 22; and Yashar, 17. The men bowed, shook my hand, and retreated. I could detect a particular affection the old man had for the youngest, a modest boy who wouldn't look me in the eye. His name, Yashar, means "he lives!"—a name the Turks often gave to a baby who appeared dead when it was born, before they smacked its bottom.

Baba offered me a Turkish cigarette, and I offered him a Pall Mall. I offered cigarettes to the sons, but they all refused, placing their left hands over their breasts and bowing. I was bewildered. Didn't any of them smoke? Then I remembered that Suleyman had accepted a cigarette at the shop. I later learned that a Turkish son does not smoke or drink in the presence of his father. It has nothing to do with concealing the fact; it is some inexplicable form of respect. So Baba and I smoked and drank tea, which Yashar brought us, and talked Turkey.

Finally, dinner was announced by Yashar. I had noticed him padding in and out of the room. He had placed a huge copper tray on the floor in the middle of the room and put a number of pillows on the floor around it.

We all sat down cross-legged like American Indians, and I surveyed the tray. It was full of bowls of food, some of which I could recognize: cucumbers in yoghurt, dried beans in oil, lamb stew—each bowl with a spoon in it. Although there were eight of us, the tray was set for seven. I could tell by the triangular-folded napkins in front of us. I soon learned that Yashar, the youngest, didn't eat with us. He was the servant.

I became alarmed when I noticed that there were no individual plates in front of each person. No knives, no forks, no spoons! How on earth were we to eat this stuff without plates and utensils? I began to panic because I knew the inevitable Turkish *"Buyurun!"*[5] was coming, and I would have to be first. I had long ago learned that the "After-you-Alphonse, No! After-you-Gaston" routine absolutely did not work in Turkey. I tried to stall for time by shaking out my napkin. Yipes! It was bread. Thin, flat, round, dark bread, folded like a napkin.

"Buyurun," said Baba, gesturing to the bowls.

There was no getting out of it. I took a deep breath, grabbed the bowl nearest me, shoved a spoonful into my mouth, and passed it on to Baba. I took a bite of bread, smiled at everyone, and said, *"Choke guzel!"* I then took another bowl, put a spoonful in my mouth, passed the bowl on to Baba, bit some bread, and smiled. And so on and so on. We cleaned up the entire tray.

It was only after I got back to Diyarbakir and was explaining my experience to Dr. Tosun that I learned, to my humiliation, that I was supposed to put a spoonful of each delicacy on a piece of bread and eat it like a canape. (Oh, how Cadillac laughed!) But Baba and his sons were too polite to say anything to me, and each of them did exactly as I had done in order not to embarrass me. I'm sure they were thinking, "These barbarians! Is this the way they eat in America?"

But the dinner was pleasant and cheerful with plenty of *raki* for Baba and me. We even got a little *sarhosh* (happy-headed).

After dinner and Turkish coffee, everyone except Yashar said good night to me, shook my hand, and left the room. Yashar took two of the mattress pads off the benches, piled them on the floor, threw a blanket over them, and indicated that this was where I was to sleep. He bowed politely and

---

5. A commonly used polite command. Depending on context, it can mean "welcome," "be my guest," "after you," "please come in," "if you please," etc.

disappeared. I was alone.

Well, the bed he had prepared for me suited me fine, but I had to go to the bathroom. I fretted about this for a while, considered watering the potted plants on the windowsills, but then bravely decided to go outside. I furtively opened the door—it was pitch black—and stepped on Yashar, who was sleeping across the threshold. After much apology, I whispered to him that I wanted to make water.

"*Hi, hi!*" he said, and led me to an outhouse at the end of the orchard. It was not unfamiliar to me, but in the dark I was afraid of falling in. So I asked Yashar's permission to water a peach tree.

"*Buyurun!*"

The next morning I had breakfast in the orchard under an apple tree with Baba and a crony of his. Yashar served us (I never saw a woman the whole time I was there) the usual breakfast of goat cheese, black olives, fruit-flavored honey, and tea. Baba kept telling his friend he never knew an American who could speak so much Turkish. I acted very modest—with good reason—and suspected that Baba had never met an American before. The crony took out an antique silver box, the size of a cigarette packet, exquisitely carved, and opened it. It was full of shredded tobacco, with a sheaf of cigarette papers. He rolled a cigarette, licked the paper, twisted the ends, and handed it to me.

"You're not going to give him one of *those,* are you?" shrieked Baba.

"Sure."

"Allah! Allah! Allah!"

I took it graciously and offered him a Pall Mall, which he accepted. Baba also helped himself.

I took one drag and started coughing for 20 minutes.

"You see!" said Baba.

As they were slapping me on the back, I realized that I had destroyed years of good Turkish-American relations that had been carefully nurtured by our State Department. I had just enough tea left to bring the spasm under control and surreptitiously dropped the cigarette in the grass.

The Van Adventure / 77

Yashar accompanied me to Suleyman's shop and smoked a Pall Mall on the way. I didn't; I was thinking strongly of giving up cigarettes altogether. Soon Nerghiz and I were on a bus back to Van. He stayed in town to peddle hats, and I went back to the hotel.

The desk clerk was upset that we had not slept in our beds the night before. I explained the situation, showed him my rock and some pictures I had salvaged, but it was only when I said we would pay for the room the night before that he relaxed and smiled.

A minor, untoward incident occurred that day. While I was walking around the town, I came to a girls' school at recess. I strolled into the schoolyard and struck up a conversation with the teacher, who was very pretty and shy. I got so excited that I rushed back to the hotel to get my camera—I had loaded it that morning— and returned in three minutes. The teacher lined all the girls up on the steps of the school. I took what I considered to be a glorious picture, reminding me of the days when I stood on the steps of my grade school. When I pulled the picture through the camera it jammed. I tugged and tugged and began sweating. Everyone was crowded around me, except the lady schoolteacher who was standing modestly in the background. Finally the paper tore. I opened the camera carefully and found all the film crinkled and rolled up in a ball inside. It was immediately obvious to me what had happened: the desk clerk and the boys at the hotel had fiddled with my magic camera, hoping to take a picture of themselves. I made a hasty retreat from the schoolyard in shame. I looked back and saw the lady schoolteacher smiling and interpreted her smile to mean, "Well, that was typically American—all fuss and exuberance and nothing to show for it."

I glared at the desk clerk when I got back to the hotel but didn't dream of accusing him of any wrongdoing. He proved his guilt by not asking me to take a picture of himself.

I left Van the next day, having arrived at the airport in the battered blue bus in plenty of time. No one in Diyarbakir was upset that I had been missing for two days. They listened to my explanation with blank faces. Life on the base was so dull, repetitious, and boring that red-blooded Americans turned into glassy-eyed zombies shortly after arrival. And they lived out their 18-month tour that way like vegetables, mostly cabbages.

About a week later, as I was waiting at the airport for a new employee to arrive, I was approached by Mahmud of the Secret Police. Naturally he never admitted he was with the Secret Police, but it was obvious to me. He was always at the airport when a plane arrived or departed. I often saw him at the hotel going through the guest register. He made the rounds of the bars every night. He would simply survey the patrons and leave. He never took a drink. When I would see him at the airport we never spoke, but nodded to each other. I wouldn't dream of blowing his cover, which everyone in Diyarbakir knew. He was a sphinx, and just as bald.

"We have a telegram about you," he said in a very low voice, gazing nonchalantly into the sky.

"You do??"

"From Van."

"Van?"

"You stole something out of the museum there." I was astonished.

"I did not! I didn't even go to the museum!" I was furious. "I don't think they even have a museum in Van!"

"A rock. You'd better come in to see the Chief of Police. And bring the rock." Then he strolled away.

I was seething but tried to appear calm. I knew immediately it was the scrollwork stone, and it flashed into my mind that that damned little desk clerk had ratted on me. Mahmud hadn't mentioned when I was to come to the police station, but I decided to get it over with as soon as possible.

The next day I left the base on the pretext of having some company business in town. I went first to pick up my friend Kerim at his paint store to act as my interpreter. I didn't trust my Turkish in such a serious situation, and I didn't want anyone at the base to know I was already involved with the police. We went to my hotel room to pick up the stone. I explained the full circumstances to Kerim. We took hundreds of Polaroid pictures of it (well, several) because I had a feeling I was going to lose it forever. I told Kerim that I *would* give it up, but that I was going to fight for it! I put it in a brown paper bag, and we drove to the provincial government building.

We were ushered in *immediately* to the office of the Chief of Police—an ill omen since I was used to waiting hours to see government officials. The office itself was surprisingly elegant, with a faded but handsome carpet on the floor, dusty draperies, deep leather armchairs, and a huge desk behind which sat roly-poly Hikmet Bey with his little Hitler mustache—the police chief himself. I had met Hikmet only once before, at a party, and he very cordially told me that if I *ever, ever* needed any help, I was to come straight to him. He was anything but cordial today.

"What's the meaning of this?" he said, shaking the telegram over his head.

I explained carefully and truthfully where I had found the rock, holding my head high. Kerim translated politely and subserviently, holding his head low. I couldn't tell whether Hikmet believed me or not, but he screamed that I had to give it back! I told him the stone wasn't worth anything to anyone, except me—as a souvenir. I took it out of the paper bag and walked over to show it to him more closely. He tried to grab it from me, but I snatched it away.

He drew back from it in obvious distaste. Mahmud, who had been lurking in the far corner, came forward and curled his lip at it. I could tell they were thinking: Is this what all the fuss is about? Why, there were all kinds of stones like that all over Diyarbakir.

"You see," I said, "it has no archeological value whatsoever. Why, the Metropolitan Museum in New York wouldn't give you five dollars for it." I began wondering if they would even give 50 cents—or might they be intrigued by it?

"I don't care anything about museums in New York," he

screamed, "you have to give it back!"

I sat down and tried the buddy-buddy approach. "Hikmet, you once told me if I was ever in trouble, you'd help me. Well, now I'm in trouble. I want to keep this stone—as a remembrance of my wonderful trip to Van. Believe me, the stone has no value to anyone but me." I smiled wistfully, or so I thought.

"Enough of this nonsense!!!" He crashed his fist down on the desk.

Everyone froze.

"You have to give it back," he snarled. "I have orders from Ankara," shaking the telegram at me. He was miserable and angry. I'm sure he wasn't used to anyone talking back to him. "Mahmud! Do your duty," he commanded, pointing at me.

Mahmud started to approach me. I stuck the stone under my coat and shouted in Turkish, *"Makbuz! Makbuz! Makbuz istiyorum!"* (Receipt! Receipt! I want a receipt!)

"A what?" said Hikmet, flabbergasted.

"A receipt. I won't give it up unless I get a receipt."

"Allah! Allah! Allah!" said Hikmet, raising his arms to heaven. Then he fired off a series of orders. To Mahmud: "Go get Abdullah!" To the tea-boy: "Open that window! Bring me some tea! Where are my cigarettes?" I definitely needed a cigarette and wanted tea, but I didn't dare ask.

Abdullah turned out to be the regional director of education. Presumably it was one of his additional duties to see that no one walked off with the Roman bridge which spanned the Tigris River a few miles below Diyarbakir. He was thin, scholarly, stooped, and, at the moment, wringing his hands. Hikmet let loose a barrage of instructions, and Abdullah scurried out.

Tea came, cigarettes came, and Abdullah came with a little portable typewriter which he set on his knees and began attacking as Hikmet dictated. In less than two minutes Abdullah handed the document to Hikmet.

"Sign it!" he screamed at Abdullah. Then he waved it at me. "You! You sign it, too!" he said, a little less loudly.

Kerim quickly okayed it and I signed. I handed the stone to Abdullah like a sacrificial offering. He looked at it in terror and then at Hikmet in bewilderment. "Just get it out of here!" said Hikmet.

I tucked the receipt in my wallet (a gesture that I know irritated Hikmet) and shook his hand.

"We commend you to God," I said. But only God and I got the sarcasm because in Turkish *Allaha ismarladik* has no more significance than our "Goodbye."

Outside, I felt relieved but sad. I took Kerim back to his shop and drove furiously to the base, where I immediately made 20 thermofax copies of the receipt.

"What's that?" asked our male secretary.

"Never mind," I said. I didn't want anyone at the base to know my shame.

The next day the whole bit was overblown when I got a radio call from my brother in Ankara, our beloved General Manager.

"What's the big idea about stealing something out of the museum at Van??? Over!" It was a bad connection, as usual, but he didn't help by yelling at the top of his lungs. I could have heard him better if I had leaned out the window.

"I didn't steal anything out of the museum at Van. Over."

"Well, the Turkish police came to me and said *I* stole something from the museum at Van and I told them it must be my goddamned brother. Over."

"I didn't *steal* anything! I found it. A rock. Anyway, I gave it back to them. Yesterday. I got a receipt. Over."

"You'd better send me a full report, you understand? Over."

"Okay. Over."

"As if I didn't have enough problems. Jeez!" And he switched off without saying "over."

My full report was a copy of the receipt. Just to bedevil him I wrote on the bottom, "Have Sedat translate it for you—it explains everything."

I have only one regret. A few weeks before I had bought a piece of white marble in the square in front of the big mosque in Diyarbakir. On Fridays, all the junk sellers spread their wares out on a mat: old keys, batteries, pots and pans, gears, spark plugs, vinegar bottles, and once in a while something antique, or at least ancient. The marble piece that caught my eye was the size of an overturned soup bowl, sculptured with a lotus blossom motif. It had a hole in the middle and five holes around the sides. It was part of a fountain, probably Roman. I tried it under the kitchen faucet and it worked beautifully—sending out five delicate pencil-thin sprays. I paid five lira for it (50¢). Why hadn't I taken that piece to the police station?!! It meant nothing to me. Oh, it was charming, but when I looked at it I saw 50¢ and perhaps some hazy Roman villa with a fountain in the middle of a rose garden. My scrollwork stone would have reminded me forever of a wonderful wacky weekend in Van. No one would have known the difference—not Hikmet or Mahmud or Abdullah or Kerim. And it would have been so much more convincing as a stolen object. Oh well.

To this day, I have a feeling that my lovely scrollwork rock is being used as a doorstop in the office of the Regional Director of Education in Diyarbakir. Abdullah is probably dead (he was doddering at the time) and his replacement probably curses it every time he stubs his toe on it, wondering where on earth that stupid thing came from.

But *I*, to this *day*, have in my safe deposit box at the Bank of America a fading thermofax copy of a receipt which reads, if anyone at the Bank of America knows Turkish:

September 30, 1958

Received from the undersigned by the Regional Director of Education in the presence of the Chief of Police of the Province of Diyarbakir: one old Van stone.

signed: Mr. Abdullah
signed: Mr. John

The Icon

≈

I went to the base every Sunday morning to go to Mass, as well as to have an American breakfast of eggs, sausage, bacon, and hotcakes with Father Bloch. He always said Mass in the tiny chapel without an altar boy until I got up enough nerve to ask him if he would like me to serve. I hadn't served at Mass since I was 12 years old. "Of course!" he said, genuinely delighted. It all came back to me and I only tripped once.

One Sunday after Mass he said, "I can't have breakfast yet. I have to go to Diyarbakir to say Mass at the Chaldean church. Would you like to go with me?"

"Yes!" I had no idea there was a Catholic church in Diyarbakir. As we roared into town in Father Bloch's jeep, he told me about it. There were about 40 Chaldean families in Diyarbakir. They had no priest and hadn't had one in years. The nearest one was in Mardin on the Syrian border. That priest was old and came to Diyarbakir only once a month if he was feeling well enough. Father Bloch had heard about the church from a previous chaplain, ferreted it out, and told the families he would say Mass every Sunday.

We roared through the Harput Gate into the Old City and sped down twisting, winding, cobblestone streets, chickens flying (what possesses gentle priests to drive like cowboys when they get behind the wheel of a jeep?), and pulled up to a forbidding, nondescript building that simply looked like a wall. We knocked on a narrow wooden door which was opened shortly by a tall thin old man who looked like a stork.

"*Merhaba,* Yunus," said Father Bloch jovially. Yunus greeted Father Bloch warmly and welcomed me. His name meant Jonah. No wonder the whale spit him out—he was so scrawny.

The church was dark in spite of a few naked lightbulbs hanging from the ceiling and three clear-glass windows on one side looking onto an interior courtyard. It was absolutely square with no niches, nooks, or crannies. There were several interior pillars, two sections of wooden pews in the middle of the floor, no kneelers, some paintings on the walls, and two candelabras. At one end was a raised stage, about five feet off the floor. It had a wooden altar with tiers on it made of flat boards painted green. There were dusty artificial flowers in vases on the altar, and above, a festoon of Christmas tree ornaments covered with centuries of grime. The church was called *Aya Meryam* (St. Mary's). Father Bloch and I went backstage to get ready for Mass.

I could hardly pay attention to my duties at Mass because I was so busy sneaking glances at the congregation. There were about 20 people, mostly old. The women (who outnumbered the men, naturally) sat on one side, the men on the other. During the sermon, which was given by Yunus in Chaldean, I had an opportunity to observe the parishioners more closely. One woman was kneeling on a small rug (hers?), bowing to the floor and rocking back on her haunches, just like the Moslems. Another woman was lighting candles. She struck a match, lit a candle, blew it out, lit it again, blew it out, and lit it again before the match burned her fingers. Presumably, she got three souls into heaven on one match. She went on and on like that, getting droves and droves of Chaldeans through the pearly gates until all the candles were lit. Then she dropped one coin in the slot.

After Mass I began inspecting the church more carefully, particularly the paintings. I was admiring one of them when a young man came up behind me and said, "Hello, Mister John." It was Kerim who ran the paint store in town.

"Kerim! What are you doing here?"

"What are *you* doing here, Mister John?"

"I was helping Father Bloch say Mass."

"I was helping my father Yunus collect the money from the boxes."

I pointed out the painting I was admiring. It was about 16″ x 20″ and hanging so high on a pillar you could hardly see it in the gloom. But it was obviously Thomas putting his finger into Christ's side while the other apostles looked on sadly. And the charming thing was they all looked like Turks! I fell in love with it at first sight. I gently maneuvered the conversation around to the possibility of my buying it— "a donation to the church, of course"—a handsome donation, I implied. I pointed out that the picture was torn in one spot, trying to give the impression that it wasn't worth much and hating myself at the same time. But I was captivated, in the throes of temptation and lust. Kerim said he would ask his father and let me know the following week. He was aptly named: *Kerim* means "dear one."

I met Father Bloch at St. Mary's the following Sunday and could hardly concentrate on my duties during the Mass. He prompted me gently several times and afterward asked me if I was sick. Kerim was waiting for me under the pillar and came straight to the point.

"My father called the elders of the church together and they said no."

My heart sank, but in a way I was glad. My conscience felt better and I was glad there was someone left in this world who could resist the crass American dollar.

"Well, ask your father if I can take it home and clean it."

"*Hi, hi!*" said Yunus.

I took it back to my hotel room and studied it for days before tackling the job. I knew how to repair the canvas from all the scenery I had built for college dramatic productions. It was a triangular tear, about two inches in each direction, the easiest type to repair. Also, it was near the bottom of the picture in a relatively unnoticeable spot in the dark red folds of St. Peter's robes—or was that Jude the Obscure?

Kerim helped me find the materials, the same kind we had used in school: dried glue pellets (horses' hooves?) and linen canvas. I cooked the glue on a hotplate and cut a round piece of linen about four inches in diameter, and glued it on the back of the painting over the tear. Before the glue was dry, I used a stylus to arrange the threads on the front of the canvas so that they would line up properly. I used a dab of iodine to color the white ends of the threads. It looked good.

I waited several days before I attempted to clean the painting. I tried Ivory soap on a patch near the lower right-hand corner and it appeared to do no damage to the paint, so I gently cleaned the whole picture. It was a revelation. Fortunately, there appeared to be no varnish over the painting. Christ was holding a staff with a white banner, on top of which was a cross. The white was white, the haloes glistened, and the red-and-blue robes were warm and rich.

An inscription came to light at the bottom of the painting. It was written in Chaldean and Kerim's father translated it for me later: "This painting was donated to the Church of St. Mary's by Yakub Urfali in the Year of our Lord 1825." I had removed 133 years of dirt and candle grease, maybe more because there was no artist's signature nor a date when it was painted. It could have been much, much older.

I then took the painting to a shop and had a new frame made for it. They only had wild baroque gold frames, which I hated, but which I knew the elders of the church would love. Still, I was pleased with the results.

I couldn't bear to take it back the following Sunday, or the Sunday after that. Each week I kept expecting Kerim or his father to question me about it, but they never did. One day under the influence of temptation and booze, I ordered a bellboy to bring me a hammer and a nail and I hung it over my bed.

"*Choke guzel tablo*" (very beautiful painting) he said. "Did you do it?"

"Of course!" I said brazenly.

I got more nervous every time I went to Aya Meryam. Finally, when I convinced myself that they had forgotten all about it, I knew it was time to take it back, or give up my religion!

They were so pleased with it that I was embarrassed. They thanked me and shook my hand and inspected the frame so closely I wondered if they even noticed the picture. I suggested that it would look better hanging on one of the walls rather than on a pillar. They readily agreed and insisted on my professional opinion as to where. The best spot was already occupied—you could see it as you entered the door—and it suddenly occurred to me to take that painting home and clean it.

"*Hi, hi!*" they said.

Thus began my career as an art restorer. Each week I would take a new painting home after Mass, clean it, and bring it back the following week. I would hang them over my bed and enjoy them till Sunday. My bellboy wanted to know where my *atelye* (studio) was.

"In the old city."

"Where? I'd like to visit you, to watch."

"It's very difficult to find."

Each painting presented a new problem. On some the paint was flaking and even water would lift the paint. I flicked them lightly with a brush dipped in lighter fluid. Some were varnished, and some were shellacked, and some had layers of both. Soon I had all kinds of potions, remedies, and medications in my hotel room: lighter fluid, turpentine, benzene, fingernail polish remover, Windex, Mr. Clean, gin, vodka, *raki*. I was always very careful to try the weakest solution first, and if that didn't work, move on to something stronger. One painting gave me particular trouble— nothing seemed to work. One of my friends who visited me—my room was the Guggenheim Museum of Diyarbakir—said that he had read that the French use cognac to clean paintings. I rejected the idea of using Turkish firewater (*kanyak*) and bought a bottle of 75-year-old Napoleon brandy from the PX. I fortified myself and tried it on a small patch near the bottom. In front of my eyes, it turned the surface milky. I was furious! I abandoned all efforts to do anything at all with that painting except to remove the grime. I didn't, however, abandon the cognac.

One painting was a charming triptych, except that one panel was missing, so it was a diptych. It was painted on wood. The center panel was about two feet high, shaped like a Gothic window, depicting the Virgin and Child. The background was a velvety olive green. The Virgin's robe was blue, trimmed in gold, the Child was in white with a gold cord around His waist, and each had a fragile gold filigree halo. The painting was so delicate I used only Ivory Snow suds on it.

One large painting (4' x 6') made me laugh, but I took such a fancy to it that I held it over for a second week by popular demand. It was St. John baptizing Jesus. Jesus looked quite traditional with long brown hair and a loose white robe. But John was naked except for a bright red silk cloth wrapped around his loins and a magnificent red silk turban on his head. He was clean-shaven except for a long black pencil-thin mustache that stuck out over both sides of his cheeks, and looked like it had been waxed. Several people offered to buy it from me.

It was a joy going to church every Sunday—I didn't mean that the way it sounded—it was an *extra* joy.

One Sunday, just before Christmas, Kerim told me that the elders of the church had had a meeting and decided that I could have one of two icons that were hanging side by side in the back of the church. I had seen them many times, but they were both in excellent condition and didn't need my ministrations right away, so I was saving them for last—for dessert.

"I can have one of these?" I said incredulously.

"Yes," said Kerim beaming.

His father was standing beside him, not understanding a single word of the English we were speaking, but understanding only too well the situation because he kept gesturing to the icons, urging me to take one, quickly, as if the elders might change their mind. They were small (9" x 12") paintings on canvas over a slab of wood. One was Jesus healing the sick and the other was Lazarus being raised from the dead. I chose Lazarus.

I choked up as I thanked them and took the painting home. It shows Lazarus rising up out of his coffin like a ghost, swathed in white except for his face. A little boy is holding the wooden lid of the coffin. Lazarus's sisters are groveling on the ground, imploring Jesus. Jesus is standing in front of 10 apostles (who's missing?), looking like a deputation that has just arrived on the scene. His right hand is outstretched in blessing; in his left hand is a rolled-up scroll (?). Jesus is dressed no differently from his apostles, but all are wearing gorgeous brocades of dark red, green, and gold. Every figure in the picture has a wide gold halo, like a dinner plate: Jesus, the apostles, Lazarus, his sisters—all except the little boy (the poor thing).

I decided to do nothing to this painting except wipe it off with a damp cloth. It wasn't that I didn't trust myself as an art restorer (I didn't), but it was in such excellent condition it needed nothing. I hung it over my bed.

It's still over my bed. I carried it with me every time I moved and the first thing to go up on the walls was the icon—over my bed.

Thirty Below Zero

≈

In December the snows arrived along with a multi-addressee TWX[6] from our central office:

"MSG CO-12 -16-33
ADANA, TUSLOG DETACHMENT 10
ANKARA, TUSLOG DETACHMENT 30
DIYARBAKIR, TUSLOG DETACHMENT 8
ISTANBUL, TUSLOG DETACHMENT 28
IZMIR, TUSLOG DETACHMENT 20
KARAMURSEL TUSLOG DETACHMENT 3
SAMSUN, TUSLOG DETACHMENT 3-1
SINOP, TUSLOG DETACHMENT 4
TRABZON, TUSLOG DETACHMENT 3-2

"TAKE NEWLY ACQUIRED COMPANY VEHICLE TO NEAREST CUSTOMS OFFICE AND REGISTER IT IN OUR COMPANY'S NAME. ASAP. REPORT WHEN MISSION ACCOMPLISHED."

Our newly acquired vehicle was a clunker which we had bought from the previous contractor. It was a 1956 Plymouth station wagon that had over 100,000 miles on it, innumerable dents, and several coats of revolting brown paint in various shades. Still, it ran. I showed the TWX to Abdul. He

---

6. TWX = Teletypewriter Exchange Service, or Telex. Telex was a major method of sending written messages electronically after World War II. Its use declined as the fax machine grew in popularity in the 1980s.

inquired at government offices in Diyarbakir and was told that Erzurum was the nearest custom-house.

"Erzurum!" I exclaimed. "That's 450 miles away! Up in the mountains! Nowhere near any border!"

"It's the main custom-house on the East-West route from Iran."

"But what about Mardin? That's only 60 miles away—on the Syrian border."

"Oh, sir, that's only a village. They only handle smugglers."

"*Olur,* Erzurum, so be it. We'll leave Saturday afternoon." I got out my maps and *Blue Guide.* "We can stay overnight in Elazig at the Murat Palas—they have 26 rooms. Telephone 47—call now for reservations."

"Oh, sir, they don't know what reservations are."

"Call!"

"Yes, sir," he said just to humor me.

"Then we can drive to Erzurum on Sunday, have a good night's sleep, conduct our business early Monday morning, and be back here Monday night or Tuesday at the latest. Get going!"

"Yes, sir," said Abdul, rolling his eyes.

Our Site Manager was against the idea—the weather was too uncertain. But I convinced him that it wouldn't get any better, and an order from the central office was an order. As Administrative Supervisor it was one of my jobs to handle customs, and I was trying to make a good impression.

"A set of chains and a bottle of Johnnie Walker will get us through," I said. "We'll only miss one day of work."

We got started much later than I had planned. Little administrative crises kept popping up—like the arrival of a truckload of bricks, which the driver wouldn't unload until he was paid. It was four o'clock when we left Diyarbakir in a light flurry of snow. By five it was a storm. By six we put on the chains. By seven we had our first flat tire. We reached Ergani at eight and had dinner while the tire was being repaired. By that time we had travelled exactly 40 miles in four hours, but at least it had stopped snowing.

Ten miles outside of Ergani we had our second flat tire. I decided to go back to Ergani to have it repaired rather than go on to Elazig without a spare. By ten o'clock we had located the owner of the service station and dragged him out of bed to fix the tire. By midnight we came to a fork in the road with a sign reading: Elazig 60 km straight ahead, Maden 2 km left.

"We're going to Maden," I said as I pulled off the highway and started up a narrow road on the side of a mountain.

"But there won't be a hotel in Maden," said Abdul. "It's only a village."

"We'll wake up the village shopkeeper and sleep at his house on the floor."

Maden was the center of the copper mining district. The name *Maden* means "metal." There were steep mountains all around us, and the road got narrower and more precarious, wide enough for only one car. I was starting to get apprehensive about having to back down this mountain if the road got any narrower, when a black building loomed out of the snow.

"Look!" I said triumphantly. There was a sign on the building: Maden Palas.

The Maden Palas was made of wood, jutting out over the street like an Alpine chalet, but very black and weatherbeaten. We parked the car under it and climbed the outside steps to the lobby, a room about six feet square with a lantern, two chairs, and a pot-bellied stove—stone cold.

We called and yodeled, and finally a grizzled old man appeared rubbing his eyes. I'm sure he thought he was seeing ghosts—Abdul in his navy blue overcoat, and me in my fleece-lined trenchcoat. The old man said all four rooms were empty, but he wouldn't put us in the front room which projected out over the street on stilts—that room was too cold. Instead he led us to the back room, which he assured us was much warmer.

It had two beds with thick comforters, one night table with a candle, and nothing else. Three walls were bare wood.

The fourth was the mountain! Bare rock! I could see veins running through it and wondered if they were copper.

The old man lit the candle and left. The temperature in the room was probably a cozy 10 below zero. I opened my overnight bag and took a healthy swig of Johnnie Walker right out of the bottle. I offered some to Abdul, but he refused—a strict Moslem.

"You may need it—it's antifreeze."[7]

He clicked his tongue. He stood in the middle of the room hugging himself in his overcoat. He seemed to be trying to disassociate himself from my choice of a hotel.

After a few more swigs I decided to take the plunge. I ripped off my trenchcoat, threw it on the bed, ripped off my jacket, shirt, pants, shoes and socks, and leaped under the comforter moaning, "Allah save me, save me," as I shivered waiting for my body heat and alcohol fumes to warm the bed.

Abdul still didn't seem to know what to do. Finally he sat down and slowly removed his shoes, placing them neatly under his bed. Then he leaned over, blew out the candle, and slipped under the comforter fully dressed, overcoat and all! Why hadn't I thought of that? Oh, the power of childhood training when Mother always said, "Now you must get undressed, dear, and go to bed."

The next morning (yes, we survived) we were served breakfast of tea, bread, and honey around the pot-bellied stove, which was roaring cheerily. After a second glass of tea, we took our leave. I insisted on picking up the tab for our room and breakfast since this was my idea. It was three lira, about 30¢, for both of us!

We started off for Elazig, 40 miles away. It took us three hours to get there, up and down mountains, and the road was snowy and slick, even with chains. We had lunch in Elazig, then started off for Erzurum, 150 miles to the north.

We drove all afternoon and into the evening, up one mountain and down another. In between there were stretches of bare asphalt, and I had to take the chains off. I was

---

7. Spirits give the feeling of warmth but in fact lower the body temperature.

afraid they'd break, and also we could make better time. Each mountain we came to had that damn sign: *Zinjir Lazim* (Chains Necessary). And each time I would try to get up without them, but always failed. I began to hate the man who had invented these diabolical devices and took no satisfaction in thinking that at that very moment he was probably ice-skating in heaven.

On the last mountain, I got all the way to the top *without chains!* It was a triumph of art, skill, dexterity, and cunning, and I was shamelessly proud of myself. And *then* we started down the other side! The road curved sharply to the left. I gently turned the steering wheel to the left, but the car kept going straight, sliding down the snow-slick highway. I panicked and jammed on the brakes, which locked. I spun the steering wheel all the way to the left but the old miserable Plymouth kept going straight ahead. It went off the highway and over the shoulder and came to an abrupt stop in a 10-foot wall of snow. Snow buried the windshield and half the car. I turned off the ignition and pulled on the emergency brake, but the car wasn't going anywhere. I was able to force the door open just wide enough to slither out. Abdul had a wall of snow on his side and had to get out on mine. We struggled up to the rear of the car and surveyed the situation. We were miles from nowhere, 10,000 feet high in the Pontus Mountains of northeastern Turkey, it was ten o'clock at night, and the temperature was 30 below zero.

Abdul and I then proceeded to do everything wrong, according to any book on survival. I jacked up the rear of the station wagon and put on the chains while Abdul helplessly tried to help. He knew nothing about cars or driving in snow—he didn't even know how to drive. Since I had spent half of my life in snow country in upstate New York, I took charge of the rescue operation. I lowered the car, removed the jack, and instructed Abdul to push as I got into the car and put it in reverse. I accelerated slowly at first but the car didn't move an inch. Then I gunned it madly. The rear of the car simply sank deeper into the snow. Then smoke started choking Abdul as the wheels spun and rubber burned. We still hadn't moved an inch backward but we had buried the rear end of the car up to the axle in snow. It was hopeless.

I could think of nothing else to do but get into the car and wait for a passing car, though we hadn't seen one in the last two hours. Our hands were frozen, our shoes were full of snow, our socks were soaking. I started the motor to get the heater working. We lowered the front windows about two inches—the only thing we did right. The heater put out such meager heat that I could hardly feel the difference. And then we made a pact. Abdul would sleep for one hour while I watched for a car, then I would sleep. The sleeping one was allowed the luxury of putting his wet stockinged feet under the butt of the wide-awake one.

As I sat there on Abdul's bony feet, I cursed myself for not thinking to put the chains on before we started down. But who would have thought of such a thing? Sir Edmund Hillary? St. John the Divine? At 11:30 I woke Abdul, though I don't believe he really slept. We switched feet, but his thin little bottom was almost as cold as my feet.

I tried desperately to sleep but couldn't. I kept thinking I ought to review my past life and sort out the good from the bad, but I was too cold and wet and miserable.

I must have fallen off because at 1:05 Abdul shook me violently and I woke to see the glare of headlights in the rearview mirror. Abdul jumped out and ran into the middle of the highway, waving wildly. I switched on the lights and jumped out too—in my stocking feet. The car came to a stop. In the glare of its blinding headlights I couldn't see what it was. Finally my eyes adjusted and I saw it was an enormous highway truck, painted bright orange, with a snowplow on the front. The wheels were bigger than I was! Allah be praised!

While Abdul spoke to the driver I ran back to the car to put on my shoes. I was confused at the length of the discussion between them until Abdul came to me and said sharply in English, "Give me 50 lira!"

He rarely spoke English and never in that tone of voice. I fumbled through my wallet and fished out a wet 50-lira note. He gave it to the man and they hooked a steel cable to the bumper. I put the Plymouth in reverse to assist in getting out, but it was totally unnecessary. The truck pulled out the Plymouth as easily and smoothly as a pair of tweezers removing a splinter.

I got out to thank the guy, but Abdul pushed me aside as the truck roared down the mountain.

"That was a godsend," I said as I started creeping down the mountain, even with the chains on.

"Pich!" said Abdul under his breath.

"What did you say?"

"Pich! Bastard!"

"Who?"

"That driver."

"Why?"

"He didn't want to pull us out. He said he had no tow rope."

"But he did! You saw that—a steel cable, no less."

"I know. That's when I offered him 50 lira. And he took it, the bastard!" Abdul went on muttering all the Turkish swear words in the book, which I barely knew.

"What would we have done if he had refused to pull us out?"

"I wasn't worried," Abdul said as he reached into an inside pocket and drew out a small revolver.

"My God! Is that thing loaded?"

"Naturally."

"What on earth did you bring a gun for?"

"There are many wolves in these mountains, Mister John. They can be very dangerous in wintertime."

We reached Erzurum at two o'clock in the morning—we had only been 10 miles away. We stopped at the Temelli Palas (45 rooms) with hot water heating. I told Abdul to tell the sleepy bellboy to turn on the radiators.

"They're on!" said the bellboy.

I didn't believe him—the room was frigid and I could

see my breath. I walked over and put my hand on one of the radiators and got a nasty burn. Abdul and I slept in our overcoats that night.

The next morning we argued with Customs officials for three hours, but they flatly refused to have anything to do with the transfer of our vehicle. They insisted the transfer had to be accomplished in Ankara, where the vehicle was originally registered. I demanded to see the Governor, but this too was refused. I abandoned my principles long enough to suggest to Abdul, "50 lira? 500? Salems? Half a bottle of Johnnie Walker?" But Abdul knew it was hopeless.

When we got back to Diyarbakir two days later, there was a TWX waiting for us:

"DISREGARD MESSAGE CO-12-16-33.
ALL TRANSFERS OF COMPANY VEHICLES WILL BE ACCOMPLISHED IN ANKARA.
NO FURTHER ACTION REQUIRED."

It was from my favorite brother. I didn't have the nerve to send back this message to him: "Thanks a lot."

Christmas in Chaldea

≈

I WAS STILL living in the Turistik Palas Otel when Christmas came, but I was determined to have a Christmas tree in my tiny room. Nobody was going to feel sorry for me, by God!

In the outdoor garden restaurant (which was unused in winter) I had previously admired a six-foot blue spruce which looked as if it had come straight from Colorado. It was in a wooden pot, so I asked the manager if I could have the tree hauled up to my room. He thought I was mad, naturally, but threw up his hands and said, *"Buyurun!"* That meant "help yourself" but it implied that I had already taken over his whole hotel and his staff, so why not take a tree from his garden, too! "Will you give it back?"

"Of course! After Baby Jesus' birthday, I promise."

I rounded up my work crew—the doorman and all the bellboys (two of them). I first asked for a hose to wash off the tree.

Blank expressions.

"Su! Su!" I screamed. (Water! Water!)

One of the bellboys ran inside and came out carrying a glass and a bottle of spring water. I poured the water over the tree and asked for more. They all ran in and came out handing me bottle after bottle of spring water which they had previously filled up from the tap in the basement and capped with aluminum foil seals. I poured each bottle over the tree, sprinkling and scattering like a bishop from Dubuque.

Then I turned to them and started barking orders like a drill sergeant. (My Turkish improved by leaps and bounds every time I got excited.)

"Lift!" They did.

"Follow me!" They did. The desk clerk, several cooks from the kitchen, and a handful of guests were very impressed with our procession.

"Up the stairs!" They went up.

"Oh God, don't put it down in the middle of these steps, we've got three more flights!"

I thought about unstrapping my belt and lashing them, but they juggled it onto their shoulders and almost raced past me.

"Easy! Careful! Good! Now, down the hall! In here! Set it down! There, in the corner! Aaaaaah! Beautiful!"

I greased their out-stretched palms, but they wouldn't leave. They were all very excited about the project and wanted to know what was next.

"Toz ol!" I barked. It meant literally "become dust," and they did.

The next day I went to the PX to buy ornaments which I had seen the week before. I bought two boxes of six each—their entire supply! Wiped them out! Orhan, the PX manager, was delighted since no one on the base wanted them, and he was afraid he'd be stuck with them.

Knowing that 12 ornaments do not a Christmas tree make, I bought a variety of cigarettes, chewing gum, and candy bars and went home to trim my tree the night before Christmas.

Kerim, from the Chaldean church, helped me.

"Why do you do this?" he asked as we hung the ornaments, cigarettes, chewing gum, and candy bars on the tree (with U.S. government paper clips for hangers). "Does it have something to do with our Catholic religion—the birth of *Jesu?*"

"Well, no."

"I haven't read in my Bible about a tree. I know about the three very intelligent men who came from the East."

"Well, a Christmas tree is just a way we have of celebrating the birth of Christ in our homes. It's not religious, it's just fun."

As we were tying on the Pall Malls, Salems, Camels, Lucky Strikes, Hershey Bars, Baby Ruths, Snickers, Juicy Fruit, and DoubleMint, Kerim said that an American sergeant had given the Chaldean church several boxes of ornaments two years before. "We didn't know what their purpose was, so we strung them all across the top of the altar at the church—did you notice?"

"Yes, I noticed." They looked cheap and vulgar on the altar and were covered with dust, but I didn't say anything more.

When we finished trimming the tree, it looked as beautiful to me as any tree I had ever trimmed at home.

I got out my Polaroid camera and had Kerim take pictures of me under the tree with all the Christmas presents, which had arrived weeks before. My beloved baby sister had sent me a Steuben air-twist cocktail glass because I told her I was collecting a set of them and I only had two. I filled the glass with real gin and put a real olive in it. Kerim took several pictures of me raising my martini glass in a toast with a seraphic smile on my face, under the most beautiful Christmas tree in the whole Moslem world.

The next morning I zipped down to the Chaldean church to serve Mass for Father Bloch on Christmas morning. Kerim was waiting for me outside the church. I knew from the glint in his eyes that something was up. He beckoned me into the church and there, right in the middle of the altar where Father Bloch was to do most of his praying, was a scrawny Christmas "tree"—three fir branches lashed together. The tree was decorated with the ornaments from the sergeant plus Yeni Harman (new blend) Turkish cigarettes and little bags of netting with Jordan almonds and Turkish Delight in them.

I laughed. Oh, how I laughed!

"Is something wrong, Mister John?"

"No, no, it's beautiful—beautiful!"

Father Bloch was aghast when he saw it, but I persuaded him to work his way around the tree as he said Mass. He did, but it was all I could do to keep from giggling out loud during the service.

When I got back to the hotel, my room was already made up. A few minutes later there was a tap on my door. It was the maid, and she was beaming at me and covering her face and giggling about "the tree, the tree." I invited her in and she stared at the tree in astonishment, holding her cheeks, as I explained in my best Turkish the symbolism of it all.

"Bir daka, bir daka!" (One moment, one moment) she said, patting my belly, and rushed out of the room.

One moment later she was back again with her girl friend, another wizened crone. Their eyes sparkled like little girls as they jibber-jabbered in hushed tones as if they were in a cathedral. Magnanimously, I told them it was our custom that each person could take something off the tree. I kept wishing the tree had gingerbread men, candy canes, and popcorn balls, instead of Chesterfields, Tootsie Rolls, and Dentyne.

"Are you *sure?*" they asked, as if I were feeble-minded.

"Of course! *Buyurun!* Help yourselves!"

They each rushed to the tree, wrenched off an ornament, and held it up to the light to watch it twirl and sparkle.

I had an instinctive urge to grab the ornaments out of their hands—"That's not what I meant!"—but I quickly realized the glittering balls were so much more exciting to them than a dumb package of cigarettes. They thanked me and thanked me—I gave them a tight-lipped smile—and they kissed my hand and pressed it to their forehead as they bowed out of the room backward with their sparklers.

I was pouring myself a little nip in my Steuben stemware to calm my nerves when there was another knock on the door. It was the two bellboys who had carried the tree up, grinning from ear to ear, knowing full well that I knew why they were there.

"Come in! Come in! Help yourselves!" I said stoically.

They helped themselves not only to an ornament but a package of Salems, too.

Then came the desk clerk, the laundry boy, two waiters,

the chef, the doorman, the manager, and two strangers who were apparently guests in the hotel. In less than an hour I was wiped out. The tree was bare except for a Juicy Fruit or two. But it was a wonderful, if short, Christmas season, and I think of it every time I see a Christmas tree or a package of Lucky Strikes or a Tootsie Roll.

My beloved baby sister *loved* the Polaroid picture of me under my Turkish Christmas tree. Mother wrote back, "You poor thing!"

That Rascal Ibrahim

≈

IN THE DEAD OF WINTER, I moved into my new apartment. The building was four floors of still-wet concrete—and I was the first tenant. Each apartment covered an entire floor. I chose the third floor. I bought a pot bellied stove, had it installed between the dining room and living room, and stoked it with wood—morning, noon, and night. All of my waking hours were spent feeding that stove—when I wasn't at work—and still I was cold. I took to wearing an electric blanket with a long extension cord. I could go from the living room to the dining room to the kitchen and got pretty good at wielding the cord behind me like an old duchess flicking her train. I had to unplug to go to the bathroom.

All my social life revolved about the stove. Meals were eaten, guests were entertained, magazines were read, and letters home were written around that stove.

One night I offered a visiting Turk a Pall Mall. He took it and offered me a Yeni Harman cigarette. I took it and prayed I wouldn't start coughing. He laid the Pall Mall on the edge of the stove and started rolling it over and over.

"What are you doing?" I said, horrified.

"I'm drying it out. Your cigarettes are too wet."

"But we put cellophane on the package just to keep them moist!"

"And we put cellophane on ours just to keep them dry."

"*Touché.*"

"What?"

"Never mind."

Mercifully, spring came. Not a warm spring, but at least I could discard the electric blanket. It was time to spruce up the apartment. Actually, I had put a lot of work into it and I was very pleased with my effort. My apartment was modern, stark, and striking. The walls were chalk white, the furniture was black, and the draperies were an orange-and-black hounds-tooth corduroy. The drapes covered two complete walls, floor-to-ceiling. The two sofas, made to my own specifications (I simply ran a tape measure up the back of my leg and under my hams), were black wood, upholstered with a black-and-white plaid corduroy. I had a round coffee table, six feet in diameter, made of black wood. I was in the process of covering the top with half-inch glass tiles in every imaginable shade of blue and green to give it a turquoise look. My guests would help me glue down the tiles with Dupont cement. I winced as I watched one Turk make a two-foot patch of pea green. He was so proud of having matched the color, I didn't have the heart to say anything. I pried them up as soon as he left.

The floor was parquet, the only one in Diyarbakir, and I was the envy of all my friends who had terrazzo floors. I scattered the floor with goatskin rugs, white with black-and-brown designs. I had black shelves made for my stereo and records. The dining room, which opened onto the living room, had a large archway (I had removed four frosted-glass doors). The dining table was round, black, and poker-sized, with black captain's chairs. I decorated the walls with copper trays, old keys, and Turkish prayer rugs.

Copper was very cheap in Diyarbakir because there were copper mines nearby. *Diyarbakir* means "Land of Copper." I had copper ashtrays, vases, pitchers, and even a cauldron, which I stacked with wood.

Turkish rugs were cheap and of excellent quality. My "family" prayer rug was a yard wide and three yards long. It had seven different colored panels, each in the shape of a *Mihrab*. The *Mihrab* is the niche in the mosque toward which all Moslems pray—assuring them that they are facing Mecca. Since my prayer rug had seven *Mihrabs,* I always thought of it as a father-mother-five-kids rug, though they'd have to squeeze in rather tightly.

Narcissus came to visit me one day. In the course of his roaming around the apartment on an inspection tour, he stopped in front of the prayer rug and began questioning me about it. I didn't think he was complimenting me on it, but I said *"Choke guzel"* anyway. Was he asking the price? "900 lira," I said. Finally he waved me aside, disgusted at my limited Turkish. He took off his jacket, laid it on the floor, and knelt down to pray. I immediately realized he had been asking if it had been walked on. Moslems must pray on something that has never been stepped on with shoe leather.

I withdrew to the sofa and watched him in fascination, trying to get the gist of the ritual. He bent all the way to the floor, touching his forehead, then sat back on his haunches, his head thrown back, eyes closed, lips moving. Then back to the floor, a pattern he repeated three times. Ella Fitzgerald was singing Cole Porter on the phonograph, but Narcissus didn't seem to mind. Once, while his forehead was on the floor, he opened his eyes and turned to see if I was watching. I was staring. He winked at me, which broke the spell, and went back to his prayers.

When he was finished, he put on his coat, smoked a cigarette, and drank a scotch. He also casually strolled to the phone and made a long-distance call to Ankara without even asking permission. Oh, well, he was, after all, a blood relative.

Both the Turks and the Americans were bowled over by the striking modernity of my apartment, here on the edges of Kurdistan. One of the best touches was the lamps, all made from differently shaped wicker baskets, with clear glass bulbs inside. At night, the shadows they threw on the walls and ceiling were shamefully theatrical.

Only one thing was missing—plants! Greenery!

Diyarbakir had no florists and no nurseries. People started everything from seeds saved year after year, or from cuttings they took from their neighbors' yards by moonlight. But I had seen a large oleander bush in a clay pot, just inside the entrance of the Regional Headquarters of the Democratic Party when I went to a ball with Dr. Tosun and Cadillac one night. It would look nice in my apartment, and I began deciding where I would place it.

One Saturday morning, I explained the proposition to my houseboy, Shaban. He was not exactly the brightest person in the world—an example, perhaps, of a person growing to be like his name. To the Turks, anyone named *Shaban* was stupid, like our Mortimer Snerd. The word was actually Arabic, one of the three holy months of the Moslem calendar: Shaban, Muharram, and Ramadan.

"Come on, let's go and buy it. I'll pay 100 lira."

"Oh, sir, that's too much."

"Okay, you do the bargaining. But don't fail! I must have that plant."

The headquarters was closed and Shaban was delighted. He took a dim view of the whole project, mostly because it was such a bizarre thing to do and he might be exposed to ridicule, a commodity he could well do without. I banged on the front door and rattled hell out of it while Shaban tried to look invisible. I finally managed to stir up the *kapiji*, the building's resident janitor. Shaban insisted on speaking to the *Mudur*, the director, and after a lot of haranguing, the *kapiji* let us in and said, "Wait here." We were standing right next to my coveted oleander. It was covered with dust.

The manager appeared. He had bushy eyebrows, piercing black eyes, a bristling mustache, and a shiny bald pate. He also barked.

"Yes! What is it?"

Shaban bowed and expressed his hope that the *Mudur* was in good health, and also his family and relatives.

"Yes, yes! What do you want?"

Shaban squirmed and gulped and said, "This gentleman would like to buy this tree." He pointed to the oleander. The Turks have no word for plant or bush.[8]

The *Mudur* looked at the tree as if he had never seen

---

8. In fact oleander can be described as either plant (*bitki*) or tree (*ağaç*).

it before, then looked at me in astonishment. I smiled—a mistake.

"This *zikkim?*" *Zikkim* means poison tree in Turkish.

"Yes," said Shaban apologetically. *My master is mad,* he might as well have added.

"How much?" said the *Mudur* menacingly.

"Fifty lira!" said Shaban firmly. He was happy that the bout had begun.

"Fifty lira?!" screamed the *Mudur*, clutching his heart. "I'm bankrupt!" He turned his back to Shaban and staggered to a corner of the vestibule, resting his head in the angle of the walls.

Shaban was impassive.

The *Mudur* slowly pulled himself together and came back to the center of the ring. He eyed Shaban for a second, then spat out *"Yuz elli!"* (150)

Shaban threw up his hands, spun around, and went to his corner calling on Allah to save him.

I stood in the ring feeling very stupid.

With great visible effort, Shaban composed himself and came back to the middle of the ring. *"Yetmish besh!"* (75) he said with a washing-of-the-hands finality.

The *Mudur* had what seemed to be the start of an epileptic seizure. He rolled his eyes and his head fell back on his neck. Mouth open, he rocked dizzily back and forth on his heels. Suddenly he stiffened and said, like the crack of a bullet, *"Yuz!"* (100)

"Sold!" I shouted, handing the *Mudur* the sweaty 100-lira note I had in the palm of my hand all the time. Shaban glared at me and grabbed the oleander pot so he could hide his face in shame. The *Mudur* clapped me on the back as if I were the winner of the match. He laughed and pumped my hand and said I was welcome anytime at the Regional Democratic Headquarters.

Shaban sulked all the way home. "I could have got it for 90." But I was happy. My oleander was beautiful. I washed the leaves, watered it, and placed it in the archway between the dining and living rooms, enhancing both. Then I sat down with some sipping scotch to enjoy it.

My Turkish friends were amazed at it. They had never seen so large a plant *inside* a house. They all warned me it was poisonous. "I know. I didn't really plan to eat the leaves."

"How much did you pay for that?"

The Turks always ask the price of everything (and the value of nothing, as Oscar Wilde used to say). I tried to avoid answering because they always said I paid too much and gave me a lecture about how the rich Americans were spoiling everything for the poor Turks. But I had learned if you drove too hard a bargain with the Turks, they got you in the end. One American lady who loved to go shopping in the bazaar—to get pinched on the fanny—bought a copper pot for 35 lira, identical to the one I had paid 50 lira for. Oh, how she gloated. The next time I saw the coppersmith, I tore into him. He remembered her well and told me hers weighed one kilo less than mine. He simply used thinner-gauge metal.

"How much did you pay for that *zikkim?*"

"*Yuz,*" I said stony-faced.

"100 lira!!? I could get you two for that price!"

"Do it!" I said, whipping out my wallet and thrusting a 100-lira note at him.

He glared at me (you smartass), then recovered his dignity and took the money. A week later he came back with a single pot of oleander. It was much smaller than the one I had bought, and scrawny.

"It was all I could get for 100 lira," he said sheepishly. "I bought it from a neighbor lady; her husband died last week."

"But it's white!" I said, to ease his embarrassment. "White *zikkims* are very rare. They're usually red."

He perked up and began to feel proud of himself.

"Would you like a scotch?" I asked.

"No. I'll have whiskey."

And then that rascal Ibrahim came. It was the Saturday before Easter. The doorbell rang and I opened the door. There was this man: muddy old shoes, no socks, baggy black trousers, and black shirt. He was unshaven, grinning with all front teeth missing, fierce mustache, yellow eyes, and black hair matted with dust and sweat.

"*Chichek,* mister?" he said, grinning ingratiatingly. He was holding three small plants in pots. They were hardly *chicheks* (flowers); they looked more like herbs: small and puny and rather pathetic, but they *were* green. I pretended not to be interested and said scornfully, "How much?"

He quickly eyed me up and down, trying to decide how much I was worth. "One lira!" he said bravely.

"For all three?"

"No, no!" he screamed, fearful that he had made a bargain. "One lira for each! Three lira for all three."

I pulled out my wallet and fished out a 2½ lira note. *"Iki buchuk* (25¢) is all I'll give you," I said.

He snatched the bill out of my hand and practically threw the pots into my arms. I closed the door and brightened up. Each of them had a smell, especially when I crushed the leaves. The Turks love any plant with a smell, even marigolds and geraniums. It was not unusual to see a fierce, dark, bandit type with a rifle slung over his shoulder walking down a road smelling a rose. I washed the leaves, watered them, and put one on the dining table, one under the lamp on the end table between the L-shaped sofas, and one on the unfinished coffee table.

A few hours later the doorbell rang again. I opened the door and reeled backward. There were plants all the way up and down the staircase. Solid! You couldn't walk! And in the middle of it all stood Ibrahim, beaming and covered with mud.

"Chichek, mister?"

I was overwhelmed. There must have been 50 plants. I realized I mustn't show too much emotion.

"Well, maybe," I said. I stepped gingerly out into the hall and started selecting. Some were hopeless, but I ended up taking 30 of them. Ibrahim helped me carry them into the apartment and madly tried to arrange them, in corners, on the windowsills, on tables and shelves. It was all I could do to restrain him. I gave him 30 lira.

"Anything else, Mister John?" We had learned each other's names during the interior-decorating session.

Well, I was feeling heady. It was such a lovely spring day, and Easter was coming, so I said, "Can you bring me some tulips?"

"What?"

"*Laleh.*"

"Ah, *laleh!* Hi, hi, Mister John." He saluted and dashed out the door.

One hour later he arrived with a potted tulip—a lovely Red Emperor. It was glorious.

"Perfect," I said. "How much?"

"For you, Mister John, five lira," he said, bowing almost to the ground to indicate he was my slave forever.

I gave him the money then noticed that the tulip looked a little sick. Its head was drooping, and its neck was tied to a stick stuck in the pot. "Is this tulip all right?"

"Oh yes, Mister John!" Then he lapsed into a furious explanation, half in Turkish, half in Kurdish, which I couldn't understand but took to mean he had dug it up from his garden (did he have a nursery?) and potted it, and naturally the shock of transplant affected it. "You understand, Mister John, tomorrow it will stand up just like you know what!" He winked and made a gesture with his finger. We parted on the best of terms.

The next day the tulip was limper. I watered it like mad.

The third day it expired.

I grieved over it for a moment, then pulled it out of the pot. There was no bulb! It was just a cut-off flower, jammed into a pot of dirt. I fumed for days afterward, waiting for Ibrahim to visit again so that I could strangle him with the piece of string he had strung up my poor Red Emperor with. But he didn't show.

I had forgotten about him until he appeared several weeks later. "You!" I shouted. "You have no face! How dare you come back here!"

"Please, Mister John, let me explain—"

"No, no! No explanations! Deception! That's what it is, nothing but deception!" I really let him have it. When I got angry my Turkish was majestical. Not swear words and gutter language, but full of righteous indignation and self-pity, overflowing with words like "ingratitude" and "retribution." I called on Allah to be my witness and avenger.

"Please, Mister John, just listen to me."

Since I had exhausted my vocabulary of martyr language, I calmed down, giving the impression of a rational human being willing to listen to the other side of the story.

"Well?"

"Mister John, would you like to buy a stone lion?" He gave me an angelically wicked toothless smile. I was deflated, defused.

"A stone lion?"

"Yes, Mister John, a beautiful stone lion. Very cheap."

Hmm. I knew that Diyarbakir abounded in stone artifacts—could Ibrahim know of one I could buy?

"How much?"

"*Yuz.*"

Hmm. Same price as my oleander. I could certainly afford that. "Okay, let's go see this stone lion."

"Oh no, Mister John, *olmaz! olmaz!*" (it must not be). *Olmaz* was the opposite of *olur*.

"Why not?"

"The family is very poor, very modest. It would be *ayip* (shameful) of you to go to their house and see them in all their abject poverty, you a stranger, a rich American."

"Yeah, yeah." Still, he did have a point, and he stuck it in again.

"*Ayip! Ayip!*" (shame, shame)

"Well, okay."

"You give me the money and I will buy it for you. They are very good friends of mine—but poor."

He folded his hands on his breast and lowered his head. What a sucker I am. Still, it was worth a chance. After all, it was only 10 dollars. He took my 100-lira note humbly, folded it solemnly, and tucked it in his pocket as if it were a sacred trust. He patted it to show me how secure it was. Then he brightened up.

"Mister John, have you seen the Diyarbakir wall?"
"Of course, many times."
"From the *outside?*"
"No, from the inside. I've driven around the inside of the wall many times. I even took my driver's test there."
"No, no, Mister John. You must see it from the *outside!* It is truly extraordinary! Pictures! Writing! Animals! You must come with me, Mister John, now!" He started tugging me. "We will walk all around the *outside* of the wall—it's the only way to see it! Trust me! You won't regret it!"
"Okay, okay. Just let me get my camera."
So without much enthusiasm, but with two packs of film and my Polaroid, I started on the excursion with that rascal Ibrahim.
It turned out to be everything he claimed, and more. The old city of Diyarbakir is built on a bluff overlooking the Tigris River. It is completely surrounded by a wall 30 feet thick, 60 feet high, and five miles round. Among ancient walls in existence today, it is second only to the Great Wall of China. We started at the Urfa Gate, just opposite my apartment, and proceeded east. The ground began dropping away until soon there was only a path at the base of the wall wide enough for two donkeys. The wall was made of black basalt which gave it a very forbidding appearance and probably accounted for Diyarbakir's ancient name: Black Amida. There were 80 towers, each connected by a curtain wall.
"Look!" said Ibrahim, pointing to the wall towering above us. It was covered from top to bottom with a deeply etched inscription.
"My God, It's Latin!" I had studied it madly for four years in high school; now I began cursing myself for forgetting it. The *Blue Guide* came to my rescue: "These walls were constructed by the Emperor Constantine in the year 394 in memory of the Emperor Valens and his brother Valentian who valiantly gave their lives in securing the kingdom against the forces of the infidel."
I took a Polaroid picture of Ibrahim pointing to the inscription. I always had to have a human in my pictures to

show size and proportion. Ibrahim hooted with joy when he saw the instant results. He tried to wheedle the picture out of me, but I promised to take a picture of him later.

The Turks were very strange about having their picture taken. The men loved it—an innate vanity, perhaps. The women always refused, hysterically hiding their heads in their black shawls. They thought it stole their souls, a mixture of superstition and the interdiction in the Koran: "no graven images."

Next we came upon a tower, 80 feet in diameter, called the Seven Brothers. Ibrahim told me a spooky story, with gestures, about seven brothers, Turks of course, who were captured by an unspecified enemy, sealed up in the tower, and starved to death. On certain nights when the moon was full you could still hear their screams. I put my right index finger under my eye and pulled the skin down—a very effective Turkish gesture meaning, "You're pulling my leg."

Ibrahim laughed and laughed, and slapped me on the back. "I love you, Mister John."

"Yeah, yeah," I said, extricating myself. He reeked of garlic.

But the tower was beautiful. An Arabic inscription, chiseled in bas-relief in regal Kufic[9] letters, was surrounded by an embossed frame of acanthus leaves. Above the frame was a two-headed eagle with outspread wings, every feather showing. On either side of the eagle were two life-size lions with human heads which extended from the wall in three dimensions. However, one of the heads was gone.

Around the frame were reliefs of animals, birds, and humans. I was puzzled, for images are expressly forbidden by the Koran. Once again my *Blue Guide* came to my rescue. (Ibrahim became very suspicious of my *Blue Guide*, instinctively sensing that it was the enemy, unmasking his tall tales.)

Black Amida—Diyarkbakir—had a flaming history.

---

9. Kufic is the oldest calligraphic form of the various Arabic scripts. Kufic developed around the end of the 7th century in and around Kufa, Iraq.

Connected to the Persian Gulf by the Tigris, it was a strategic location. The earliest existing section of the wall, the citadel, was built by the Scythians in the 4th century B.C. But archeologists discovered that the citadel was built on an artificial mound constructed by the Assyrians in the 7th century B.C. Thereafter, the town was overrun by the Persians, Greeks, Parthians, Romans, Byzantines, Armenians, Hamdanids, Abbasids, Marwanids, Seljuks, Ortokids, Mongols, and finally, the Ottomans.

Each time Black Amida was conquered, or reconquered, the walls had to be repaired. And each conqueror left his own inscription in hieroglyphics, cuneiform, Armenian, Greek, Roman, Arabic, Turkish, or some still-undeciphered language. Often the conquerors simply removed the blocks of writing of the vanquished and inserted their own inscriptions, leaving the animals, reliefs, and frames in place. That explained the combination of writing and reliefs on the Seven Brothers Tower. Actually the inscription was Turkish, using the Arabic alphabet, and said: "These walls were restored by Mohammed the Ortokid in 579 Hijra (1183 A.D.). God is great. There is no God but God, and Mohammed is his messenger." I marveled at the beautiful symmetry of these disparate cultures.

Then I began wondering what had happened to the head that was missing from one of the lions. Vandalism? No, it was too high off the ground. An earthquake? Perhaps. Diyarbakir was in the notorious Turkish earthquake zone. I had been through a quake just a few weeks before—my first! I didn't even know what it was. I was paralyzed, unable to move. I was just ready to swear off Johnnie Walker when it stopped, but my basket lamps were still swinging.

I caught Ibrahim's attention and pointed to the lion with the broken-off head. *"Zelzeleh?"* (earthquake?) I said.

"Galibah" (probably), he said nonchalantly like a true tourist guide who lived in constant danger and was immune to the ravages of nature and marauding hordes of transient dynasties.

The embankment right behind us sloped down at a

dizzying angle of about 60°. At the bottom were rocks and stones which had obviously tumbled down the embankment and piled up around the trunk of a large mulberry tree. I had a brainstorm.

"Let's go down and see if we can find the head," I said.

"*Hi, hi!*"

We slid down on the seat of our pants and turned over rocks for half an hour. We didn't find the head. We didn't find anything! I felt foolish. Getting back up wasn't nearly as easy as getting down.

We started on our way again, and as we rounded a corner we came face-to-face with a bear—alive! I yelped and almost fell off the path. It stood about eight feet tall on its hind legs, but had an iron ring around its neck and a chain leading to the hand of its keeper, a wizened old man who looked to be about 969 years old. For one lira, Methuselah[10] said the bear would dance for us. I coughed up the money and the old man started beating a tiny drum the size of a can of baked beans. The bear slowly raised itself on its hind legs and lifted one foot after another about two inches off the ground. It, too, was so old I thought it was going to have a heart attack during the performance. A little beastie and her mother came around the corner and stopped to watch the show. The beastie was delighted and clapped her hands. The mother had drawn her black veil over her face with only a slit for the eyes. I knew if I raised my camera to my eye, the mother would grab the child and flee. Then I had a real brainstorm. My camera was open, slung around my neck and resting on my belly. I sneakily aimed the camera with my belly-button and snapped the picture. No one heard the click because of the drum. Then the bear started moaning and sank to the ground, an indication that our one lira had run out or arteriosclerosis had set in.

A little farther along the way, when we were alone, I pulled out the picture. It was a triumph. I patted my belly.

---

10. Methuselah is the man with the longest life-span in the Bible (969 years).

Ibrahim patted his too and said, "Now me!"

"Later."

Each turn of the wall brought new delights: a sphinx, a birdman holding an ax (Hittite?), a Greek inscription framed by dragons, a section of cuneiform writing which fascinated me and bored Ibrahim.

We came to the Mardin Gate, on the opposite side of the city, through which all the great conquerors from the East had passed. There was a little tea stand at the gate. I sat down on a rickety stool at a rickety table and ordered tea. I was getting hungry and Ibrahim offered to go into the city to get us some shish kebab.

It was a scenic spot. Below was the Tigris with a 2nd century Roman bridge spanning it. It was still in use, the only road to Van and Persia beyond. It too was made of black basalt, with 10 arches of different sizes. In the middle of the bridge was a jog—two 90° angles—a real shock when you're driving. The purpose of the zig-zag was to prevent the storming of the bridge. It was easy to imagine what a jam-up of men, horses, chariots, and carts that jog could cause.

I walked down the road about 100 yards to get a picture of the bridge, with a grove of poplars in the right side of the picture. Just then I noticed a young man coming up the road. As he approached, I saw that he was astonishingly handsome, wearing a brilliant blue shirt (turquoise, naturally) open at the throat, and black baggy trousers. The baggy trousers that old Turks and Kurds wore were ugly things, usually dirty, with tight legs and a floppy piece of cloth that went from their waist down through the legs and up the back. The explanation for this bizarre costume was equally bizarre—God is coming down to earth someday and will be born of a man! This droopy loop was to catch the baby when it falls. But this young man's trousers had no loop. His hair was black and curly, glistening in the sun; his skin was bronzed; he was clean and neat and looked like he had just stepped out of the pages of an oriental romance. I *had* to get a picture of him!

I held up my camera as he approached and asked him

in my most polite Turkish if I could take a picture of him. He brushed me aside without stopping. I ran ahead of him and started walking backward, still imploring. "If you love God...," I said, an expression that usually worked wonders. He stopped dead.

"Why do you want to take my picture?"

"Because...because...well..."

He started moving again. "You just want a picture of me so you can take it back to your friends in America and laugh at me."

"No, no," I protested, trying to keep up with him. "You are very *yakashikli*." (handsome)

He gave me a sneer.

"I'll give *you* a picture. Look!" I whipped out the picture of the Roman bridge. He glanced at it over his shoulder without stopping. "Look! That's you in the corner of the picture. I took it just a few minutes ago."

His face clouded and he slowed to a stop. He took the picture in his hands and studied it carefully. Then he took my camera and examined it, turning it over and over and upside down.

"You'll give *me* the picture?" he said, still skeptical.

"Yes, yes, absolutely."

"*Olur*." (so be it)

I backed up and focused carefully. I didn't want to make a mess of this picture, *and* I had a plan in mind!

"Smile!" I said, demonstrating.

He clicked his tongue, throwing his head back—a very emphatic way of saying "no" in Turkish. He stared steadily and broodingly at the camera. The Turks never smile when they're being photographed. They want to look fierce and forbidding. I've even had some of them tear up a picture if I caught them smiling. I have no explanation, except maybe they want to look like Genghis Khan or Attila the Hun.

I clicked. "Oh, *bir daka! bir daka!*" (one moment! one moment!) I shouted, as if something went wrong. I ripped the picture through the camera and snapped the shutter again. He was a bit suspicious of this maneuver, but he waited patiently. After one minute I opened the back case and peeled off the picture. I handed it to him. Slowly a smile appeared on his face, then his gorgeous white teeth, and finally he threw his head back and laughed to the skies. I "fixed" the picture and gave it to him. He shook my hand and thanked me solemnly and went on his way into the city, still looking at his picture.

I felt a little guilty because I knew I still had his soul captured inside my camera. I walked back to my wobbly tea table and pulled the picture through. It was a beauty.

Ibrahim returned with the shish kebab, muttering about the price of everything going up and up and up. I'm sure this was to let me know I would get no change from the money I had given him. "Robbers!" he said, laying it on thick as he chomped his meat sideways with his molars.

We continued on our round. The path became narrower and narrower on the riverside until it finally disappeared at the steep walls of the citadel. We had to squeeze inside on our hands and knees through an opening where four or five blocks had been removed from the wall. The citadel was a little city by itself, with a high wall separating it from the rest of the city. The most interesting feature was a water distribution system. Water came from an aqueduct built by the Romans and arrived at the top of the wall. From there it was ingeniously directed down four stories to cisterns below the citadel.

We came at last to the Harput Gate, the main gate to the city. The name is Armenian for "deliverance," though it was through this gate that all the conquerors from the west entered. It was the most decorated of all the gates, with strange birds and mythical animals. A Latin inscription gives directions to a new hotel built by Appius in the 5th century A.D. Ibrahim pointed to a swastika and said, "Look! Even the Germans have been here." It was about two feet square and beautifully carved. I didn't have the heart to tell Ibrahim that it was really the Sanskrit sign of good luck, but I decided it was time to give him his reward—a picture. He arranged the picture himself, posing like Napoleon in the middle of the gate, stopping cars and hissing bystanders out of the shot. He tried to kiss me when he saw his picture, but I resisted his advances.

The sun was setting as we got back to my apartment. I thanked Ibrahim and even began to think kindly toward him—without his insistence I might never have seen the outside of the wall.

"Don't forget the lion," I said as we shook hands.

"Lion?"

"The stone lion! I gave you 100 lira this morning—"

"Oh yes, Mister John, yes. Next Saturday."

I climbed the stairs, took a shower, fixed myself a reward of scotch and water, sat on my balcony, and watched the sun sink slowly behind the walls of Black Amida.

The following week I had visions of stone lions dancing in my head. My conscience panged me several times when I thought of my depriving poor Turks of family heirlooms, or even archeological treasures, but I squelched the pangs with the thought that I was being honest and above-board about the whole thing—I was paying hard cash. I wondered if I should get a receipt.

Saturday came and went. Ibrahim didn't.

I wrote off the 100 lira to experience and punishment for my greed. But several Saturdays later, the doorbell rang and there stood Ibrahim, holding a sick geranium.

"*Chichek*, Mister John?"

"Where's my *arslan?*"

"*Arslan*, Mister John?" he said in yellow-eyed innocence.

"Yes, lion!" I said, lapsing into English. "You know goddamned well what I mean!"

"Oh, *arslan*, yes. Well, Mister John, it takes time. It's very difficult. I'm working on it. You like *chichek?*"

"No, I don't want *chichek!* I want my stone lion! I gave you 100 lira for it! Don't you come back here till you have my stone lion!" I didn't exactly slam the door in his face, but the windows in my apartment reverberated.

The doorbell rang immediately. I wrenched the door open.

"Please, Mister John, let me talk to you. It's such a sad story."

"I bet it is!"

"A long story—"

"I have lots of patience."

"May I come in?"

"No."

He started describing the great lengths he had gone to on my behalf. "These things are not simple in Turkey, Mister John. You Americans are very cold-blooded—you just walk right up to someone and say, 'How much?' but we Turks have our pride—"

"You mean there is no lion? You were just making up that story?"

"No, no, no, Mister John! There is! There is!" Then he described how he talked to the father, who said he had to consult his wife, who said they should consult their son, who was in the army and thus was very educated about these things.

"And the son's in the army for two years?" I said sarcastically.

"No, no! He got out last week."

"And he said no."

"No, he said yes!"

"Well?"

"Alas, the grandmother said no."

"Why?"

He spread his arms and looked toward heaven, meaning only Allah can understand women.

"Okay, give me back my 100 lira."

He gave me his winning grin and bowed his head.

"You mean you spent it."

He looked up at me, grateful that I was so understanding. "I love you, Mister John."

"Okay, go! *Git!*"

"Please, Mister John." He started pushing himself in the door.

"No! Never mind! Forget it! It's all right," I said in my

best martyr voice.

"Please, Mister John, I'll make it up to you!" I had a hand on his chest, but he was disconsolate, desperate, and strong. "I have an idea, listen to me, I'll do anything for you! Just listen to me—"

"No, no, just go, *git!*" I had decided to be impervious to his wiles. We struggled while Ibrahim poured out his idea, half in Turkish, half in Kurdish, and little by little certain words came through to me:

"—difficult—"

"—dangerous—"

"—late at night—"

"—hammer—"

"—a tall ladder—"

"—the wall—"

"—lion—"

"—don't you remember—"

"—the other head!"

I stiffened. I spun him around by his shoulders and almost threw him down the stairs.

"*Git!*"

"But Mister John—"

"*Git!!!*" He was falling down the stairs backward. I pursued him down to the second floor, "*Git!*" Down to the first floor, "*Git!*" Out to the gate, "*Git!*" Even in my distraught condition, I knew it was shameful for him to be seen being thrown out of my apartment, but I stood in the street with my hand raised to Allah until that rascal Ibrahim disappeared around the corner and out of my life forever.

Making Babies— Turkish Style

≈

WHEN I FELT my brand-new apartment was presentable, I put an invitation up on the company bulletin board:

> OPEN HOUSE
> Sunday, March 21, 1959
> 10 am to 4 p.m.
> EVERYBODY WELCOME*
> Address: Sarafian Apartments, 3rd Floor, outside the wall
> near the Urfa Gate, Diyarbakir
>
> Mr. John
>
> P.S. *Including wives

I might never have learned how to make babies— Turkish style—if I had not put the P.S. on the invitation.

"Everybody???" said Smitty, our Site Manager.
"Yes."
"All the *Turks?*"
"Yes."
"But John, we've got 254 Turks! How are you going to get them all into that apartment of yours? Plus the Americans! Plus the Germans! Plus the French! Plus the Italians! Plus their *wives!*"
"I'm sure they'll all be staggered," I said airily. "Some of the Turks have to work shifts on Sunday—guards, pow-

er plant operators, food service personnel, firefighters—so they'll come early. Everyone will seek his own level."

"You've gone ape, John. And we've only been here nine months!"

Abdul helped me compose the Turkish version.

"All the Turks?" he said with his eyes popping.

"Yes."

"The Cadre?"

"Yes."

"The craftsmen?"

"Yes."

"The laborers??!"

"Yes. *And* their wives!"

"Allah! Allah! Allah!"

"Those are my wishes."

"Oh sir, no one will bring his wife. Why don't you just have a party for the Americans and the foreign nationals—that's what the other contractor used to do."

My nostrils flared. "This is a party for *everyone* who works for *our* company—an *Open* House! Do you understand???"

"Yes, sir," he said, long-suffering, "but no Turk will bring his wife."

And none did, thank Allah! The party was a fiasco.

It started off badly when the doorbell rang at 9 a.m. and I was still in the shower. It was Oscar and Ruby Johnson, each carrying an empty stem glass.

"Hi John!" said Ruby, bubbling with excitement and pinching my cheek. "Are we early? We've been up since 5:30 this morning drinking martinis. Do you have any gin?" She barged past me into the living room.

Oscar, our Maintenance and Repair Supervisor, spread his hands and rolled his eyes to heaven.

"Oh, dear, there's no one here!" said Ruby in amazement. "I *told* Oscar we were too early, but he insisted we come right then and there. I hadn't even finished my martini! Never mind, John, don't fret! Just point me in the direction of your liquor supply, and we'll help ourselves. Do you have plenty of ice?"

"The gin is in the freezer."

"What a cunning place to keep it! Did you hear that, Oscar?"

"The drink stays colder that way."

"Oh, ours never get warm."

"Help yourselves," I said through clenched teeth as I clutched my bathrobe around me and disappeared to my bathroom to shave and pull myself together. It was an ominous beginning.

Three Turks punched the bell exactly at ten o'clock. Ruby rushed to the door to let them in, bowing deeply like a grand duchess. She tried desperately to force a martini down their throats, but they would have only *Koka-Kola*. The Germans arrived. The French arrived. The Americans arrived last. Ruby appointed herself hostess and did her best to try to get them all as drunk as she. She succeeded with nearly everyone but the Turks. One German tried to throw one of his countrymen off the balcony—in anger, not in jest—and everyone was furious because someone stopped him. Howard started a poker game in the dining room and took everyone's money. Giselle turned up the phonograph and danced with every available male except the Turks, who were gaga but declined. Oscar tried to choke Ruby. Jenny said it was "just a little family tiff" and put Ruby to bed—mine!

The Turks, all dressed in blue serge suits, sat upright like schoolboys with their knees together. Nobody went home except the Turks, but more kept coming. Four o'clock came and went. The Americans started raiding my icebox. One couple went home to eat and came back. At six o'clock I announced that the movie *Gigi* was playing at the base, but nobody took the bait. At eight o'clock the Germans carried Udo out feet-first. At ten o'clock I said good night to everyone, then found Ruby still in my bed. Oscar had gone home without her. I started to go to pieces, but Jenny took over, hauled Ruby to her wobbly feet, and supported her down the hall. They crashed from side to side and went out the front door. Howard stuffed his pockets with lira and dollar bills and declared that the bank was now closed. I collapsed on "Ruby's" bed and moaned, "Allah doesn't love me anymore."

All week long, everyone—*even* Ruby and Oscar—told me what a great party it was, and wanted to know when the next one was. I accepted the compliments graciously and thought, "Heh, heh!"

The following Sunday at noon, the doorbell rang.

"What fresh hell is this?" I wondered. (I had been reading a biography of Dorothy Parker.)

It was Yilmaz, our chief electrician, with a very pretty dark-haired girl wearing a navy blue jumper with a simple white blouse.

"This is my wife, Mister John. I wanted to bring her to your Open House last week since you said that wives were invited, but the other Turks would have objected. I hope you don't mind that we came one week late."

"No, no, come in, come in! I'm glad you came!"

I ushered them into the living room and they perched on the sofa, the wife looking around at my bizarre Turkish decor.

"Let me fix you a drink."

I overdid it by reeling off the gamut of potables available for their pleasure—gin, scotch, bourbon, vodka, wine. Then inspiration hit me.

"Raki?" I suggested inspirationally.

"Koka-Kola," said Yilmaz, to put me at ease.

I rushed to the kitchen and fixed them huge tumblers of Coke and myself a Johnnie Walker and water. Yilmaz asked for the ice to be removed.

"But—?"

"Ice is very bad for you in the wintertime, Mister John. It gives you cancer of the stomach."

"Well—er—yes, if you say so." I scooped up their drinks, flicked the offending ice into the sink, and added more cola to their glasses.

"Thank you, Mister John." They sipped theirs slowly

while I gulped mine. "I am very sorry I had to leave your open house so early last Sunday. I had the noon shift."

God is merciful, I thought. "How long have you been married?"

"Three weeks," he said with an adoring smile for his wife. She giggled and covered her face with her hands. She didn't speak one word of English, but she was bright and alert, and Yilmaz translated everything for her like lightning. "We are very backward here in Diyarbakir, Mister John. Some men make their wives wear the veil all the time, even though it is against the law. Ataturk, the father of our country, forbade women to wear the veil. He was a great man, just like your George Washington. But I want to be modern. I read books and magazines and newspapers. I won't let my wife wear the veil—she goes bareheaded, just like they do in Hollywood. I wanted to bring my wife to the party last week, but the other Turks would tell everyone she was *oruspu*. How do you say that in English, Mister John?"

I hesitated between "whore" and "slut" and decided on "prostitute."

"Yes, prostitute. But a woman isn't a prostitute just because she doesn't wear a veil. Look at all those foreign ladies at your party—they were not prostitutes!"

The *Koka-Kola* seemed to have gone to Yilmaz's head. He talked on and on. He told me about the wedding-night customs. The groom's mother stands outside the bridal chamber, waiting for visual evidence that the bride is a virgin. They hand out a bloodied handkerchief, then she goes away and leaves them alone.

I was unnerved by the description and tried to lighten the situation by saying, "And now are you trying real hard to make babies?"

"Oh no, Mister John, it's too expensive."

"I don't mean *lots* of babies, but surely you want one?"

"Oh yes, a boy! But a girl would be all right, too. We pray for one, but it's very expensive."

"Not one child. Surely you can afford to have one child on your salary."

"No, no, I mean *making* them is very expensive!"

I was bewildered. Surely *that* part of marriage was free—one of the few pleasures the poor can enjoy.

"Oh no, Mister John. Each time after we have *sikmek*—how do you call it in English? F—"

"Intercourse," I said hastily.

"Yes—intercourse—well, we Moslems have to wash all over immediately. That is a sacred rule. We don't have running water in our apartment—It's only one room, really—so we have to go to the *hamam*—the public baths. She goes to the ladies' *hamam,* and I go to the men's *hamam*. It costs an *iki buchuk* (25¢) for each of us. So you see it's very expensive!"

I was miserable. I felt like giving them a handful of quarters and saying, "Enjoy yourselves!" but, of course, I couldn't.

They left after about two hours, Yilmaz pumping my hand for having received his bride, who blushed beguilingly, and with promises that they would come back again.

The next day, I said to Udo (the German who almost got thrown over the balcony), "How is Yilmaz doing?" Udo was his boss.

"Vich vun is dat?"

"Yilmaz! Your chief electrician!"

"Oh yes, fantastic! He iss my best man. I couldn't get along vithout Yilmaz."

"Well, why don't you put him in for a raise?"

"No, no! I don't vant to spoil him. I chust kick him in the ess, and he does good vork!"

I suggested that a raise may be a little more of an incentive, but Udo said, "Look, Mister John, you vant to give raise? You give Udo raise."

I decided to speak to Oscar, who was Udo's boss. We worked out a raise for Yilmaz, along with other deserving Turks, so that no one would suspect my motives.

Yilmaz and his wife visited me many times after that,

but one Sunday morning when I opened the door, I could tell by the look on their faces and the bulge in her belly that their prayers had been answered. We celebrated. But the baby—a boy—was born dead.

They rarely visited me after that. Then one beautiful sunny spring morning, Yilmaz appeared at my door with his wife carrying a blue bundle. I peeked in at the little dark wrinkled thing, and it burst into tears. I have that effect on children.

After we were settled with our drinks, I asked the baby's name.

"*Satilmish!*" said Yilmaz beaming.

"*Satilmish?* What a strange name! That means 'sold'— I've seen the word in shop windows."

"Yes, we sold him to my wife's sister for one lira. She has nine children."

"One lira? That's 10 cents in American money."

"Yes," he said happily.

"And she already has nine children?!! I don't understand."

"Oh, we sold the baby when he was still in my wife's belly. That keeps the evil eye away. My wife's sister has nine healthy babies, so you see it worked. And now I have a healthy son!"

I looked into the blue bundle again and tickled the baby's double chin. "Hi, Sold! How are you?"

He burped.

Mr. Isn't-It

≈

I FIRST MET Mr. Isn't-It at the airport in Diyarbakir. He was the Mobil-Turk representative, responsible for seeing that the plane that came from Ankara three times a week was properly refueled. Since I had to meet every new employee, I spent many an hour sitting with Mr. Isn't-It at the tiny terminal building (it was the size of a two-car garage), waiting for tardy airplanes and sipping tea.

Mr. Isn't-It's real name was Attila. He was about 40 years old, a big man with a barrel chest, a full head of slick black hair, a bushy but neat mustache—good looking in that dark, fierce Mongolian way of so many Turks. He was always wearing a white shirt, tie, and a blue serge suit—a strange costume, I thought, for supervising the refueling of an airplane with high-octane gas—but he was more like the overseer of a plantation. Each time the plane landed, we would walk out to the gate (two free-standing posts on the tarmac with a rope in between) and watch the passengers disembark. I was looking for some forlorn, anxious person, and Attila was looking at the airline hostesses who disembarked. He spent more time inspecting the girls than he did the gasoline that went into their planes.

"Ah! This one is very beautiful, isn't it?" he would say as one of them approached us across the tarmac.

"Yes, it is," I would say appreciatively.

He always spoke to me in English, in order to practice I felt sure, and to impress the airport employees (all two of them). I always answered him in English, out of respect, but my Turkish was much better than his English. Sometimes I corrected him, gently, for which he thanked me profusely. But on the subject of "isn't it" I never corrected him. It was too delicious to spoil, especially when he was commenting on the ladies who got off the plane. He loved the ladies, as the Turks do.

"This one is very ugly, isn't it?"

I was quite surprised. I thought she was one of the more attractive ones. "Is it?" I said.

"Oh yes. Too skinny! All those bones sticking out. Not comfortable. But you Americans like skinny girls, isn't it?"

I knew the Turkish word *degilmi* was the same as *n'est-ce pas*, and I could have easily taught him to say, "Isn't it so?" but I also knew the Turks had no gender and made no distinction between *he, she,* or *it*. The only third person singular pronoun was *o*. *O geldi* (he came), *o gitti* (she went), *o oldu* (it died). It isn't at all confusing, because once the Turk announces that he's talking about his uncle, there's no need for the pronoun after that. It was only when they spoke English that they got into trouble, like: "My uncle died last night, she was killed in an automobile accident." So I didn't correct him on "isn't it." It was too comical.

One day, sitting under the acacia tree outside the terminal, Mr. Isn't-It said to me, "Let's have a party!"

"Wonderful idea!"

"At your apartment."

"Fine!" All my friends were dying to meet Mr. Isn't-It.

"You bring whiskey from radar station." (The Turks don't have the definite article either, but never mind.)

"Okay."

"And American cigarettes—Salem!"

"You bet."

"And Hershey chocolates!"

"Whatever you like."

Then he drew himself up to his full height and said, "*I* bring Turkish hostesses!"

"Great!"

"And lobsters!"

"Lobsters???"

"From Istanbul. Alive!"

Well, I was wild about the idea and invited all my friends, especially the ones with wives because I knew they would love Mr. Isn't-It, to say nothing of the live lobsters. The party was set for the following Saturday at 4 p.m.

The day came. Attila and I were at the gate when the plane arrived, on time!

"Aha!" he said, as a blonde hostess got off the plane. "This one is new, isn't it?"

"Yes, I think it is."

"Verrrrry beautiful, isn't it?"

"It certainly is!"

When the baggage was unloaded, Attila climbed all over it like a large monkey. "Ah! Here's the lobster," he said dragging off a huge ice chest. "Let's go!"

He rounded up the pilot, the co-pilot, a steward, and *four* hostesses, and we took off in two Land Rovers to my apartment in town.

"Four hostesses on a DC-3?" I said to the blonde.

"Oh, we just came for the party," she said sweetly. *"Turkcheh biliyormusun?"* (Do you speak Turkish?)

"Az buchuk," I said with a wink. It means "a little and a half."

"You're cute!"

My American friends were already waiting, with plenty of PX whiskey under their belts. We marched in with Attila leading the procession and carrying the lobster chest. The American ladies took over in the kitchen and started boiling pots of water all over the stove. They squealed at the lobsters, which were clacking in the ice chest. The Turkish girls, who were much smarter, were entertaining the men in the living room, sipping gin-and-tonics and batting their beautiful black eyelashes.

I asked Attila what time the crew had to leave—knowing that they only stopped 45 minutes in Diyarbakir—and he told me they had already radioed Ankara that the weather was bad, so they would have to stay overnight in Diyarbakir.

He had even made hotel reservations the day before at the Turistik Palas. I was shocked at his mendacity but delighted that we were going to have a long, relaxed party.

The scotch flowed, the smoke from the Salems billowed through the air, Billy Vaughn played the theme from *A Summer Place* over and over again, the hostesses danced like angels with all the American men, and Attila came through as promised.

"Elizabeth Taylor is a pig, isn't it?" he said to one of my startled guests.

"Er—ah—yes, it is."

"Brigitte Bardot is a fish, isn't it?"

Not knowing this was a great compliment in Turkish, she said, "Er—I don't know—is it???"

The party was a roaring success. The lobsters were delicious, the hostesses were delicious, and Mr. Isn't-It was the hero of the day.

It was almost three months before I saw Attila again. Our workforce had stabilized, and we had very few newcomers. But one day I was meeting a VIP and ran into Attila. I was genuinely happy to see him, and he slapped me on the back like an old army buddy. We sat down to tea, and he lowered his voice. "Look at that one over there."

It was a very stylish woman, perhaps a foreigner meeting someone or taking the plane to Ankara.

"Very beautiful, isn't it?"

Well, I burst out laughing. I had been away from him too long and I was caught off guard.

"What is it? What is the matter? Why are you laughing, Mister John?"

I could see he was upset, so I *had* to explain. I couldn't possibly get out of it. The game was over, and I was very sorry. I began slowly and patiently and gently. I didn't want to hurt his feelings since I could have corrected him many months before.

"Well, Attila, I must tell you something about English."

"Yes, yes! Please, what is it?"

"Well, in English we say, 'she is very beautiful, isn't *she?*'

Not isn't *it?* It depends on the gender—masculine, feminine, or neuter." I could tell by the look on his face he didn't understand any of those words, and I began to get discouraged and depressed. "It depends on whether it's a man, a woman, or a thing. For example: 'He is a bad man, isn't *he?*' Or: 'This coffee is very good, isn't *it?*'"

I felt miserable, but he grabbed my hand and pumped it violently.

"Oh, thank you, Mr. John, thank you, thank you, thank you! You are my true friend!"

I smiled, but I was actually sad.

Then suddenly, he pulled himself up to his full height, clapped his hand on his breast with a loud thump, stuck out his chin so I could see his profile, and said, "I am very handsome, isn't *he!!!*"

I said, "Well—yes, he is."

Selma

≈

THE LARGE SIGN on the wall behind the orchestra read:

DANS MEJBURI DEGILDIR

I remember the first time I was able to figure out what it meant: "It is not obligatory to dance." I thought it a very strange sign to have in a nightclub, but it was in all three of the bars in Diyarbakir: the Londra (London) Bar, the Dijleh (Tigris), and the Nil (Nile) Pavyon. Every bar had essentially the same set up: a dance floor (concrete) with tables surrounding it; a raised stage at one end with a live orchestra of five or six instruments; and below the orchestra, just off the dance floor, a line of straight-backed chairs on which sat the bar girls, on display like merchandise, waiting to be asked to dance or to join a customer at his table. The bars were the size of a basketball floor.

All around the room was an enclosed balcony with arched windows. They were, in effect, booths where you could sit with a girl in semi-privacy. The arches were quite open, high enough so you could look down on the dance floor, but low enough so the waiter could serve drinks through the window. There was also a long passageway behind the booths where you entered, and where the waiters also served drinks. The booths were called *Konsumasyon, the French* word "consummation," which means simply a repast, a little something to eat or drink, but which had a double meaning to the Americans. Still, the *Konsumasyon* was just private enough for a little intimacy or hanky-panky, but not enough for *in flagrante delicto!*[11]

The sign meant it was not obligatory *for the girls* to dance, if you asked them. And I saw many a poor slob being refused. An unshaven Turk, or a Kurd with a thick black mustache and black baggy trousers, was often refused. Part of the fun of bar-hopping in Diyarbakir was watching customers stroll the long mile across the empty dance floor, bow, and ask a girl to dance. It was worth making a bet on. The dance floor was never crowded. If the girl accepted him, he would pump her hand up and down a few times around the floor to the unfamiliar Western music and then invite her to his table (if he didn't have very much money) or to the *Konsumasyon* (if he had just sold a hundred sheep that day). At first I was very smug, knowing that I'd never be refused with my clean white face, my neat white shirt, tie, and Western jacket; but one time I got refused, in no uncertain terms. She not only said no, she warded me off with a slicing gesture of her down-turned palm, which everyone understood, and I had to slink back to my table and order another drink. "A *dubleh* (double)!" I learned later that her *berdush* was present, somewhere in the nightclub—perhaps at a table, perhaps in a booth, or perhaps just surveying the scene in his job as a policeman. *Berdush* is a very difficult word to translate.

Every bar girl has three loves. One is a sugar daddy, like me, usually an American or a Westerner, rich (by Turkish standards), who could buy her lots of drinks. She gets a commission on all drinks he buys her—a little round plastic disc, like a Las Vegas chip—which she cashes in at the end of the evening. The more discs she turns in at the end of the evening, the more her stock goes up with the manager. I remember the first girl I invited to the *Konsumasyon* gulped down three Kool-Aid colored drinks before I had finished one cognac. The waiter never left us. He stood at the door of the

---

11. Latin for (literally) "in flagrant delight" or (colloquially) "in the middle of full sex."

booth, practically in attendance on her majesty. When her fourth drink arrived, I waved the waiter away and grabbed the drink before she could, to taste it. It *was* Kool-Aid!

"That's not *kanyak*," I said in my impeccable Turkish.

"Of course not!" she said. "We're not allowed to get drunk like you! Except champagne!" She pronounced it *"shampanya,"* exactly as it was spelled in Turkish, and her eyes lit up inquiringly.

"Have another Kool-Aid."

The second love was her *berdush*. He was her bad guy, her gangster, her Marquis de Sade, perhaps her pimp. He controlled her, he dominated her, he beat her, and she worshipped him. She bought him silk shirts and got him scotch whiskey and American cigarettes from her sugar daddy. He took her money and sometimes her gold bracelets when he was desperate. (Every time a bar girl got 200 lira ($20), she would buy a thin 24-carat gold bracelet and put it on her arm. Her arm was her safe-deposit box, her savings account.)

Her third love was a boy back home. A sweet, pure, handsome, clean boy she grew up with. He was her dream of a good life, an escape from the sordid bar life, back to her sweet childhood. This third lover never knew it, or hardly ever.

All the girls said they were from Istanbul, though their accents often betrayed them. I once pressed a girl unmercifully on this subject and she said, "Well, I *visited* Istanbul once!"

"Then I'm *Istanbuli*, too," I said. "I've visited there many times." She glared at me and ordered another drink without asking if I would pay for it or not.

When bar girls were no longer young, or could no longer attract men to the *Konsumasyon*, the Istanbul managers would fire them, and they would drift to the provinces: Sinop, Samsun, Trabzon, Adana. Diyarbakir was the end of the line. The girls were mostly fat, stuffed like sausages into baby-pink silk dresses with lots of frills to camouflage the bulges. They had spit curls, flamboyant blue eye shadow, hot rouge spots, flaming lipstick smeared across their mouths, and spiky satin shoes with straps, several sizes too small, which they teetered on precariously as they made their way across the floor to the *Yuz Numera*, the toilet serving both sexes. (*Yuz Numera* means "Number 100." I don't know the origin of the expression, but Room 100 in every public building was the toilet.)

Once I was standing at the urinal relieving myself of some filtered cognac when one of the girls rushed in.

"Oh, hello *shekerim* (my sugar), how are you? I haven't seen you in a long time." She pulled her skirt off over her head. "Here, hold this." She rushed over to the commode, threw up, came back, and retrieved her skirt. "Thank you, dear," she said, and put it on. "See you later, *shekerim*." She rushed out.

The bar life of Diyarbakir fascinated me. When I first arrived, I went out nearly every night. The first bar I went to was the Londra, in the basement of the hotel where I first stayed. I sat in a corner at a rickety wooden table covered with a red-checked tablecloth. The tiny ashtray was overflowing with cigarette butts. A waiter came up to me.

"Efendim?" (Sir?)

I pointed to the ashtray reprovingly.

"Oh yes, of course." He picked it up and dumped it on the floor right at my feet. "What would you like to drink?"

"Kanyak." It was a Turkish corruption of the French word *cognac*. The Turks thought it was an original Turkish word because they always pointed out that *kan* means "blood" and *yak* means "to set fire to." But *kanyak* was good, a little sweeter than French cognac, but very smooth.

I took a nice deep swallow, then lit up a cigarette. As I looked, my drink started sinking. My god, what was in that drink? I watched, mesmerized, as the glass started disappearing, taking the tablecloth with it. I grabbed the glass just in time and raised the tablecloth. The table had a very sizable knothole; the knot had fallen out. It wasn't too difficult to avoid that pitfall for the rest of the evening.

I noticed a baggy-trousered Turk who looked like a bandit. The waiter had just presented him his bill for the evening and went to serve someone else. The man looked at the first item on the bill, picked up an empty beer bottle, and smashed it on the floor beside him, without taking his eye off the check. The second item apparently displeased him too, and he smashed another bottle. By that time a couple of waiters converged on him and tried to hustle him toward the door. He fought like a baby bull and threw one waiter halfway across the dance floor. Then all the waiters rushed into the fray, some with chairs over their heads. They brought the chairs crashing down, obviously on the heads of other waiters since the bottle-smasher was quite insulated in the middle of the pack. Unlike in the movies, they were glancing blows off the neck of one waiter into the side of another. The group, like a bunch of enraged black bees, started moving slowly toward the door as the police rushed in. (There were always police outside every bar for just such disagreements.) In less than a minute, it was all over and life went smoothly on; the orchestra hadn't even stopped playing.

One night, as I was entering the Dijleh Bar, two burly waiters were bouncing a customer. They had him under the arms about two feet off the floor. He was kicking his feet like a bicyclist, demanding (in English) to be put down, insisting on another drink, and declaring, "This is an outrage!" It was actually one of our employees, a red-headed British fellow who had always struck me as rather meek and mild. I asked Baba, the manager, what had happened.

"Oh, you know the Americans," he said blithely.

The Americans *were* always getting into trouble. About once a week some American would come in from the base (usually for the first time), get drunk, and then take two or three girls with him into the *Konsumasyon. Shampanya* would flow; the girls would squeal and giggle from the pinching and squeezing; a steady stream of waiters would invade the nest carrying drinks, cigarettes, chocolates; and then the evening would come to an end. The girls would slip out of his drunken embraces and disappear like smoke. The waiters would surround the poor slob and present him with an astronomical bill he couldn't possibly pay. They would take whatever money he had, lira or dollars, and try to get him to sign an IOU. He would accuse them of cheating him, and the fight would begin. The waiters always won, and they would throw him out onto the street, bloodied and minus his watch.

After two or three such incidents, the Base Commander would declare such-and-such bar off-limits and put pressure on Hikmet Bey, the Chief of Police, to close it. I once tried to persuade Baba, the Dijleh's manager, not to let the girls and the waiters fleece every American who came in for the first time or he never would come back again. His philosophy was, if the sucker was that dumb, you might as well get him while you've got him.

The three bars were forever closing (for bankruptcy) or being closed (by the police for reasons never disclosed). (One time all *three* were closed! I was desperate—I had to stay home and read a book.) But then they would open again, sometimes under new management, but nothing ever changed.

I was sitting in the Londra Bar one night after it had just reopened. Sipping a cognac, I scanned the room. The plump chickens in front of the stage looked the same; the orchestra sounded the same. And suddenly I saw Selma!

She was standing at the cash register, making change. I had never seen her before. I had never seen a girl cashier in any of the Turkish nightclubs. She didn't look anything like the other girls. She was absolutely from a different world. She was wearing a forest green turtleneck sweater and a green plaid skirt. Her black hair was brushed straight back from her broad forehead and held by a headband of the same plaid material as her skirt. She was wearing absolutely no make-up. Her face was pale and strong, with classic bones. I judged her to be about 27.

I had become rather jaded about the bar girls and had even contemplated giving up my nighttime prowling, but one look at Selma and I was hooked.

I ordered another cognac and studied her; no need to rush. She rang up the customers' tabs quickly and coolly, and even smiled at them when she gave them their change.

She spoke a few words to each of them. Could she possibly be saying, Please come back again?

I finally got up enough confidence (my third cognac) to go over to speak to her. I prayed that the Turkish language god wouldn't desert me.

"*Iyi akshamlar.*" (Good evenings) I always thought it was curious that it was in the plural, but it had a pleasant ring to it.

"*Size-de.*" (And to you.)

"*Yeni yiliniz kutlu olsun!*" (May your New Year be salubrious!) It was March, but I thought the expression lovely and flowery.

She suppressed a smile and said, "*Mersi.*"

"You're new here, aren't you?" I continued in Turkish.

"Yes."

"I'm an American."

"I know."

"Really? How do you know?"

"It shows."

"Are you a Turk?" I said incredulously.

"Naturally."

"What is your name, if it pleases your grace?" (Oh, Turkish is so ornate!)

"Selma."

"Selma!" I had never heard it before, and yet it sounded so familiar. "A beautiful name."

"Thank you."

"My name is Mehmet Ali."

She smiled.

"Demirbajak," I added as my last name. I had adopted it from the janitor of my apartment building who had one leg shot off during some war and used a crutch made of scrap metal. It meant "Iron Leg."

She actually laughed and looked me over for the first time.

"Would you be so kind as to dance with me?"

"Oh, it cannot be! I have my work to do. Please forgive me." She had, indeed, very efficiently totaled up customers' bills and given them change while I was standing there.

"Perhaps later?" I said.

"Perhaps." And she gave me an enigmatic smile.

I went back to my table and sipped slowly and happily on my fourth *kanyak*. It fired my blood warmly.

At 12:45—the bar would close in 15 minutes—I went up to Selma and said, "*Shimdi?*" (Now?). The bar was practically empty.

She glanced around the room and said, "*Olur.*" (So be it.)

I took her in my arms, gently. She was quite relaxed. The music was slow, thank God, draggy but dreamy. Selma danced like an angel, and I told her so. I was even emboldened to use the familiar second person singular form of the verb, hoping she wouldn't slap me.

"Thou danceth like an angel."

She didn't slap me. She looked up at me and said with a little laugh, "You, too." (Damn, second person plural!)

"I never saw a woman worker in a bar before. Bar girls, yes, but not a woman accountant."

Selma smiled and said very modestly, "I'm the manager."

"Oh my God, how wonderful. I—I—congratulate you."

"Thank you."

We danced for 15 minutes to ancient American popular songs. There were lots of wrong notes, but no sour ones. I almost laughed out loud when this scruffy orchestra finally swung into "Goodnight, Irene."

"Good night, Mehmet Ali."

"Good night, Selma. May I see you again?"

"We're open every night."

I became a regular late, late customer at the Londra Bar. My work didn't suffer because of a trick I learned from an old Norwegian sailor who worked for us. Gustav had loved bar girls all over the world before he gave up the sea.

"Now, Chonnie," he would say to me, "when you get home from vork, you go right to bed. Don't eat anything or you'll sleep all night long. Then about 9 p.m. you get up, you shower, you shave, you go out to dinner, and you have a nice meal. Then about 11 or 12 p.m. you go to the bars. All the young bucks will have spent all their money and gone home, and you can have all the girls. They'll all be a little bit drunk so you won't have to spend much money on them. You can stay up all night if you like."

I followed his advice. Selma never sat with me, nor would she allow me to buy her a drink, but we always talked by the cash register, and I always had the last dance. She never let me take her home—she lived at the Bakir (Copper) Hotel—the police were very strict about that.

Every month we had a party at the Officers Club on the Diyarbakir base. These parties were highlights, even milestones, for the military who lived there. They were not permitted to have wives or families at the base since there were no services to support them—no hospital, commissary, or school. Some of the military never set foot off the base for their entire 18-month tour. They became like zombies. The parties were the only thing that brought them to life. The Base Commander always invited prominent Turks and their wives (Dr. Tosun and Cadillac loved these parties) and the wives of contract employees who were living in Diyarbakir, although there were only a handful. Cadillac danced all night and giggled charmingly because she couldn't understand a single word her partners were saying to her.

One month the entertainment committee decided to have a belly dancer. The Base Commander approved, and I was selected to make the arrangements since I had a reputation, exaggerated, of being the greatest living authority on nightlife in Diyarbakir. However, no one trusted my judgment to select the particular belly dancer since they felt I had gone native and had begun to find even the fat ones with gold teeth beautiful. So I was assigned a handsome young bachelor lieutenant to accompany me to the bars and make the selection.

Lt. Bobrink came to my apartment every night and we started making the rounds. The floor shows usually went on at the same time and overlapped, but since all three bars were within one square block, it was easy to race from one to another. The lieutenant became so enchanted with the animal excitement of the bar life that I think he deliberately procrastinated in making his choice. He felt so safe with me because I knew the language and the waiters and the managers. He even broke down and ordered a *kanyak* on the rocks instead of *gazoz* (soda pop).

"The water they use to make this ice is not boiled, is it?"

"No."

"Or chlorinated?"

"No."

"Where does it come from?"

From the river, I was dying to say. The Tigris flowed right by Diyarbakir. "From artesian wells. Don't worry, the cognac will kill the germs."

After his blood got fired up, he started asking the girls to dance, and then brought one to our table. I insisted she drink *only* Kool-Aid and left them alone. We were at the Londra, so I went to talk to Selma.

After a week he lost all of his shyness and began hustling the girls off to the *Konsumasyon*. "Don't worry," he said, "I'm a fast learner. I only let 'em have Kool-Aid." He always came back flushed and tousled, and raring to hit another bar.

I began feeling old and finally pressed him for a decision about a belly dancer for our Officers Club party.

"Okay, Laleh!"

"Laleh? Who's she?"

"You know, that terrific one at the Londra Bar! Let's go and talk to her!"

I was delighted that he had selected one of Selma's girls. I had been very scrupulous and didn't try to influence him at all, but I knew I'd have no trouble getting Selma to agree. Faruk or Baba, the managers, might have given me a very hard time.

"Look! She's on!" he shouted as we entered the Londra. He dragged me to a table right down front.

"That one???"

"Yes, isn't she something else?"

Something else she was. I almost died. She couldn't have been more than 16 years old, thin, skinny, emaciated—you

could count her ribs. She looked like a tubercular boy.
"That one?! Are you sure?"
"Sure! Isn't she terrific! Look at that."

She was wiggling and bumping her way around the dance floor in a pink spotlight. She looked like a pink worm to me. She gave Lt. Bobrink a very special bump in the eye as she went by. He applauded madly as she did the traditional whirl at the end of the dance and ran off.

"Let's have her over to the table, let's go to the consummation, let's ask her—"

"Take it easy, take it easy. I'll have to talk to the manager. You order us a cognac."

I went over to talk to Selma. There was always a flurry of customers leaving after the *attraksyon*, so I waited till she wasn't busy.

"Please, Selma, may I talk to you? It's urgent. Could we sit down at this table right here, just for once? It'll only take a minute."

Without hesitation, she motioned one of the waiters to take over the cash register and sat down with me.

"Now, what is it, Mehmet Ali Demirbajak?"

"May we have a drink?"

"You may. I won't. Jemal, one cognac."

"Well, we're having a party at the Radar Station this Saturday night, and we want a belly dancer as the *attraksyon*."

"*Olur.*"

"We want Laleh, that child who just danced."

"*Olur.*"

"Great!"

"*If* Laleh wants to."

"Oh."

"It's just for the belly dance you want her, isn't it?"

"Yes, yes, nothing else. I swear. No hanky-panky. No *zig-zig*."

"You must pay her 250 lira."

"Fine, fine!" That was only about $25.

"Do you have an orchestra?"

"Yes."

"Turkish?"

"Yes, some Turks who work at the base always play for our parties."

"All right, I'll ask her. I'll let you know later." She got up and went back to the cash register.

I went back to Lt. Bobrink, who was squirming.

"What happened? Is it okay?"

"They'll let us know later."

"Later when?"

"Later tonight." He was miserable. He couldn't find Laleh. He was sure she was in one of the booths with some old Turk pawing her. "Why don't you dance with that one?" I said, nodding toward a buxom beauty sashaying across the floor, flashing a gold smile at us.

"You're sick."

Late in the evening, Selma gave me a high sign. I went over to her.

"Laleh agrees."

"Great! We want her to be our guest for the rest of the evening, naturally."

Selma nodded.

Then I took a breath. "You too, Selma. I'd like you to come. As *my* guest. If you could arrange to get away from this place."

She nodded again, with a strange sideward movement of her head.

"Thank you," I said humbly.

"Saturday is a political holiday," she said with a twinkle in her eye. "All the bars will be closed."

"Marvelous! I'll pick you up at your hotel at nine o'clock. The *attraksyon* goes on at 10."

I collected Lt. Bobrink, told him the good news, and dragged him out like a bouncer.

The next day I told our Site Manager that we had found a belly dancer. Everything was all set.

"Are you sure it was one that Lt. Bobrink selected?"

"I swear! *Wait* till you see her!!!"

During the week I began worrying about the repercussions of having a belly dancer at the base. I knew all the gossip in Diyarbakir—that we had girls out to the base every night; we had whiskey; we had orgies. Would this confirm it? On Friday, I had a brainstorm. We would invite Hikmet Bey to the party. He could see for himself that everything was above-board. I talked it over with Abdul. "Isn't that a good idea? To invite the Chief of Police himself?"

Abdul shrugged but sat down at the Turkish typewriter to type the letter. It said, "Most Esteemed Hikmet Bey, Chief of Police, etc. etc. etc. Greetings to you. Pray God you are in good health and all your family too. May God etc. etc. etc." (Abdul put all this flowery business in, insisting it was necessary. Finally, we got down to brass tacks.) "We have invited a belly dancer to perform at a party we are having at the base. We would like you to be our guest Saturday night at eight o'clock." (Abdul then added another full paragraph of a complimentary close. It seemed to me to be a ridiculously long letter.)

Saturday morning I went to Selma's hotel. I wanted her to read the letter and approve it. I was told to wait in the inner courtyard. I sat under a mulberry tree. It was always such a surprise to find these courtyards in the middle of the old city of Diyarbakir. From the street the buildings look so old and dusty, but once inside the courtyard it was cool and green. Invariably there was a pool. This one had a fountain and was surrounded with pots of geraniums.

Selma appeared looking perfectly beautiful. I had never seen her in the daytime. She had a pink band around her brushed-back hair, a pink pullover, a pink cardigan, and a pink skirt. She ordered tea, and I chafed until it arrived and we were alone.

I took out the letter and handed it to Selma. She took it out of the envelope and glanced at it. She moved her eyes across the paper, then handed it back to me. I was bewildered. She couldn't possibly have read it so fast. She had a blank look on her face and casually glanced up at the sky. Suddenly it dawned on me that she couldn't read.

"Er—ah—would you like me to read it to you?"
She nodded.
Oh God, I thought, I'll never be able to do it. Look at all that formal language Abdul had used! And I knew Turkish was an agglutinative language: they take a simple word like *ev* (house) and start sticking on endings: *evler* (houses), *evlerim* (my houses), *evlerimiz* (our houses), *evlerimizden* (from our houses). A simple two-letter word could grow into a 26-letter word in no time at all. I began to get vertigo as I looked at all those long formal words, which looked like caterpillars. Then I pulled myself together. I knew I could do it. Turkish was completely and gloriously phonetic, and even though I couldn't understand half of it, I could read it to Selma, haltingly but clearly, like a first-grader. I was determined not to embarrass her.

"*Sayin Hikmet Kababuyukoglu,*
Mudur, Diyarbakirdaki Polis—"
By the time I was finished, I was sweating like a stuck pig. I pulled out my handkerchief, mopped my brow, and said to Selma, "Is it all right?"
Again the cool nod. Did I detect an affectionate look in her eyes for the Hades I had just been through? "Well, then, I'll take the letter over to Hikmet Bey right now. See you tonight at nine."

I was ushered into Hikmet Bey's office almost immediately. He shook my hand effusively, and I was glad there were no hard feelings from the Van incident. I gave him the letter, but he didn't look at it until we had the inevitable tea. Finally he opened the letter. I watched his face intently as he read it. It was as impassive as the Sphinx's.
He stood up, thrust out his hand; I jumped to my feet and grasped it.
"*Teshekkur ederiz*" (we thank you) he said, and gestured to the exit.
The party started nicely. Cadillac and Dr. Tosun were the first to arrive. All the officers, young and old, were lined up in a receiving line. Cadillac giggled her way through the

line, then swung young Lt. Bobrink off the end onto the dance floor, laughing gaily. Next came the Turkish Air Force General, his wife, and their beautiful daughter. Then came Ruby and Oscar, Howard and Sevim, Dewey and Giselle, the Engineer Sarafian and his girlfriend, several Turkish officers and their wives, and soon the party was swinging.

I left the party at 8:30 and drove to Diyarbakir in the faithful Plymouth. At the hotel I asked for Selma and was flabbergasted when the clerk said, "Go right up, the first door on the right." I climbed the stairs. There was a 14-year-old boy at the door who bowed to me, opened the door, and gestured me to enter.

I walked into a scene! Selma was near the door, Laleh was seated in the middle of a very rumpled bed, wearing nothing but a white silk slip and looking godawful. A dark policeman was standing on the other side of the bed, buckling up his belt. I tried to take it all in at a glance, but it was too much for me. Selma looked worried. Laleh looked pale, dark circles under her eyes like she had been in a boxing ring, damp hair stringing down over her face. The policeman was fiercely handsome and gave me a steady, surly look as he buckled up his britches. No one said a word. The policeman slowly put on his tie, taking all the time in the world to adjust it in the mirror, then took out a comb from his hip pocket to adjust his blue-black locks (the upswept wave from his forehead took some doing before he was satisfied). Then he strapped on his pistol belt, complete with pistol and studded with bullets. Finally, he put on his jacket and his visor cap, which he adjusted till it was at the perfect angle. He nodded to each of us individually—first Laleh, then Selma, then me—and then departed. Selma rushed to Laleh and embraced her. Laleh started bawling. Oh God, I thought, what a fiasco! Laleh looked like one of those war-ravaged victims you see in films. I was on the verge of apoplexy and looked at my watch instinctively, but not really caring what happened next. Selma ordered me out of the room, along with the bug-eyed boy who was still standing at the door.

"Wait downstairs in the garden. We'll be down in a

minute."

I paced the garden wondering how on earth I could explain *this* to our Site Manager, to our Base Commander, to poor Lt. Bobrink. Oh, for a *kanyak!* And suddenly Selma appeared, coming down the steps with her arm around Laleh, who was wearing a man's raincoat. I took the small suitcase Selma was carrying and led them to the car. A crowd of hangers-on from the hotel followed us. I put Laleh and Selma into the back seat and jumped into the front seat behind the wheel. The hangers-on were crowding into the back seat, and the 14-year-old had ensconced himself happily in the right-front seat. I started throwing people out from all directions but Selma screamed, "Let *him* stay!" (the 14-year-old.) "He's Laleh's brother!"

I started down the street with all four doors open, reaching back with my right arm and knocking off into the gutter all the unwanteds. By the time we reached the gates to the city, all the doors were closed. Laleh whimpered all the way to the base, but I didn't care. I had given up. No one spoke a word during the 12-mile ride to the base.

I took Laleh and Selma to the chaplain's office, which was just down the hall from the Officers Club, to use as Laleh's dressing room. I was no longer amused at the irony and went to the bar and ordered a double scotch.

After less than 10 minutes, Selma joined me and said, "*Her shey hazir.*" (Everything's ready.) It was exactly ten o'clock.

The Base Commander came over to me with his arm around Burhan, the orchestra leader. "Everything ready, John?"

"You bet," I said, hoping he wouldn't see my crossed eyes.

Burhan conversed briefly with Selma, then went back to the orchestra. A big drum roll started. Spotlights came on. The guests plopped into chairs surrounding the dance floor. Unattached lieutenants squatted on the floor. Laleh burst through the double swinging doors and onto the dance floor, bumping and humping and grinding and clacking brass castanets with her fingers over her head. And she looked beautiful! Sensational! Fresh face, fluffed out hair—what magic had Selma performed? I couldn't believe it was the same girl. I looked at Selma; she squeezed my arm.

Laleh's costume, if you could call it that, consisted of skimpy beads across her boyish bosom, and a beaded skirt that concealed only one thing. She twirled and whirled filmy scarves and looked like a butterfly gone berserk. The audience went wild.

Laleh danced for half an hour like a demon possessed. Flashbulbs were popping everywhere. Officers were crawling around on their hands and knees trying to get better angles for their snapshots. Then Laleh started twirling like a mad whirling dervish, a signal that she was about to stop. The drummer went into a frenzied drum roll and finally—boom! But the audience screamed for more, and Laleh quickly complied. Finally, after almost an hour, she ran off the dance floor into the arms of Selma who hustled her through the double doors to the chaplain's office, followed by a wave of lieutenants with an inexhaustible supply of flashbulbs. Selma locked them all out.

Everyone started congratulating me and slapping me on the back. "Boy, you sure picked a great one, John!" Cadillac smacked me with her fan and said *"Sheytan!"* (Devil!)

I began wondering if Laleh had survived—she surely lost 10 pounds which she could ill afford—when Selma and Laleh emerged. Laleh looked radiant. She was wearing a simple white cotton dress with thin shoulder straps, bordered with painted tulips around the hem. Wouldn't you know—her name means "Tulip" in Turkish. She was quickly whisked away by a band of admirers.

I began to relax for the first time that evening and looked at Selma for the first time too. She was wearing a strapless turquoise silk dress (she had apparently taken off the jacket) and no makeup, no jewelry. She didn't need it. She looked beautiful to me. And I had Selma in *my* world for the first time.

"What would you like to drink?
"Gazoz."

"Not whiskey? Gin? Vodka?"

"*Gazoz.*"

"Bartender, a 7-Up, please."

We went to the buffet table. It was typical American food—frozen shrimp, frozen chicken, frozen beef, canned olives, processed cheese, Ritz crackers—awful, really, but I was curious to get Selma's reaction to it. I pointed out the pig meat (ham) to her in case she wanted to avoid it. She did.

We sat in a corner and started eating.

"Do you like the food?" I asked.

"It's very clean." What a curious remark, I thought, but I didn't press it. Then she said, "Pig meat is delicious, isn't it?"

"Do you want to try some?" I said, offering her a slice of ham.

"No, no, no! But it is delicious, isn't it?"

Just then the Base Commander came striding up to me, his face clouded. "Get that slut out of here! All my officers are sniffing around her!" And then he strode away.

Damn! I started to follow him, but Selma touched my arm gently. She understood everything.

"Let's go," she said kindly,

She deftly extricated Laleh from the sniffing officers over the protests of both Laleh and the officers. We retrieved her beads and butterflies from the chaplain's office and gloomily left the base.

As we were going out the main gate, two Turkish police cars roared in with Hikmet Bey leaning out the back window of one, waving the guard aside. They never stopped. The dirty bastard!

I learned later that they roared up to the Officers Club, leapt out, charged in, and stopped dead. There was nothing to raid. The Base Commander was very cordial (having been warned by the gate guard), and tried to persuade Hikmet and his henchmen to stay. But Hikmet refused and slunk out.

The next night the Londra Bar was closed. I went to the Nil Pavyon and asked Faruk if he knew what had happened. He gave me a gesture, a scoop of his right hand, meaning,

"So it's closed. So what." Baba at the Dijleh knew nothing either.

I worried all week long. The following Saturday afternoon I went to Selma's hotel. She was not there. "*Gitmish,*" said the clerk. I noticed the peculiar expression he used: "It is said that she has gone," meaning that he had gotten the information second-hand. I knew that it was useless to question him further.

"And Laleh?"

"*Gitmish.*"

~

Several weeks later I was sitting in the Dijleh Bar when a waiter came up to me, leaned over and said, "Selma wants to sit with you."

"Selma?"

"Yes."

"Where is she?" I said, looking wildly around the room.

"Right over there." He pointed to a plump, painted girl in a baby-blue satin dress who was smiling at me.

"That's not Selma!"

"Yes, it's Selma. I'll bring her over."

She came teetering across the floor toward me, and it was not just the spiked shoes. She was drunk.

She sat down with difficulty and said, "Greetings, Mehmet Ali."

"*Shampanya?*" the waiter asked, and rushed off to fetch it without waiting for an answer.

I couldn't believe my eyes—the smeared scarlet lips, the eye shadow, the spit curls, the dangling earrings, the sausage curls hanging down the back of her neck, and all of her squeezed into a blue satin dress, two sizes too small for her.

"Mehmet Ali, let's go to the *Konsumasyon.*" Selma got up and started staggering toward the booths. I grabbed her around the waist and escorted her, trying to look as casual as possible. In the booth she insisted I sit beside her, rather than opposite. I still had my arm around her.

"Selma! Selma! What *happened?*" I meant to her, to the

bar, to everything.

She looked up at me sadly and passed out on my chest.

The arrival of the *shampanya* aroused her. The waiters always made a big scene by shaking the bottle vigorously so the cork would explode out the window and the bubbly would come pouring out like a gusher. This barbarous ritual served two purposes—reminding other customers they were cheapskates for not ordering *their* girls champagne, and emptying half the bottle so the girl would not have to drink so much before ordering another bottle.

Selma took a sip.

"Selma, tell me what happened! Please."

"Oh, Mehmet Ali," she said, and went to sleep on my chest again.

We sat that way for the rest of the evening. Several times the waiter came and wanted to rouse her to bring more champagne, but I put him out. Finally I put my foot up across the doorway.

At closing time another girl came and led Selma away.

I went back the next night hoping to find her sober, but I couldn't find her at all. I asked Baba.

"*Hasta.*" (Sick.)

I went back night after night. She was still *hasta* and then *gitmish.* (gone)

That summer I was transferred to Izmir and forgot about Selma—almost.

~

Izmir is a lovely city on the Aegean Sea, as modern and sparkling as Diyarbakir was backward and dingy. And I had a whole new set of nightclubs to explore.

After I had been in Izmir about a year, I came out of the THY (Turkish Air Lines) office one Friday morning and saw Selma coming up the street. Or was it? My eyes had been deceived so many times since I last saw her. As she drew closer, I became more and more convinced it *was* Selma— her hair brushed back from her forehead, wearing a simple light blue raincoat. She was holding by the hand a little boy about six years old. I stood stock still as she passed by. No look, no flicker of the eye. She stared straight ahead, so intently and with a trace of anxiety that I was sure it was Selma saying, "Please don't stop me. I'm living another life now. The past is past."

About three months later I stepped out of my apartment house on the Kordon, the seaside promenade. It was a warm evening, and I really hadn't decided where I was going. The sun was just beginning to set over the Bay of Izmir. Suddenly I saw a man and a woman approaching. It was Selma again. The man was about 45. He had a small thick mustache, was slightly bald, and looked rather gentle for a Turk. Was it *his* son I had seen Selma with? Was she married to him before she came to Diyarbakir? Was he a widower who had taken her and her son in, and married her?

The man looked at me idly as they passed. Selma did not. She stared straight ahead like a sleepwalker. She was wearing a thin black coat, the outward sign of a good Moslem woman in Turkey.

A few paces beyond my doorway the man stopped at a tobacco stand to buy cigarettes. Selma stood behind him, profile to me. Slowly she turned and looked directly at me. Her expression didn't change. Neither did mine. We simply looked at each other, each with our own thought waves. Then she turned back to her man and they went on their way. I watched them for blocks, getting smaller and smaller, until they disappeared.

I was content to put her out of my mind. The life of a Turkish bar girl is a hard one. Her sugar daddy gets transferred to some other country, her *berdush* gets tired of her and finds someone younger, and her boy back home won't have her any more—she's too soiled. The lucky ones find a good, honest, older man, like the one who had just passed, to take care of her and give her a home.

∼

Two years later, I was transferred again—this time to Ankara. On my last night in Izmir, I decided to make the rounds of all the bars—the New Moon, the Kapris, the Sibel, the New York Pavyon, and the Londra. Yes, there was a Londra in Izmir. I had one last *kanyak* in each bar. Near the end of the evening at the Londra, I was starting to get very drunk and a little bit sentimental when a voice whispered in my ear, "Selma would like to sit at your table." I pulled myself together and tried to shake it off. I looked and there was a waiter saying, "Selma would like to sit with you." I thought it was a trick. I thought he was trying to torment me. I grabbed him by the shoulder pad.

"Selma? What do you mean, Selma?"

"Right there, look!"

And weaving, wobbling, high as a kite and smashed to the gills, came Selma over to my table.

"Mehmet Ali!" she squealed. "How are you, Mehmet Ali, my sugar, my soul, my spirit!!! Waiter! *Shampanya!* Come on, Mehmet Ali Demirbajak, let's dance! You dance like an angel!" She dragged me to the dance floor, bumping into tables and knocking over chairs on the way. Even smashed, she was a good dancer. She laughed and talked a blue streak about absolutely nothing. She didn't answer any of my questions, perhaps purposely.

When the orchestra stopped, she dragged me back to the table and poured champagne into my cognac and insisted on toasting with every drink. "To your honor, my sweet! To your honor, my soul! To your honor, my spirit!" She kissed me after every toast, on my cheek, on my forehead, on my nose, on my chin, on my ear, but never on my mouth.

She invited all the other girls to our table (most of the customers had gone) and kept urging me to dance with them. "Mehmet Ali dances like an angel! (Kiss, kiss.) Waiter, more *shampanya!*"

That night as I was preparing for bed, I got a shock when I looked in the mirror. I looked like a red Indian. I felt very sad, but not sorry, as I washed Selma's lipstick off my face.

Genghis Khan Rides Again

≈

A DINNER INVITATION with Genghis Khan! Who could resist? Well, it wasn't exactly Genghis Khan who had invited me to dinner but a bank clerk in Diyarbakir named Jengiz. Except for his profession, Jengiz could have been the reincarnation of his famous namesake. He was young, vigorous, brooding, and broad-shouldered. He had a nose chiseled out of granite and an absolutely Biblical jawbone—just a simple bank clerk by day, but a marauding barhound by night. Oh! I forgot to mention one thing about Jengiz—every tooth in his head was gold. God, he was dazzling! Blinding when he smiled—fortunately not often because he was very businesslike at the bank and just as intense about his monkey-business at night. (I had seen him many times at the nightclubs in Diyarbakir, but he was always too preoccupied to notice me sitting in my corner. And he was always on the go. I felt it was very polite of me never to notice him or speak to him out of his element.)

When I opened the company bank account, the manager grandly assigned Jengiz to us as our very personal representative. He would see to it that we had all the bills and coins we needed to meet our payroll, since I had indicated to the manager that payrolls were our most pressing concern. Every month we gave Jengiz, two days in advance, our requirements for paper money and coins. Jengiz was very cooperative and I looked forward to seeing his dazzling display of gold teeth each time we went to pick up the payroll.

But soon afterward, a coin shortage struck Turkey and

every payday became a crisis. Jengiz started collecting coins for us during the month. He kept a white cloth bag under his counter at his feet, and each month when we went to collect the payroll, Jengiz would zap us with his golden smile then haul up his golden hoard. But each month the bag contained fewer coins.

Our Site Manager just pooh-poohed the problem. "Look, John, the Turks have paper money all the way down to an *iki buchuk*—25¢! So any shortage is a mere nothing."

To the Turks it was *not* a mere nothing—it was at least five glasses of tea and a grudge against the cheap Americans who failed to pay honest wages for honest work. When we were short of coins, I instructed Abdul to give each employee an IOU. He was mortified. He said he would simply keep a list of the shortages, but I was adamant. Our laborers were mystified, but our clerks assured them that this was the modern western way of doing business.

The following month, a week before payday, I instructed Abdul to pass out *iki buchuks* to all his friends and have them go to the coffeehouses all over town and order *one* glass of tea (coffee was too expensive) and bring back the change. "The company will absorb the cost of the tea," I said magnanimously. "Do you understand the meaning of the word 'absorb'?"

"*Bosh ver,*" he said, which can roughly be translated as, "Who cares?"

Operation Teahouse was a flaming success until the shopkeepers got wise to Abdul's gang and refused to serve them.

The next month I had another one of my brilliant ideas: we would give postage stamps. Surely *they* were legal tender! But that was a worse fiasco. The laborers kept turning over the little bits of colored paper sticking to their sweaty thumbs as the clerks smugly explained their purpose. We abandoned that program abruptly when I had a letter returned to me from the PTT (post office)—Turkish commemoratives were good only for a limited time, and afterward were worthless.

During our coin crisis, I attended a Mass at the Armenian church with our interpreter, Fehmi. I was eager to compare it with the Chaldean church. (The Armenian church was vastly different—gaudy and gorgeous.) The sermon, which I expected not to understand at all, was in Turkish and all about money. I heard the words *lira, kurush, para* (money), *ayip* (shameful). When we got out, I said to Fehmi, "Your Armenian priests are just like our American priests—always asking for money!"

"Oh, sir," he said reproachfully, "he wasn't asking for money. He said the collection basket wasn't the place to make change. Didn't you notice the men who put in big bills and then took out change? Very shameful!"

I realized that they were hapless businessmen like me, strapped for coins. I was furious that *I* hadn't thought of the idea.

"The priest threatened to throw them out of the church," Fehmi said, "like Christ threw the money-changers out of the temple. Do you have that story in *your* Bible?"

"Well, er, yes." I was ashamed to tell him it was the same Bible, and that I envied the change-makers in church.

The following payday caught me completely unprepared. Abdul came to me and spread his empty hands: "Not enough coins."

My brain started racing frantically. I jumped up, ran to the first aid cabinet, and grabbed a bottle of 1000 aspirins. "Give 'em these!"

It was the first time I saw Abdul express any emotion. His eyes widened and he beamed. I knew the Turks *loved* aspirin. Operation Aspirin was not only a heady success, but there was also jubilation and dancing as the word spread down the payroll line. The laborers swallowed them on the spot, without water. The clerks went to the water cooler and downed them in a civilized manner with a paper folder of water. One out of five employees came into my office to shake my hand. "*Your* aspirin is so much better than *ours!*" With or without a headache, the Turks swallow aspirin by the handful. The power they attribute to aspirin is magical, almost mystical.

The following month, after Jengiz had counted out our paper money, he reached down and waved an empty bag in front of me like a white flag.

"Oh, Mister John, please don't look at my faults! I am very, very sorry, but we have no coins at all this month. Would you please do me the favor of having dinner with me tonight at the Turistik Palas Restaurant?"

"Well—er—yes. That would be nice." I knew he was just trying to save face.

"Oh, thank you, thank you, Mister John. Eight o'clock!" He blinded me with his metallic smile and tried to kiss my hand.

On the way back to the base, Abdul said to me, "Aspirin again?"

"What else?" I said resignedly.

Jengiz was already at the table when I strolled into the courtyard of the garden restaurant at five minutes to eight. The table was completely covered with hors d'oeuvres. A bottle of *raki* stood in the middle.

"You must try our national drink, *raki*," said Jengiz, pouring me a glass and plunking two ice cubes into it. "Be careful, it's very powerful. We call it lion's milk!"

I didn't bother to tell him I called it mother's milk, and that I was already addicted to it.

"To your honor, Mister John!"

"And to yours, Genghis Khan!"

"What?"

"Oh, sorry. Bottoms up!"

Jengiz wolfed down half of every dish on the table while talking non-stop about the wonders of Diyarbakir nightlife. "Have you ever been to the *pavyons*, Mister John?"

"Er—once or twice."

"I'll show you tonight."

The waiter arrived with an enormous platter of mixed grilled meats. It was enough to feed Jengiz's hoard of gold teeth, but I was grateful that I could pick and choose. (Turkish food was still very strange and somewhat intimidating to me.) Jengiz stabbed all the meats with his fork as he reeled them off to me—Shish kebab, baby lamb chops, lamb liver, beef fillet, lamb kidneys, and *koch yumurta* (literally ram's eggs, but plainly they were testicles!). Well, I had never eaten "mountain oysters" in America, and I had no intention of eating them in Turkey, no matter how much I offended my host.

Jengiz ate with gusto and talked a blue streak about his conquests at the *pavyons*. At one point he leaned into the rose garden and neatly regurgitated a chunk of shish kebab. Urp! It was all over in a second! "There was a fly on that piece," he said airily, and continued chomping and chattering without losing his train of thought.

Suddenly he sat up straight.

"MISTER JOHN!!!"

"My God, what is it?"

"You haven't had any *koch yumurta!*" And he ladled four of them onto my plate.

I stared at them in horror but smiled and started to eat around them. I gulped down my *raki*, my mind whizzing around wondering what to do about them. I told Jengiz I wanted some more *raki*, and he was so pleased. While he had his head turned to call the waiter, I catapulted all four of the *yumurtas* into the rose bushes. I covered the empty spot on my plate with shish kebabs, hoping Jengiz wouldn't notice. By that time the cats had arrived, threatening to give me away. They even put their paws on my lap and begged for more; Jengiz shooed them away with a horrible hiss and a swipe of his knife, almost decapitating me.

After Jengiz had polished off several pounds of meat, he belched grandly, bared his glittering teeth, and said it was time to invade the *pavyons*. We hit all three bars, Jengiz dancing up a storm and disappearing into the *Konsumasyon* booths while I nursed cognacs.

At the Londra Bar a girl came up to me and said, "Hello sugar, I love you. You buy me drink?"

"You *love* me? Why, you don't even know me."

"Yes, I do! You drive that red *motosiklet!*"

"Waiter, give this girl a drink."

I *had* bought a Lambretta motor scooter just a few weeks before because it was a convenient way to scoot around town (there was *no* place to park in the walled city), but mostly because it was a zany thing to do. I didn't realize I was so famous.

Then Jengiz came back declaring that the Londra Bar was very boring and we should go back to the Nil Pavyon. As we were walking through the long, rose-covered arbor next to the garden restaurant where we had eaten and urped, a man came up behind Jengiz and stopped him. I moved on a little way so they could talk privately. Suddenly fists started flying, and Jengiz and the man were crashing into rose bushes. Other men jumped into the fray without a moment's hesitation, not knowing who they were helping or why, apparently choosing sides by determining which army needed the most help. I moved even further away, not wishing to interfere in the internal affairs of another country. As the clash escalated into a battle, I considered climbing the rose arbor.

Mercifully, the police arrived and started banging heads equitably with billy clubs. The whole flailing, flogging, floundering mob moved lugubriously toward the street. When the coast was clear, I moved cautiously after them. The police dumped the assailant on his head into the back seat of a jeep (I was glad they got the right one!), and Jengiz jumped into a horse-and-buggy right behind. He knocked the decrepit driver out of the front seat, grabbed the reins and, standing there triumphantly restraining the rearing horses, he spotted me cowering on the edge of crowd.

"Come on, John, we're going to jail!" he shouted.

I mumbled something stupid like, "Some other time!" Or, "You go along, I'll see you later!" The jeep started off and Jengiz cracked the reins and went galloping behind them, shouting like a modern Ben Hur.

I went straight home and said my prayers.

I saw Jengiz a few days later—I had to deposit a check. Abdul wanted to take care of it for me, but I wanted an excuse to see Jengiz alone. He looked surprisingly good. The bruise under his right eye had turned yellow and the angry gash across his jutting jaw only made him look more handsome. But when he opened his mouth I saw that all of his fabulous gold teeth were gone!!!

"Jengiz! What on earth happened that night? Who *was* that guy?"

"I have no idea. I never saw him before."

"But—but—"

"He said we were talking to his girl at the Londra Bar!"

Well! I knew *I* wasn't talking to his girl! Or was I?

"I think I'll get white teeth this time," said Jengiz enthusiastically. "White teeth are very *moderne*, don't you think?"

"Oh yes, *very moderne*," I said without enthusiasm.

He did.

Payday lost some of its luster after that.

Smitty and the Sergeant

≈

THE SERVICE CALL PHONE was ringing off the hook as I unlocked the door to our office early one Monday morning. I picked it up and acted like a clerk: "Service Call desk, may I help you?"

"This is an emergency! Cut a 55-gallon drum in half! Fill it with ice! Bring it to the Dispensary! Quick!!!"

Although I could scarcely believe my ears, I responded with the true spirit of the Service Call section. I personally supervised the cutting of a 55-gallon drum in half, ordered it filled with ice from the dining hall ice machine, and had it delivered to the Dispensary. I went along. Everyone thought I had gone mad.

Two white-coated medical corpsmen knocked me out of the way, grabbed the drum, and rushed it into the emergency room, where they tried to immerse a fat, naked sergeant into it. He looked half dead. His head flopped back, his mouth flopped open. His body was as red as a newborn baby's. He didn't resist when they jammed his feet into the tub, but when his rump hit the ice, he started screaming like a madman. Ice cubes flew all over the room! The doctor joined the two corpsmen and pushed the sergeant down to his armpits in ice cubes.

I was bug-eyed.

After a few minutes in the ice drum, the sergeant stopped resisting and started turning blue. They pulled him out—teeth chattering, body quaking—and wrapped him in an army blanket. They hauled him into the ward, threw him in a bed, stuck a thermometer in his mouth, and started piling more blankets on him. The sergeant bit the thermometer in half, the doctor said "damn," and one of the corpsmen pried his jaw open while the doctor extracted the other half from his throat.

"Never mind the thermometer," said the doctor as he staggered wearily toward his office. I followed him.

"What on earth happened to that sergeant??" I asked.

"Heatstroke!" said the doctor, holding his head as if he too were having some kind of stroke. "Damn fool spent all day yesterday out in the sun! It's 120° in the shade! Out there, it's 140°!

It was August, hell-month in Diyarbakir. No one went out in the sun in August, not even mad dogs or Englishmen. It took courage to walk from one building on the base to another. If anyone stopped you on the way, you knew he was a newcomer. Even at night it never cooled off. We often slept between wet sheets.

"Smitty, too," said the doctor.

"What do you mean?"

"Smitty! Your Site Manager! He was out in the sun with the sergeant. He's back there, too. Same thing, heatstroke! Damn fools!"

I rushed back to the wardroom. Sure enough, in a corner on the other side of the room was Smitty, covered in sweat, eyes glazed.

"Smitty! Smitty! What happened?"

He turned his head slowly toward me. I could see messages scrambling around in his brain, trying to get out. Finally his eyes focused, and he said, "Oh, Joooooohnnn!"

"Smitty, tell me what happened! Can you talk?"

Little by little, I got the story out of him. For weeks, he and the sergeant had been planning to build a golf course on the base beyond the radar screens. Every year a course had been proposed in the military construction program, and every year headquarters had turned it down. Smitty, who was a scratch golfer, and the Special Services Sergeant, who claimed he was better, decided they would build the course themselves, as a self-help program. The Base Commander was so pleased with the idea that he promised to divert funds from *any* source for what was a completely insane project. The entire area surrounding the radar screens was a moonscape of black volcanic rocks the size of watermelons—some the size of baby bears. There was not a single tree, shrub, or bush anywhere. There wasn't even any dirt—only rocks! But Smitty and the sergeant were unfazed. They spent every evening surveying the topography, making diagrams, and daubing rocks with paint. Yesterday they started laying out the course and hauling boulders around to mark off the tees and greens. Both of them ended up in the Dispensary in the middle of the night when their roommates could no longer stand their moaning and groaning.

"You damn fool!" I said sympathetically, "It's a wonder you didn't end up with a heart attack!"

"It was only to be a three-hole course, John," he said like a naughty boy. Then he grabbed my hand and rose up in his bed like Lazarus, "Oh, John, please don't let them put me in a 55-gallon drum of ice!"

"It was only 27½ gallons!"

"Please, John, promise me!"

"Well, I don't know anything about heatstroke, but I'll talk to the doctor."

Smitty sank back on the pillow and started moaning. "I once made a record with Doris Day. Did you know that, John?"

"Er—no, I didn't."

"During the war."

I decided to speak to the doctor at once. He informed me, in case I didn't know, that I was not a doctor, and didn't I have any productive work to do that day? I went back to Smitty and told him without much conviction that he was in good hands.

"Oh, John, I think I'm dying."

"Now, now, Smitty, don't talk like that. Doris Day wouldn't like it, would she? Heh, heh."

"It was in Hawaii."

"What was?"

"When I made the record with Doris Day."

"Oh, yeah, yeah."

There was a towel beside his pillow, so I mopped his face and told him I had to go.

"Krogden will have to take over my job, won't he, John?"

"Yes."

"That's company policy—when the Site Manager is gone or incapacitated, the Base Engineering Superintendent takes over, doesn't he?"

"Yes."

"I wish I could make *you* Site Manager, John—Krogden's only been here a month. But that's against company policy, isn't it?"

"Yes, it is."

"You tell him, will you?"

"Yes, I'll tell him. I'll prepare a letter for your signature making Krogden the Acting Site Manager. I'll bring it down this afternoon. Do you think you can sign it?"

"I'm going to leave you my golf clubs, John."

"Oh my God, don't do that! I'm a terrible golfer! I've got to get back to the office now. I'll see you this afternoon, Smitty."

In spite of the sun, I walked slowly back to the office. I *dreaded* telling Krogden. If I live to be 936 years old, I'll never forget the day Krogden arrived at the base, only a month before.

"Well, here I am!" he said, cockily standing in front of my desk with his hands on his hips.

"Who are *you?*"

"Krogden! The new Base Engineering Superintendent! What's the big problem?"

"Well, as far as I know, we don't *have* any big problem."

"Then how come I get this urgent message from the Ankara office to get here ASAP? I was up in Samsun—on the Black Sea! No way to get here, so I took a taxi!"

A taxi from Samsun! I gasped. It must have been 300 or 400 miles—on unpaved roads—over the Pontus Mountains.

But I decided not to question his judgment on that point at this moment.

"Well, we do have an opening for a Base Engineering Superintendent, but Smitty, our Site Manager, has been covering the position. He's an engineer, too. He's at a staff meeting right now, but I'll introduce you when he gets back."

"Where's my office?"

"That far room, where the drafting tables are."

When he left, I thought it was most peculiar that he had responded so impulsively to what was probably a very routine message that he was being transferred to Diyarbakir. "ASAP" surely meant that he was to clear up his affairs at Samsun, take a plane to Ankara for a briefing, and then fly to Diyarbakir. In any case, I sent a TWX to Ankara informing them that Krogden had arrived.

The very next day he barged into my office while I was busy with an accountant and barked, "Do I have any mail?"

I looked at him wondering if he were mad, but I decided to be gentle. "Well, the mail doesn't arrive until after lunch, but I doubt if there will be any for you since you only arrived here yesterday."

He stalked out, slamming the door.

After lunch, he came in again. "Did I get any mail?"

"No."

The next day after lunch he came in and demanded, "Do I have any mail?"

"Look, the mail only comes from Ankara three times a week via Turkish Airlines—Sunday, Tuesday, and Friday. There was no plane today. The next plane is Friday. Once a month we get packages by the MAC plane—the Military Air Command plane out of Spain."

He stalked out while my mouth was still open.

Friday after lunch: "Do I have any mail?"

"No."

"Look, you little cocksucker, I'm tired of you fuckin' around with my mail! You'd better get me some fuckin' mail, and goddamned quick, or I'm going to ream your fuckin' ass!" And he stormed out of the building.

I was flabbergasted. I'm sure my mouth fell open. Did I hear properly? I banged my ear with the heel of my hand. Yes, I heard— but I had never heard anything like it in my life! Oh, I had heard the words, but never all strung together and directed at *me!* I wasn't offended; I was too surprised. I started to laugh—a giggle that turned into a belly laugh. I walked into Smitty's office.

"What's so funny?"

I related the outburst as well as I could remember. Smitty didn't think it was funny.

"I'll speak to him," said Smitty, uncomfortably shuffling papers.

I knew he wouldn't. Smitty couldn't bear to speak to anyone when discipline was required—he was too nice a guy.

"We don't use language like that around here," he continued in his deep Texan voice. "Besides, the mail here to Diyarbakir is very slow, and he's just got to get used to it!" Then he added plaintively, "Did *I* get any, John?"

"No."

I went back to my office and sat down wondering what I had done to Krogden. There had been very few times in my life when people took an instant dislike to me, and I was always baffled. In Krogden's case, I decided it was chemical, and I certainly wasn't going to add any hydrochloric acid to the mixture. I went straight to the telex machine and fired off a priority message to the personnel manager in Ankara to "forward all Krogden's mail ASAP—repeat, ASAP!" (Even if you have to write him a letter yourself, I wanted to add, but that wouldn't look too good going out over the military grapevine.)

Krogden finally got one letter. I dashed into his office, dropped it like a ticking letter bomb on his desk, and ran. From then on, the only words I ever spoke to him were "Good morning" and "Good night." He never answered either.

About two weeks later, I was sipping a martini alone at the Officers Club one afternoon after work when Krogden came in and sat down next to me. I stiffened. He ordered a boilermaker, tossed the whiskey down, and demanded another shot before even chasing the first one with the beer.

"Did I get any mail today?" he said menacingly.

"No. I would have put it on your desk if you had."

"Look, you little..." And he let go again with his inexhaustible supply of obscenities. His vendetta with me appeared to be only over his mail.

I streaked out of the club, jumped into the Plymouth, and drove recklessly back to Diyarbakir. I grumbled to myself all the way home: The man's insane! What is this obsession he has with mail? He doesn't seem the type to write very many letters, so why did he expect to receive any? I bet he isn't even literate! And furthermore, why does he always call me "little"? I'm a head taller than he is. Still, he looks awfully tough and stringy—all those taut muscles and steel tendons. I decided not to tangle with him physically or verbally. I'd lose on both counts.

The next day I got a modicum of consolation from Captain Goff, our military monitor. "John, I heard that outburst of Krogden's in the Officers Club yesterday and sent a Memorandum for Record of it to the Base Commander. Here's a copy for you. If it ever happens again, Krogden's club privileges will be withdrawn."

"Thank you, Captain."

Big deal.

I avoided the bubonic Krogden until Smitty got sunstruck. And here I was now, having to tell him he was my boss! I went straight into his office and told him he was the acting Site Manager.

"About time!" he said, plunking himself down at Smitty's desk. "Now we can start firing all those lazy sons-a-bitches who won't work! Bring me the fuckin' roster!"

I visited Smitty twice a day but never said a word about Krogden. Smitty had problems enough. He wasn't getting any better and he wasn't getting any worse. His temperature would soar to 105° then plummet to the freezing point. Chills and fever, fever and chills.

"Smitty, have you ever had malaria?"

"Oh John, *please* don't ask me that! The doctor asks me

that all the time. I've told him no, no, a thousand times no! But he doesn't believe me. I *was* in the South Pacific during the war—Air Force pilot—flew planes all over: Kwajalein, Guadalcanal, Bougainville—but I never caught malaria. Never! I was *never* on the ground! Except Hawaii. That's where I met Doris Day. I was on R & R and she was with a USO troupe. She was my date. We recorded 'Hey, Goodlookin'' together. I used to be good lookin' then."

"You still are, Smitty."

"No, John, no. I'm burning up."

"Did they put you in the ice drum?"

Smitty sat up like Lazarus again and grabbed me around the neck. "No, John, no! Don't let them put me in the ice drum! They put the sergeant in twice! He almost died."

I looked over at the sergeant. He nodded pitifully, his face covered with sweat. I was sweating, too. It was at least 100° in the Dispensary. All over the base we had evaporative coolers—water circulating over louvers with a fan blowing the moistened air into the room. They were supposed to be better than air-conditioners because they added humidity to the hot dry air, but they didn't lower the temperature very much.

"Sergeant, did you ever have malaria?" I asked.

"Oh God, don't *you* start that!"

I felt I wasn't bringing much solace to either of them, so I said I must go.

"Don't go, John. Stay a while. How's Krogden doing?"

"Er—okay."

I didn't tell him that Krogden had fired six Turks in five days—all of them over my objections that we didn't have sufficient grounds according to Turkish Labor Laws. ("Fuck the Turkish Labor Laws!" Krogden replied.) I got a little revenge by paying the Turks a full month's salary in lieu of notice pay to try to ease the humiliation of their undocumented dismissal.

"John, did I ever tell you I beat Sam Snead?"

"No, Smitty, you never did."

"1948—PGA—Augusta, Georgia. I'm leaving my clubs to you, John—same ones that beat Sam Snead!"

"Now, Smitty, don't start that again."

Suddenly Smitty grabbed my shirt with his two hands—I heard something rip—and pulled himself up into my face. "John, listen to me," he said in a low, conspiratorial tone. "You've *got* to get me out of here! This doctor doesn't know what's the matter with me. You must send me to the American hospital in Ankara. John, *please*, say yes, quick! Before they come in!"

Just then, a corpsman came in carrying two trays. "Chow time!" he bellowed breezily. "You guys gotta eat no matter how bad you feel."

I pried myself loose and Smitty fell back on his pallet, ignoring the tray which the orderly plopped onto his chest.

"I'll see you in the morning, Smitty, first thing. Now you eat your supper."

Smitty gave me a haunted look that made me feel like Judas Iscariot as I slipped away.

I drove home to my apartment in Diyarbakir in misery. What should I do? What could I do?

I didn't have to make any decision that night, thank God, because Dr. Tosun and Cadillac, Howard and Sevim, and Dewey and Giselle all popped in on me to announce that we were going to have a perfect poker game—seven people. "And nobody drops out," said Howard, who always won, "even if you have to borrow money from the bank—me!" And he flashed a rolled-up wad of bills the size of a hot cross bun.

I played listlessly but wound up a little ahead. Howard, who won, clapped me on the back and vowed to make a poker player of me yet.

The next morning Krogden was pacing between my office and his when I arrived. "Where the hell have you been???"

I looked at my watch—it was two minutes to eight—but I bit my tongue.

"I've just talked to Smitty, poor bastard! I'm sending him to Ankara! This fuckin' doctor doesn't know his ass from a hole in the ground! Get Smitty two first-class tickets to Ankara on that fuckin' Turkish Airlines for tomorrow's flight—ya hear???"

"*Two* tickets?"

"Yeah, two! You don't think the poor sonofabitch can travel alone, do you? Alvin's going with him!"

I rushed down to the Dispensary.

"Smitty, are you *sure* you want to go to Ankara tomorrow?"

"Yes, John. Oh yes! Krogden was here a little while ago, and he said he would see to it that I got to Ankara. He's really not such a bad guy after all, is he, John?"

"Er—no. Have you told the doctor you're leaving?"

"No."

"Did Krogden?"

"I don't know. Oh, John, what difference does it make? Can't you see I'm dying!"

"But you've *got* to tell the doctor if you're leaving *his* hospital!"

"John, this fuckin' doctor doesn't know his ass from—"

"Okay, okay!"

"Oh God, I wish I was dead!"

"Don't worry, Smitty, I'll take care of it," I said with little conviction.

I went looking for the doctor, grumbling to myself about having to do all Krogden's dirty work. The doctor was not in his office, he was not in the mess hall, he was not in his room—he was sitting in the Officers Club with the Base Commander, belting down Bloody Marys.

"Doctor—sir—excuse me, please, but may I speak to you?"

"Of course, what is it?"

"Sit down, John, and have a Bloody Mary," said the Base Commander expansively.

"No thank you, sir, I'd like to speak to the doctor—outside."

"Outside???" said the doctor. "Are you crazy???"

"Well, in the entryway, then."

He shrugged and accompanied me to the air-lock that was supposed to keep the heat out.

"Smitty wants to go to the hospital in Ankara."

"What???"

"Tomorrow."

"If I thought Smitty had to go to the hospital in Ankara, I'd be the first one to send him! That's *my* responsibility."

"Yes, sir, but Smitty insists."

"He didn't tell *me.*"

"No, sir, he asked me to tell you."

"Look! I'm the doctor on this base, and *I* make the decisions! If I thought Smitty had to—"

"Krogden told me to get Smitty a ticket on tomorrow's plane."

"Don't mention *that* man to me! We had words earlier in the week, and he has very wisely stayed away from me."

"Please, sir, Smitty really does want to go to Ankara." I was miserable. I wanted the doctor's blessing. "I know he won't hold you responsible for anything that may happen—"

"All right! Let him go! Go! But let me tell you this, you little sonofabitch, I'm *through* with your company! I'm a military doctor, and I don't have to take care of you goddamned civilians with your outrageous salaries and Officers Club privileges! You mark my words—I'll never take care of anyone from your company again! *(Oh, what would my brother think?)* I don't care if you're dying of beri-beri or cancer or syphilis or rabies—you can all just drop dead!" He turned and went back into the club, making sure to fling the swinging doors in my face.

I streaked down to the Dispensary and told Smitty that I had squared away everything with the doctor, and he'd be on the plane for Ankara the next day. He actually tried to kiss my hands.

I went back to the office and got money out of the safe. Krogden heaped an additional pile of filthy instructions on my head as I jumped into the Plymouth and roared into town, straight to the THY office. It was closed! Oh God, Saturday afternoon. The sign said it opened Sundays at 9:00 a.m. I took a sacred vow on the sidewalk to be sitting on the THY doorstep the next morning at 8:30 sharp.

As I put the key into my apartment door, I heard the phone ringing.

"Hello?"

It was Krogden.

"Did you get the tickets?"

"Well, the THY office was closed—it's Saturday afternoon—but I'll go over there tomorrow morning the first thing and—"

"Look, you little cocksucker, I told you to get those fuckin' tickets—"

I hung up!

I started pacing the apartment, grinding the edges off my teeth. As if I hadn't been through enough with the doctor, and now Krogden! Johnnie Walker was my only friend. I went to the kitchen and had just poured myself a tumblerful when the phone rang again.

I picked it up.

"Did you hang up on me???"

"Yes," I said calmly, "and if you speak to me like that again, I'll hang up again."

"Look, you goddamned motherfuc—"

I slammed the receiver down so hard I heard the legs of the telephone table crack. Krogden was a menace to society—he had to be locked up! I decided to call not the police, but Captain Goff—who, although he was only our monitor, was really in charge of our whole base engineering contract—and have him throw Krogden in the brig—even if we didn't have a brig on the base.

"Buyurun," said the sweet-voiced Diyarbakir operator.

"Two nine five four!!!"

"Oh, Mister John, you don't have to shout so! I understand you perfectly even when you speak English."

I heard her plug me in and heard the busy signal. It was

probably Krogden trying to call me again.

"*Meshgul, shekerim* (busy, my sweet). You call again later, okey-dokey?"

"Okey-dokey. *Choke naziksiniz.*" (You are very kind.)

"*Size-de.*" (You, too.)

She took the wind out of my sails. The venom drained out of my body. The phone rang almost immediately, but I didn't answer it. I stacked the phonograph with Ella, Cole, Gertie, Lorenz, and Ira and George. I also bolted the door in case that maniac might take it into his mind to come to assault me physically as well as verbally.

The next morning I was sitting on the stoop of the airline office as Mustafa arrived at 8:59 wearing his usual black threadbare overcoat—in August. I started pleading with him before he could even unlock the door.

"Mustafa, listen to me! I need two tickets to Ankara for today!" I explained Smitty's precarious condition—I decided not to say he was dying—and the need for someone to travel with him on the airplane.

"Sorry, Mister John, plane all full!" he said after shuffling through his books, files, papers, and wastebasket.

"*Please*, Mustafa, I must have two tickets for today!" I decided not to introduce Krogden into the problem. "Surely you must know the people who bought tickets for today's flight? Buy them back! I'll pay you double! I'll give you anything you want: *Viski!* Salems! Ronson! Parker Pen! Playing cards!"

"Okay, Mister John," he said as his eyes filled with greed. "You go home! I call you."

At noon the phone rang. I crossed myself and picked up the receiver gingerly. It was Mustafa, thank God.

"Mister John?"

"Yes."

"I got you one ticket for today."

"But I need two! My friend is sick—he needs someone to take care of him on the trip."

"Don't vorry, Mister John, our hostess she take care your

friend on airplane. Turkish hostess very beautiful, yes?"
"Oh, God!"
"You be at airport 3:30, okay? I meet you there."
I hung up. I was sure that Krogden wouldn't approve of the arrangement. But at least Smitty wouldn't die on the plane—maybe the pretty Turkish hostesses would cure him. I sat around nervously waiting for Krogden to call. It got later and later—time to leave the base to be at the airport on time. I checked my phone to see if I had pulled it out from the wall the day before—no. Finally, at 2:55 I couldn't stand it any longer and called him.
"Mr. Krogden?"
"Yes."
"I managed to get only one ticket for Smitty, but they assured me that the airline hostesses will take care of him on the trip and see that he is taken to the American hospital as soon as he arrives in Ankara."
"Oh, that's all off! I don't trust that fuckin' Turkish Airlines. I've made arrangements to put Smitty on the MAC[12] plane tomorrow. We don't need you!"
I hung up in a slow burn and called Mustafa. He was bewildered but bounced back when I told him I would bring him a bottle of Johnnie Walker anyway.
Smitty went out on the MAC plane the next day, grandly supervised by Krogden.
After that, I descended from purgatory into hell.
"Fire him!" said Krogden, holding a scrawny little Turk by the scruff of the neck in front of my desk.
"But what did he do?"
"None of your fuckin' business!"
I had Abdul make out the termination papers and give the fired Turk his money. We both looked sad as we shook hands.
"Now pay him!" said Krogden with his arm around a great big burly Turk.

---

12. Maine Aviation Corporation, a global aviation services company.

"What for?"

"A load of sand! Now we can finish pouring the concrete for the Base Commander's shuffleboard deck."

"Where's the invoice and the receiving report?"

"Look, you little shithead. I'm tired of your lip-flappin' every time I give a fuckin' order!"

Things blew sky-high the following Monday.

Krogden had hired eight sergeants—at $3.50 per hour—to whitewash the rocks that lined all the gravel roads on the base, but I refused to pay them. The sergeants lined up outside my office waiting for their money while Krogden almost had a cerebral hemorrhage trying to convince me to pay them. But I was not to be intimidated any longer. I had asked Krogden the previous Saturday morning if he wanted some of our Turks to work overtime (at 60¢ an hour) to whitewash the rocks because I knew that a NATO general was coming on Sunday to inspect the base, and our Base Commander wanted everything looking spic-and-span. But Krogden's response to my suggestion was for me to go home and perform an impossible act on myself.

When I refused to pay the sergeants, smoke started pouring out of Krogden's ears and nostrils. Before he could catch his breath, I said, a little snottily, "Now, Mister Krogden, I will be happy to pay you the entire amount of money that you have promised these sergeants to whitewash rocks on the base. Simply sign *here*."

Krogden almost self-destructed, but he pulled himself together, stormed out, and patted the sergeants on the back as he pushed them out the door.

That afternoon, Captain Goff sent a TWX to my brother Jim that said, "Get Krogden out of here, or John, or both!" He graciously gave me a copy of the TWX, but I never forgave him for the "or both!"

Jim arrived the next day by THY. I asked Krogden if he would like to meet him at the airport and he said no! Neither did I. I sent a car with a driver who couldn't speak a word of English. Then I started collecting my notes about Krogden.

"Where's Krogden?" snarled Jim when he arrived.

"In there," I said, pointing to Smitty's office. I heard him asking Krogden where they could talk.

"Right here."

"Privately!"

"Oh, well we could go to the Officers Club bar, it opens at—"

"No!"

"Well, my room?"

"Here on the base?"

"Yes, sir!"

"Let's go!"

Forty-five minutes later, Jim came back to my office. "Krogden has resigned. He's packing now. Get him a ticket on the same plane with me back to Ankara this afternoon. Pay the sergeants and charge it to Non-Reimbursable Public Relations. Jeez! As if I didn't have enough troubles!"

I never saw Krogden again. I heard he went to Lahore and got a job with USAID where he sold six government tractors several times over to 30 Pakistani entrepreneurs. Several years later I heard, with no particular relish, that he was in San Quentin.

Oh, what about Smitty? It was very simple—he had malaria. The doctors in Ankara diagnosed it five minutes after he arrived. They immediately informed "our" doctor, who put the sergeant on quinine and assiduously avoided me ever after. Apparently Smitty and the sergeant were bitten by malarial mosquitos when they were laying out the golf course.

I called my friend Dr. Tosun, who was amazed to hear there was malaria in Diyarbakir—the first cases in 20 years. He thanked me profusely for the information.

Ankara personnel sent us a replacement for Krogden for a few weeks, until Smitty could return to work. Then everything went back to normal—except that Smitty and the sergeant abandoned their idea for a golf course.

Theresa's Mountain

≈

IN EARLY SEPTEMBER 1960, I was notified by my favorite brother that I was being transferred to Izmir as a reward for my "long suffering" in Diyarbakir. I realized that it might be my last opportunity to see Theresa's mountain, so I started off Saturday morning of the long Labor Day weekend in the Plymouth well-equipped with maps, candy bars, and Polaroid film. I was all alone except for my friend Johnnie Walker.

Theresa was an archeologist I had met at a cocktail party at the American Embassy in Ankara two years before. Every summer she came to Turkey to excavate *her* mountain. Her mountain was actually Nemrut Dag, an 8,000-foot pinnacle overlooking the Euphrates River. On top were colossal statues erected in 69 B.C. by King Antiochus to commemorate his final resting place. Since he was half-Persian and half-Greek, he had his stonecutters execute likenesses of his ancestors: Zeus Ahuramazda the Thunder Shaker, Apollo Mithra the Sun God, Fortuna the Goddess of Fertility, Heracles Artagnes the God of Strength, and Antiochus himself. Theresa had mind-blowing pictures of the statues which I, then and there, vowed to see one day.

"The statues stood seven stories high," said Theresa, "before they were toppled by earthquakes. All except Fortuna— she was the only one who kept her head!" Theresa winked.

Theresa's mountain was only 50 miles west of Diyarbakir as the *karga* (crow) flies, but I had to make almost a complete circle of 225 miles around the headwaters of the Euphrates

179

River to get there in the Plymouth. I arrived about nine o'clock at night at Adiyaman, the largest city (pop. 12,000) near Nemrut Dag and the capital of the Province. I checked into a charming old weather-beaten hotel with a wooden porch running all around it, surrounded by sycamore trees. The desk clerk couldn't have been more than 16 (surely irresponsible), so I decided to intimidate him in my fiercest Turkish.

"What's your name?"

"Murat."

"Now look, Murat! Tomorrow morning at seven o'clock sharp, I want a guide, standing right here, ready to take me to Nemrut Dag!"

"Yes, sir."

"You've heard of Nemrut Dag?"

"Oh yes, sir," he said gesturing over his right shoulder. "Many tourists stop here on their way to Nemrut Dag:'

"Good. Seven o'clock sharp!"

"Inshallah."

"Oh, God!"

"Sir?"

"Never mind. And furthermore, I want breakfast in my room at six o'clock sharp! Write this down!"

"Yes, sir."

"Two boiled eggs, three minutes *only*, toast *with* butter, and coffee *with* milk!"

"At your service, sir."

"Now, where's the dining room?" I thumped my belly by snapping my middle finger with my thumb—Turkish sign language for "I'm starving." This won him over. He laughed, clapped me on the back calling me his *arkadash* (friend), and took me down the hall to the tiny dining room. The room was dark, but there was a light in the kitchen. Murat switched on the light, sat me down like a maitre d', and rustled up a cook. The cook came running with hors d'oeuvres.

"Lion's milk! *(raki!),*" I shouted. "Where's my lion's milk?"

"Immediately, your excellency!"

The dinner was shish kebab and delicious. (It always is in the mountains.) The lion's milk made me sleep like a cub.

The next morning I got goat cheese, black olives, bread, honey, and tea. But at least it was delivered to my room at six o'clock, and by the cook himself. At seven o'clock I went downstairs and found my guide standing at the desk. He came to attention and saluted. He looked like an unshaven gangster. Murat introduced him as Hurshit. I almost started to laugh. I had never heard the name, but I found out later that it was a Persian name meaning "sunshine."

"Okay, Hurshit, let's go!"

Murat begged to go with us since it was his day off, and he had never seen Nemrut Dag.

"You've never seen Nemrut Dag?" I said incredulously.

"No, Mister John."

"But it can't be more than 15 or 20 kilometers away, according to the map."

"I've never seen it, Mister John. Please take me with you." I readily agreed since I felt *he*, of all people, should know about it so that he could help other tourists who came after me.

"Which way, Hurshit?" I said after we got into the car. I loved the luxury of using his name without offense.

"Straight ahead."

"Okay, Hurshit, you're the boss."

We drove east in the direction of the Euphrates River over an abominable dirt road full of foot-deep ruts and potholes and came to the small village of Kahta. We stopped at a tiny tailor's shop, and Hurshit jumped out.

"What's up, Hurshit?"

"One minute, Mister John."

Hurshit conversed madly with the tailor, waving his arms and pointing at me. Finally the tailor wearily put down his needle and thread, locked his shop, and got into the car with us.

"Who's this? What's going on?"

"This is Turgut," said Hurshit. "He knows the way to Nemrut Dag. I've never been farther than here." Then he told Turgut what a wonderful friend I was. What could I do? Turgut pumped my hand and grinned handsomely—his four front teeth were missing.

As we left Kahta, Turgut said, "Turn left here."

"Where?"

"Here!!!"

There was no road, so I just pulled off into a field, and we started bouncing over the plains, heading north. Here and there were traces of tracks, probably from wagon wheels, but certainly not a road. After about half an hour of this buggy ride, we came to the village of Alut and stopped at a grocery stand. I checked my map. We were getting closer. Nemrut Dag was the next stop. Turgut shouted for bread, apples, grapes, and pomegranates. The grocer brought them and got into the car with us!

"God in heaven, now what?"

"This is my brother-in-law, Sabri. He knows the way to Nemrut Dag—I've never been farther than here." I began to feel like a tour bus driver with a carload of guides.

We drove a few miles further over the flat fields. Suddenly the plain gave way and dropped to the Euphrates River Valley, thousands of feet below. It was a breathtaking sight—ridge after ridge of brown barren mountains with the blue sky behind, and the Euphrates River in the deep valley below, looking like a silver trickle. On the left I noticed some columns and stopped the car. In the middle was obviously a man-made mound, a tumulus of rocks piled high in the shape of a pyramid with four Doric pillars at each of the corners. Three of the pillars had tumbled in varying degrees, but the fourth, still standing, was crowned by a glorious stone eagle. My heart started racing faster—surely this was a preview of what was to come. On the ground near each pillar we found the stone animal that once topped the pillar—a lion, a monkey, and a ram, each of them 10 feet high. I took a Polaroid picture of my guides with the eagle in the background, and a fight broke out as to who would get the picture. I snatched the picture and pocketed it.

"Later," I said. They became sullen.

Then we started down the mountain. A road had materialized out of nowhere, made of cobblestones, undoubtedly built by those master road-builders, the Romans. The road became steeper and steeper, going straight down! The cobblestones became looser and looser. I realized that I had pushed the brake all the way to the floor, and we were still moving, sliding over the rocks as they turned and tumbled with us. I ordered everyone out of the car, thinking that the brakes were trying to hold the weight of those bodies as well as the car. I had to speak sharply to them three times before they leapt out, but ol' man Plymouth just kept rolling. The lightened car actually seemed worse. I pulled on the emergency brake with no effect. As the road got steeper, the car began picking up speed. I swear it was a 60° slope, but my judgment may have been blurred by my growing panic. The road suddenly turned sharply to the left but the Plymouth didn't care to go that way. It kept going straight toward a cliff above the river. The cliff was now coming closer. Just as I was about to leap, the back wheels slid around, and I was on the road again, which began to level out as we paralleled the river. I finally brought the car to a halt and got out to steady my nerves. A nip of Johnnie Walker was definitely called for. I looked back at that Roman masterpiece of a road and realized that we could never climb that hill on the way back. We would have to find another route. When my guides caught up with me, I offered them some refreshment. They all refused except the child, Murat, who took a healthy swallow, acting as if the whiskey were soda pop, and almost choked to death. He hollered and fanned his mouth and pranced up and down like a red Indian. The others laughed and smacked him on the back much harder than was necessary. Murat wiped his tears, grabbed the bottle, and took another swig, just to prove he was a man. He managed to get it down, but his eyes bulged.

We piled back into the car and shortly came to a handsome stone bridge about 100 yards long. The bridge spanned a tributary that seemed to come right out of the rock cliffs on the left. The bridge was one long, simple, low arch—sleek and solid and in mint condition. On both ends there were stone eagles on columns, guarding the approaches to the bridge. Again my blood pressure went up at the thought that Nemrut Dag was near.

The road then became sandy and ran beside the river. Every few hundred yards there was a small, steep, narrow ravine, and as we dipped down roller-coaster style and jerked back up, the front bumper would dig into the upward slope and the back bumper would get caught in the downward slope behind. The car would then be suspended in the V-shaped ravine with a rivulet of water flowing beneath the axles. My guides lifted, pushed, and pulled, and we got out of each of the ravines with relatively little difficulty.

We came at last to Eskikahta (Old Kahta), where my map showed the ancient-ruin symbol and the magic words: Nemrut Dag. Eskikahta was a mud village of 10 or 12 houses, all huddled in a circle like covered wagons in a corral, as if for protection from the invaders—us. In the middle of the tiny town square was a mulberry tree. It was two o'clock in the afternoon, and we were hot, dusty and thirsty. An old man, perhaps the mayor, sitting under the tree, invited us to refresh ourselves at the municipal water supply—a huge earthen water jug with a dipper chained around its neck. My guides naturally insisted that I go first. Ugh! By that time villagers and naked beasties had crawled out to stare at us. The beasties were covered with sores and scabs. I couldn't refuse with all those eyes on me, so I mentally crossed myself, took a dipperful, swallowed it, and surprisingly didn't die on the spot. While my guides were slaking their thirst and gossiping with the locals, I slipped back to the car and took a healthy swig of Johnnie Walker disinfectant.

The mayor pointed out Nemrut Dag to us, straight above. He said it was a six-hour climb, on foot or donkey, and he would be happy to provide the donkeys. We would have to sleep on top of the mountain overnight—"the sunrise is magnificent"—and descend the next day.

I was shattered. There wasn't enough time. It was Sunday afternoon and I couldn't possibly get back to Diyarbakir by Monday night and be ready for work on Tuesday morning. What a fool I had been to have come here without planning the logistics of the trip. The beasties were all over the Plymouth because they had never seen an American luxury car before—everyone else had come in jeeps and army trucks. My guides were all looking at me, waiting for a decision. I told them sadly that we must turn back. They didn't seem upset because, I suppose, they too had livelihoods to maintain.

Since I knew we couldn't go back the way we came, I instigated a big pow-wow about an alternate route to Adiyaman. The mayor couldn't understand why we just didn't turn around—everyone else did—but finally gave us yards and yards of directions on another route back. I got lost after the first turn, but I assumed that at least *one* of my guides would remember the various twists, turns and landmarks, even if it wasn't the same guide. After breaking bread, apples, grapes, pomegranates, and some cold meat pies which the mayor's wife had brought us (I had given the mayor a Polaroid picture of himself), and a long last look at Nemrut Dag above us, our bellies full, we said an emotional goodbye to the Mayor of Eskikahta and started off on his recommended road back to Adiyaman.

The alternate route followed the river for a while and started climbing to a high meadow. After an hour we came to a farmhouse with a thatched roof and a little picket fence around the front yard. It was charming—straight out of England. A withered old man with a grey stubble on his head and chin was standing inside the gate. Each of my guides took turns screaming at the poor bewildered old man, claiming that he knew the dialect of the people in these parts, but the old man didn't understand a word. Maybe he was deaf.

Finally in desperation, I said in clear Turkish baby talk, "Please, kind sir, can you tell us the way to Adiyaman?"

"I am at your service," he said, bowing like a courtier. He then proceeded to tell us the route in more classical Turkish than I could handle.

"Now, are you *sure* you *all* understood that?" I said to my guides with a snarl.

"Yes, Mister John." But they were sullen after that and began to hate me because I had bested them with the old man.

The meadow disappeared, and the road started climbing up a rocky barren mountain. The road kept getting narrower and finally petered out to a goat trail on the side of the mountain. I stopped the car and said it wasn't possible to go any farther. They all urged me on saying that Adiyaman was just over the top of the mountain. My sense of direction told me we were on the wrong side of the river and heading toward Diyarbakir, but my mental gyroscope was hopelessly out of control. Hurshit got out and ran in front of the car, beckoning me on. When the goat trail turned into a footpath, I rebelled and backed down the mountain to the tune of bickering, quarreling, and recriminations.

And then we got stuck in a rut, up to the axle! My guides got out and pushed and heaved and I gunned the motor and we finally got out with a primeval upheaval, but the motor was still racing and I realized the accelerator pedal was stuck to the floor. I reached down with my hand and jerked it up—and off! The pedal was loose from the linkage, and the motor went dead. Murat started to cry.

By that time my nerves were sticking out all over and I ordered everyone to shut up. "If you want to do anything, *pray!* Or sing! I don't care which."

I got out and lifted up the hood—I, who know *nothing* about cars. It was starting to get dark, but I could still see enough to follow the linkages from the gas pedal to a place where a piece was hanging loose. The piece had a nipple on the end, and I found another piece with a hole that seemed happy to receive the former when I snapped it into place. I got into the car and it started again, responding nicely to my pumps on the accelerator. My guides all cheered.

We went back on the goat trail until we came to a faint fork. I took the only other choice and was buoyed up when it turned into a bona fide road. But then the road started climbing and I noticed that the car had lost a lot of its former power, which was not much in the first place. We came to a hill, and although I had the accelerator all the way to the floor, the car went slower and slower and finally crawled to a stop. My guides had to get out and push me over the crest. Downhill was no problem, but uphill—everyone had to get out and push. It was ridiculous but obvious to me that something was wrong with the Plymouth's insides. It had split a gut, or at least had a hernia.

Presently we came to a water trough, where five women were filling their water jugs. I jammed on the brakes and told my guides to find out where we were. The women pulled their veils over their faces and started scurrying away. I flipped the car in gear and started stalking them like a deer hunter. My guides were all leaning out the windows, yelling for them to stop. They did, but only after they had scurried up a small hill to their village and the poor old Plymouth couldn't make it. Their husbands ambled over to the car to see what our problem was. The ladies paused in their flight and even drew nearer to hear what was going on. The men told us we were absolutely going in the wrong direction. We should go back to the last fork in the road and take the road to the right.

At the fork, there was a Turkish soldier hitchhiking. He didn't have his thumb out—that's a shameful American custom—but I could tell by his body position that he wanted a ride. I put on the brakes. My guides all kept screaming, "Go on! Go on! Don't stop for him! We know the way! To the right! There's no room for him! Go on! Oh, Allah!"

I figured that a soldier out here in the middle of nowhere, hitching a ride, *must* know where he is and where he's going.

So I backed up.

"Do you know the way to Adiyaman?" I asked.

"Naturally! Adiyaman is my duty post. Will you transport me there, please?"

I felt like giving him a Turkish bear hug but said, "Hop in!" None of my guides would speak to him. The soldier sat in the front seat beside Murat and me and immediately took over like a general.

"Turn right, turn left, go slow, careful, straight ahead, good!" I felt that at last I was in Allah's hands. It was by now quite dark—8:05 by the clock—but the road had flattened out and we were zipping along merrily. My heart began to lighten and I actually started singing:

"Sheftali agachlari,
Sheftali agachlari,
Tin, tin, tini mini hanim—"

The others all joined in lustily, delighted that I knew one of their Turkish folk songs.

"Tin, tin, tini mini hanim,
Seni seviyorum, hanim,
Seni seviyorum, hanim."

The song made no sense to me:

"Peach trees, peach trees,
Teeny, tiny, weeny lady,
I love you, lady,
I love you, lady."

But the song had a simple melody and a lively rhythm, and everyone in the Plymouth sang at the top of his voice. We needed some cheering up.

Suddenly the soldier started talking excitedly, saying *"Chay!"* frequently.

Well, I knew that *chay* means "tea," but I couldn't understand why he was shouting so. Perhaps there was a teahouse up ahead. Good! Suddenly the road made a sharp turn through some willow trees, then it dipped, and in a second we were in the middle of the Euphrates River! Then it hit me: the second meaning of the word *chay* is "stream." Why must I always learn Turkish the hard way? Luckily this high up in the headwaters the Euphrates is only a stream.

It wasn't very deep, but naturally the motor stalled when we hit the water with a spectacular splash. The Euphrates was swirling madly all around us, and then I noticed the car was sinking. When I felt the water over my ankles, I figured it was time to abandon ship. We waded ashore and watched. How was I ever going to explain to our Site Manager (or worse, to my favorite brother) that our Plymouth was at the bottom of the Euphrates River, somewhere near Theresa's mountain?

The September full moon had just risen (Allah be praised!), so it was easy to survey the situation. I took off my pants and waded out to the Plymouth. It wasn't sinking any more. In the middle of the stream was a sandbar. I waded to it and tested it by stomping. It seemed quite solid. Beyond it was a small patch of *chay* and then the continuation of our road, rising straight up out of the water. I decided we would push the Plymouth to the sandbar, let the spark plugs dry out, and then take our chances from there.

I ordered my guides out of their pants and told them to push! I was surprised how easily the car rolled up onto the sandbar with six people pushing. The only thing half-dry on me was my undershirt, so I took it off and did my best to dry the spark plugs.

After about half an hour I tried the starter. Nothing! The sandbar was about five yards wide and twenty yards long, and ran parallel to the river, so we pushed the Plymouth back to the upstream edge of the sandbar, and I got in while everyone pushed downstream. The engine coughed once before I had to jam on the brakes to keep it from going to Babylon. We repeated this maneuver six times, my guides singing a Turkish equivalent of the "Song of the Volga Boatmen." On the seventh attempt it started. What a glorious sound! Vroom, vroom, vroom! What a glorious smell! Exhaust! Clouds of blue smoke! I jockeyed the car around on the narrow sandbar until it was facing the road opposite. The road went straight up as far as the eye could see. I knew I had to drive slowly through the last half of the *chay*, but once on dry land, I would call on Allah and gun the engine.

I got through the stream without stalling, pressed the accelerator carefully but firmly to the floor, but the car chugged to a stop about 50 yards up the mountain. My gang had waded across the stream, put on their pants and started pushing. I calculated we were doing about one mile per hour. We had to stop every five minutes while my slaves caught their breath. I kept wondering if this was how King Antiochus had gotten all those statues to the top of Nemrut Dag.

Finally the road took a turn to the left, leveled out a bit, and continued up the side of the mountain on a diagonal. The Plymouth at that point turned into a self-propelled vehicle. I left all my coolies behind and made hay while I could. Dear God, let this be the last, I was saying, when the road took a diabolical turn to the right and went straight up again. The old warhorse chugged to a halt. I kept the motor running, pulled on the emergency brake, stuck some rocks under the rear wheels, and took to the bottle.

It was really a gorgeous night—I kept wishing I could appreciate it. It was warm, the sky was clear and bright with stars, and the moon had risen higher. I could see range after range of mountains on the other side of the Euphrates with Diyarbakir just beyond. I suddenly noticed that the hills were covered with grapevines, and the grapes were ripe! I picked a bunch to complement my Johnnie Walker.

My chain gang finally caught up with me, exhausted. When I got into the car and yelled "Push!", they mutinied. Murat flung himself into a ditch and started whimpering like a wounded puppy. The others sat down on the side of

the road and refused to budge. I began getting alarmed. Suddenly the "General" started yelling god-awful sounds: "Oooooh! Ehhhhhhh! Hooooooooo!"
I thought he had gone mad. Then I heard a sound from far away. Was it an echo? Then another and another. Suddenly a man appeared out of the vineyards. The soldier turned to me and said menacingly in no uncertain Turkish, "Keep your mouth shut! Don't say a word!"

Soon seven or eight people converged on us from all directions. The "General" started barking commands, ordering me into the driver's seat and the others to start pushing. With the Plymouth's meager horsepower and all that manpower, we were soon zooming up the mountain at a speed of 10 to 15 miles per hour. I could see Murat bringing up the rear, stumbling and staggering. Finally we went over a crest, and we were back on the plains at last!

I got out to thank our saviors, but they knocked each other over trying to pump my hand and bowing deeply. One little beastie even kissed my hand and pressed it to his forehead.

When we got back into the car and started off, I asked the "General" who all those people were and where they came from.

"They're watchmen in the vineyards."

"Why were they all shaking my hand?"

"I told them you were the Governor of Adiyaman. He has white hair, too."

Within minutes we were in Alut, then Kahta. I dropped off the guides like flies and finally arrived at our hotel in Adiyaman. It was almost midnight. As we climbed the steps to the porch, weary but strangely exhilarated, Murat grabbed my hand and started pumping it.

"Oh, thank you, Mister John! Thank you for that wonderful trip! It was *better* than a movie."

When I got back to Diyarbakir, I turned the Plymouth into the repair shop. Later, our Motor Vehicle Superintendent came to me and said, "Where the hell have you been with that vehicle?? You broke two piston rods, the engine is full of sand, and we even found a dead minnow in it!"

"Theresa's Mountain," I said coolly.

Several years later when I was living in Ankara, I heard that Theresa was in town. It was late August, and she had just finished a summer at Nemrut Dag. So I threw a dinner party for her at our company penthouse and invited all my archeological friends. I personally made up the menu, selecting all the foods I knew Theresa couldn't get during her three months at Nemrut Dag—shrimp cocktail, stuffed celery stalks, chicken livers wrapped in bacon, lobster tails in hot butter, baked ham, and three kinds of ice cream with hot fudge. Theresa was delighted with the spread and dived in with gusto.

"So, you've been to Nemrut Dag!" she said between mouthfuls.

"Well, I didn't really make it to your mountain. I only got as far as Eskikahta."

"But that's almost there! What happened?"

"I ran out of time. I tried to make it over a long weekend, but I never got to the top."

"Oh, three days is not enough. You need at least a week. I'm furious you didn't let me know! Why, I could have arranged *everything* for you: permits, jeep transportation, guides..."

I didn't tell her how many guides I had.

"...donkeys, pup tents to sleep on the top of the mountain in the Throne Room of the Gods! Logistics! That's the ticket!"

"Yes, I know. Have another chicken liver."

She did and then shook her finger at me. "Now, remember! The next time you want to go to Nemrut Dag, you just let me know. Why, I can even give you a letter of introduction to the Governor of Adiyaman!"

Jimmy

≈

SHE INSISTED her name was Jimmy.
"That's not a Turkish name," I said. "What's your real name?"
"Jemileh. But you can call me Jimmy—all the Americans do."
She was my new maid, and she was enormous. A mountain of flesh—250 pounds, maybe 300. I wasn't about to ask her to step on my scales. And she was surely 60 years old.
"Jimmy is a good American name, isn't it?" she asked.
"Oh, yes it is, but—well—"
I knew the Turks loved American nicknames: Smiley for Ismail, Billy for Bulent, Howard for Ahwad, Shorty for anyone who was short, but Jimmy for a maid? Still, she seemed so pleased with it I didn't have the heart to disillusion her.
"Okay, Jimmy it is. Now, tell me, how much was Mrs. Brown paying you?" (I had already checked with Mrs. Brown.)
"400 lira a month."
I was so surprised she told the truth that I said, "How about 450 to begin with?" (Mrs. Brown had thought 400 was enough: "You rich bachelors shouldn't spoil these Turkish maids for the rest of us Americans." I had argued that the cost of living was going up every day, and how could anyone live on $40 a month?)
"Olur" (so be it) said Jimmy, and started immediately to clean the apartment.

I was new in Izmir and desperate for a maid. In those days (1961) a maid was not a luxury but a necessity. No washers, no dryers, no supermarkets. Every day the maid had to go shopping for vegetables, fruit, eggs, meat, bread, milk, even drinking water—and to a different store for each item. I had formed a passion for Turkish bread—heavy, full-bodied, made of unbleached flour, and out-of-this-world when toasted and smothered in butter. But, since it contained no preservatives, it lasted only one day. The next day it could easily be used for building blocks. So the maid was a necessity, and the daily bread was hardly a luxury at 10¢ a loaf.

In Diyarbakir I had gone through one houseboy and three maids in a little over two years. The problem was not so much honesty and trustworthiness as a difference in lifestyle. Unfamiliar with a vacuum cleaner, they would beat the rugs out on the balcony and slosh a bucket of water across the terrazzo floors. Patience and forgiveness often wore thin. Domestic help was always the number one topic of conversation at cocktail parties. Maids were bewildered by the products we would bring home from the PX. I once found a can of Drano in the refrigerator. And one of my maids had persuaded the janitor to cut off the handle of an American broom because she thought it had come from the factory in an unfinished condition.

I dreaded the prospect of finding a new maid when I moved to Izmir. I had found a lovely penthouse apartment on the seventh floor of a building right on the waterfront. Actually, the apartment complex was two separate buildings—one on the waterfront and the other, mine, on the backside. I could see the sea if someone held my feet as I leaned over the balcony. But I had a lovely view of the city of Izmir, especially at night, and of Alexander's castle on the mountain above. The two apartment towers were connected in the middle with inside balconies, staircases, and a glass-enclosed elevator in between. The elevator was charming when it worked. I found out later that it shorted out every time it rained. But at least when you got stuck, everyone could see you. The women would come to their balconies and laugh at the poor monkey (me) who was stuck, but some kind soul would finally fetch the janitor, who had mysterious ways of getting it unstuck.

The day I moved into my penthouse, the janitor asked me if I needed a maid—he knew a good one, wink, wink!

Well, I had heard all the stories I ever wanted to about American bachelors in Turkey who acquire live-in maids and the disastrous consequences thereof. The only story I liked concerned one of our young German employees. He was a tall, thin drink of water, rather goofy-looking, and he had a 45-year-old maid. One Friday she told him she couldn't come the next day but would send her daughter Sherry (Shirin). Well! Sherry turned out to be about 18 and a living, screaming doll! And Adolph, being young and healthy, and it being Saturday, well, not very much housework got done that day. She willingly agreed to stay overnight and even did some picking up around the apartment. At six o'clock the next morning, the mother appeared at the front door, accompanied by the father and three brothers. All of Sherry's male relatives were carrying guns. With no further persuasion Adolph agreed immediately to marry the girl. And they lived happily ever after!!! Adolph, who had rarely been invited to a party before, became the most sought-after guest on the Izmir cocktail circuit. Everyone adored Sherry.

But *I* was much more interested in having my dishes washed than my tensions relieved. Still, I so dreaded the thought of housework after getting home from the office that I said to the janitor, "Okay, I'll try her."

The next day, Thursday, he brought her. She was small and smiling and stacked. The janitor, holding her by the shoulders from behind, projected her into my apartment, winking. Then he went away.

She spoke no English, but this didn't bother me because of my years of Turkish maid-language in Diyarbakir. I showed her around the tiny apartment briskly, and told her she could set her own hours. All I wanted was for my apartment to be clean when I came home from work. "When you've finished your work, you can go home—even if it's one o'clock in the afternoon, or ten o'clock in the morning."

"Anything else?" she asked, raising one eyebrow.

"No. Here's the key. Your salary is 400 lira, okay?" She pouted for a second. "That's what the janitor told me," I said.

She flashed a smile and said, "Okay," in English.

Friday when I got home she was still there. She heard my key in the door and rushed to open it. Beaming, she showed me around the apartment—it looked fine to me.

"Very nice. Very good," I said. "Good night."

"Anything else?"

"No, no thank you. Good night."

"No whiskey? You have many bottles of American whiskey in the kitchen. The Americans always drink whiskey when they come home from work, I know."

"I'll help myself," I said, and gently but firmly showed her the door.

"Tomorrow?" she said in English.

"Tomorrow," I said, innocently.

The next morning, a Saturday, at exactly ten o'clock, my bedroom door flew open and she marched in, clapping her hands like a drill sergeant.

"Kalk! Kalk" she kept saying, clapping her hands insistently. I knew that it meant "get up, get up," or "rise, rise," but I was too bewildered and shook up to do anything.

"Saat on!" (ten o'clock) she announced. *"Kalk! Kalk!"*

Well! Saturday morning was the only morning I could sleep in, and I wasn't feeling too chipper after Happy Hour at the Officers Club the night before (it lasted from five till midnight), *and* my bedroom was my sanctuary. So I *kalked!* I rose in the bed holding the sheet around my naked body, pointed to the door and said, "Get out! Out!" I must have looked like Julius Caesar at his most imperious. "Out of this room! Out the front door! Out of the building! Out!"

She burst into tears and disappeared. I collapsed on the

bed, but sleep was finished. I put on a bathrobe and scurried to the shower. When I came out, somewhat refreshed, it was clear to me that she was not in the tiny apartment. I found her an hour later on the roof, still crying. I tried to soothe her by pressing two weeks' salary into her praying hands. She pleaded and begged and even knelt, but I was adamant. Sleep on Saturday is, as everyone knows, as sacred as church on Sunday.

The following Monday, one of our secretaries, Mrs. Brown, wanted to know if I would like a good maid.

"How old?"

"Oh, Jimmy must be about 60, but she's really very good and a hard worker and as honest as the day is bright. We're rotating next week, and I would like to find Jimmy a good home before I leave."

I was skeptical and disconsolate, but I said, "Okay."

The following week, Jimmy appeared at my door. I was shocked at the size of her. She was no more than five feet tall and almost as wide. She filled the doorway. I invited her in and asked her to sit down while we discussed her employment conditions. She declined to sit, perhaps because she thought my wood-frame furniture wouldn't hold her, or because there really wasn't any free place to sit. Magazines and newspapers were everywhere—the place was a shambles, a certified disaster area after a week without a maid. There were empty glasses, dirty dishes, a half-finished can of baked beans, and a gin bottle with a finger or two left in it. I had gotten so spoiled and lazy that I could hardly go a weekend without a maid, let alone a week!

When we concluded our negotiations, she took off her hat and coat and went to work immediately. She was slow and ponderous, but after an hour she had created a remarkable semblance of order out of the living room. I wasn't at all tempted to look in the kitchen where she had carted all the flotsam and jetsam because I was planning to eat out anyway.

"That's good enough for tonight, Jimmy. You can finish it up tomorrow."

"But the dishes, the kitchen, the bed—"

"No, no, no. Not necessary. Tomorrow. You come when you like, and you can go when your work is finished. You make your own hours. I just want the place clean."

"*Olur.* Good night, Mr. John."

"Good night, Jimmy."

A week went by. The place was immaculate. The refrigerator was stocked. Fresh bread every day. My shirts were washed (by hand) and beautifully ironed. And each evening she was waiting for me to give further instructions. She begged me to tell her what she was doing wrong.

"Well, you don't have to put the records back into their jackets," I said. "I'll do that." I had found Ella Fitzgerald in a Bert Lahr jacket, and vice versa. I knew both of them felt uncomfortable.

"Yes, Mr. John, that's good. I can't read."

"And when I'm reading a book, you don't have to put it back into the bookcase every day."

"Yes, Mister John. I understand. You are very clever."

By the end of the second week, I knew Mrs. Brown was right: Jimmy was a jewel!

Oh, she had her faults, but don't we all? One evening when I got home late, I noticed a broken glass in the sink. I wondered why she hadn't thrown it away. Then it dawned on me—she *wanted* me to know it got broken, not stolen. Perhaps she had knocked it over, or broken it in the damned marble sink. Other maids always got rid of the incriminating evidence, convinced that they would be fired summarily if they told you. You never really noticed any breakage until you had guests and discovered you didn't have enough highball glasses to go around. Even worse was when they would break a statue or art object and glue it back together, abominably.

"Mrs. Brown taught me this," said Jimmy, proudly pointing to a broken glass in the sink.

"God bless Mrs. Brown."

I was amused by this little scruple of hers and told my friends about it. They thought it wonderful and would always counter with some traumatic confrontation with *their* maid over a missing vase or cocktail shaker which, amidst tears and breast-beating, the maid would admit she had broken.

I even got to the point where I began to look forward to seeing what was in the sink each day, like a recorded message as to what had happened while I was at the office. But my curiosity soon changed to alarm when Jimmy started lining things up in the sink like dead soldiers. In one day: two glasses, a saucer, an ashtray, and a clay bull with a broken leg. I began having visions of being completely wiped out of crockery some day.

One Saturday morning as I was stretched out on the sofa reading *Time* magazine, I observed Jimmy using the vacuum cleaner. She ran it backward. It was a fearful sight as she backed into a table with a lamp that teetered and tottered until she caught it just short of final destruction. I suggested she run it forward, but I knew in my heart it was unnatural to run a vacuum cleaner forward. We all run it backward, but we aren't the size of baby elephants. I got so nervous I couldn't watch, so I would go up on the roof while she was vacuuming on Saturdays.

But Jimmy was fiercely protective of my property. I swear she took inventory every day.

"There's a carton of cigarettes missing!" she said accusingly, with a beady eye.

"It's all right, I took them to the office this morning."

"Where's the red book??" She asked.

"The red book?"

"It was right here on this table yesterday."

"Oh, the orange book." (The Turks make no distinction.[13]) "That wasn't mine. I returned it to Tom Curington."

Another evening a Turkish plumber, who was one of our

---

13. It is possible that John and Jimmy spoke a dialect in which red and orange are not distinguished.

employees, came to my apartment to fix a leaking sink. He refused to take any money for his services, so I gave him a beautiful blue sweater I had gotten as a Christmas present several years before and had never worn. I hate sweaters. As I was getting it out of the bottom drawer of the bureau, I wondered if Jimmy would notice.

The next day: "Where's that green sweater???"

"Don't worry, I gave it away. A gift."

And she was hard-working above and beyond the line of duty. She got so that she would wash and iron my clothes as soon as I got home from work. I would change into sport clothes, and she would grab my dress shirt and wash-and-wear trousers, take them into the bathroom, wash them, and then iron them while they were still wet, slowly and patiently.

"Jimmy, you don't have to do that now. Tomorrow's another day. Why don't you go home?"

"I have no home, Mister John, just a room. Rent is 250 lira, and the landlord says he's going to raise the rent next month. I go to the cinema once a week, with my girlfriend, on Thursdays, when the picture changes."

Sometimes she would sing softly, but mostly she talked to herself.

"What did you say, Jimmy?"

"Nothing! That wasn't meant for you."

One day I came home and found Jimmy stretched out dead on the living room floor.

Oh my God!!! Should I call the police? The hospital? An ambulance? We'll never be able to get her into that tiny elevator! Or down seven flights of stairs! How will we possibly get her out of this building?

And then I noticed the mountain of flesh was moving. I quickly grabbed her hand and started smacking it. I was surprised that she was holding a large screwdriver and I couldn't get it out of her clenched hand.

"Jimmy! Jimmy! Speak to me!"

"Oh, Mister John."

I managed to get her into a sitting position and ran for a glass of water. She was moaning and groaning, but she managed to sip it.

"Do you want some whiskey?"

"No, Mister John."

"What happened, Jimmy? What happened???"

She rolled her eyes and pointed with the screwdriver to a spot on the wall, and I knew immediately what had happened: she had electrocuted herself!

For weeks after I had moved into the apartment, I was constantly bothered by two bare wires sticking out of the wall. They were obviously intended for a wall fixture, but I finally decided I didn't want a wall lamp there. They unnerved me so much that one Sunday afternoon I decided they had to go. I got a pair of wire-cutters, but since I didn't know if the wall switch was on or off, I sensibly threw the main circuit breaker in the apartment and clipped the wires off flush with the wall. They were hardly noticeable, but Jimmy had apparently decided it was a screw and tried to remove it.

"I thought it was a screw," she said feebly.

"I know, I know," I said, feeling guilty. "Let me help you up," not having any idea how I could do it. She waved me away and in good time she rolled over on her hands and knees and managed to get to her feet surprisingly well. "Well, *I* need a drink, even if you don't."

The months went by peacefully. At cocktail parties when people began discussing their maids, I just smiled contentedly. Then one day, when Jimmy had finished her work, she came into the living room in her hat and coat and just stood there.

"What is it, Jimmy?"

I knew she was struggling to say something difficult.

"I want to go to Greece to die."

"What???"

"I want to go to Greece to die. I'm Greek, you know."

"No, I didn't know."

"Oh, yes. In 1922 when Ataturk drove the Greeks into the sea, and the sea ran red with blood, my mother and I weren't able to swim out to those British warships waiting to rescue us. Only my sister and her husband escaped. But we hid in the basement of the church while the Turks burned the whole Greek section of Smyrna to the ground.[14] It's now a park, where they have the International Fair every year. Eventually, we learned Turkish, took Turkish names, and called ourselves Turks. But I'm Greek. I want to die in Greece. My sister lives in Salonika."

I felt very sad. She had been with me almost two years. But I couldn't possibly refuse her request. "It's okay, Jimmy, if that's what you want to do."

"I have no money."

"I'll help you. How much do you need?"

"The boat from Izmir to Athens is 400 lira. And the train from Athens to Salonika is 150 lira."

I gave her the money and an extra three months' salary. "When do you want to leave?"

"Tomorrow."

"Tomorrow??"

"There's only one boat a week to Athens."

Oh, these Turks! I mean, these Greeks! They never plan ahead, just spring things on you at the last moment. Then suddenly I realized I was bereft.

"Jimmy, Jimmy, you must get me a replacement! Another maid! Someone as good as you!"

"Oh yes, don't worry. I've talked it over with my girlfriend Hattie. She'll come to work for you. I'll tell her to come to work on Monday."

She had tears in her eyes as she collected the few meager things of hers which she kept in my apartment and put them into a paper bag. She was very careful to show them to me: a brush, a comb, a bottle of Helena Rubenstein skin

---

14. Known as the Great Fire of Smyrna (or Catastrophe of Smyrna), which destroyed much of the port city of Smyrna (modern day Izmir).

cream that I had given her for Christmas, and a small picture of the Blessed Virgin, which I had never seen before.

"May I take this, for my sister?" It was a stupid bottle of after shave lotion, a birthday present I had never opened. It had a gold cap in the shape of a horse's head. She must have thought it very beautiful.

"Of course, of course."

We shook hands at the door and then impulsively she grabbed me around the waist and laid her head on my stomach. I watched her go down in the glass elevator until she disappeared from sight.

Hattie came on Monday, as promised. She was about 60 too, but tall and thin, all business, very pleasant—and I took an instant dislike to her. I didn't know why.

"Is your name really Hattie?"

"It's Hatijeh. She was the first wife of Mohammed. But the Americans can't pronounce it."

We agreed on her name and her salary, and she started to work. The maddening thing about her was that she was so pleasant, especially when I reprimanded her.

"These shirts are terrible! You've got to iron better than this! Look at that collar! All those creases and wrinkles!"

"Yes, m'sieur," she said, smiling.

"Look at these glasses! All those water spots. And look at this one—you can still see the milk ring around it. It's not even clean! You have to use hot water! Soap! Oh, God!"

"Yes, m'sieur."

I gave Hattie her walking papers after one week. To salve my conscience, I gave her two weeks' severance pay, and she left in great good spirits. She even insisted on shaking my hand. Then I got drunk on the sofa.

I was despondent. Friends and their wives tried to be sympathetic and even came to wash the dishes from time to time, but only Johnnie Walker was of any real help. After a week I had gotten to the point where I was considering taking back the *Kalk* lady. I hated to go home. Then one evening I returned to the apartment building and found the stupid elevator was out of order. Well, that did it! The final blow! The ultimate insult! I was going under, and I didn't care anymore. Seven stories! Or eight when you consider the Turks don't count the ground floor, like the French. Oh well, what's the difference! By the time I was dragging up to the 7th floor I didn't care if I lived or died.

And then I saw Jimmy!

She was leaning with her back against my door, panting and wheezing and puffing.

"Jimmy, what are you doing here???" She was a sight for sore eyes. A vision of loveliness. Had I climbed to heaven?

She couldn't answer me. All she could say was, "Oh, Mister John! Oh, Mister John! Oh, Mister John!"

I opened the door, and we both stumbled into the apartment. I collapsed on the sofa, and she plopped in one of the stronger chairs.

"Jimmy, Jimmy, why are you back? What happened? Tell me quick!"

Slowly, one by one, she got out the words.

"When I got to Salonika—"

"Yes, yes."

"My sister wasn't home—"

"Yes."

"So I came back."

As simple as that.

She slowly took off her coat and went to work. She stayed with me until I was transferred to Ankara. Kitty Curington immediately agreed to take Jimmy when I left, so I knew she was in good hands.

It was about a year later that I got a letter from Kitty:

Dear John,
Jimmy died. Not in our apartment from the electrical wiring, but in her bed, in her sleep. Her girlfriend, who suspected foul play, told the police she worked for us, so I had to go and identify the body. I did.

She looked so peaceful and plump, like always. We had her buried in the Greek Cemetery. We selected a stone, very small and simple. Since we knew so little about her—we didn't know when she was born (she didn't either, I asked her one time) or even what her real name was—we just put on the stone:

JIMMY
DIED 1965

Is it all right? We'll miss her.

Love,
Kitty

I fixed myself a drink and sipped it slowly. Yes, It's all right, I thought. God is good.

"May I Have Your Eyes?"

≈

I THOUGHT it was one of the most romantic things I had ever heard in my life. She said it as she gazed deeply into my eyes. I was sure I understood her perfectly as my Turkish was improving by leaps and bounds daily. She even repeated it: "May I have your eyes?" She gazed into them so deeply I began to get embarrassed. My eyes really aren't exceptional at all. They are small and hazel, with thin eyelashes and no lids. I remembered an old American girlfriend who once told me that my eyes were cruel, and if it weren't for my sensual mouth, I would be quite unattractive. But, here was this lovely Turkish girl gazing into them, wanting them. I could feel myself starting to fall in love.

We were having dinner together at an outdoor restaurant on a little hill overlooking the Bay of Izmir. It was a garden with tables and chairs under the olive trees. There was a small structure housing only the kitchen, but all the food was grilled outside over hot coals. The view was magnificent: the lights around the bay shined like a string of pearls, and the city of Izmir across the bay tumbled down from Alexander's Castle into the sea. In those days there were no neon or mercury vapor lamps, only incandescent ones, and they twinkled like diamonds and topaz in the crystal-clear night. It was a warm night (I'm sure there must have been a moon), and soft music floated through the silver leaves of the olive trees.

It was really my first date with Jaleh (her name meant "a flower kissed with dew"), though I had sat with her and danced with her many times at the Sibel Gazino and bought her many drinks. The bar girls never got a night off, and the only way you could get the manager to let one of them off was to pay for the number of drinks she would have hustled had she been working. But I knew the manager well, and he said it was all right, figuring I had already bought enough drinks and would probably buy a lot more. Gazing into her big dark eyes, I knew he was right.

I really didn't know the proper answer to her question, but I decided on "*Evet, janim*" (yes, my soul), and put a lot of heavy breathing into it.

She thanked me happily like a child, picked up my fish head, and sucked the eyes out. Swoop! Swoop! And they were gone.

I was sick. Then I noticed the fish skeleton on her plate. She had sucked it clean of any flesh, including the head. Ah.

The fish was indeed excellent, a trout, but since I had no intention of eating the head on mine, I had cut it off. She had apparently thought I was saving the best part till last.

I thought I felt a chill wind come up, so I suggested it was time to go.

Nuri

≈

THE DOORBELL RANG. I opened the door, and there stood the most beautiful boy I had ever seen in my life. He was about 18 years old, maybe 20, hair the color of honey, eyes the color of damp turquoise. I was sure that he was a cup-bearer of the gods, except that he was carrying a toolbox.

"Mister John?"

"Yes."

"My name is Nuri. I am a carpenter. Your Personnel Supervisor, Metin, has sent me to put up your curtain rods. May I come in, please?"

"Oh yes, yes, come in! Please! Am I glad to see you! *Hosh geldiniz!*" (You have come well.)

"*Hosh bulduk.*" (We have found it well.)

He spoke entirely in Turkish—a curious, evenly pronounced Turkish—and I answered him in my heavily accented pidgin Turkish.

Nuri went to work with great efficiency. With a chisel and a hammer he chipped out deep square holes in the concrete walls, then inserted pre-cut wooden blocks and cemented them in with white cement.

I particularly admired his work because, in the past, I had destroyed whole walls just trying to put in a nail to hang a picture. When I had to replace a light bulb in a ceiling fixture, I always prayed to the Hittite deities. Usually the old bulb had fused into the socket and, when I wrenched it out, the whole light fixture would come down on my head—to say nothing of several yards of ceiling plaster. And, as to curtain rods!—I had been through that horror two times before. Each time the rods and drapes came crashing to the floor, and I had to take to my bottle.

Nuri said to me in precisely enunciated Turkish, as if he were speaking to an idiot child, "It is necessary to wait for 15 minutes until the cement hardens. I am very sorry, Mister John."

"Okay! Okay! No problem. Let's have a drink! Would you like a beer?"

"No, thank you."

"*Viski?*"

"No, thank you."

"Do you mean 'no,' or are you just *nazlanmaking?*" (The Turkish word *nazlanmak* means to say 'no' when you really mean 'yes.' It is polite to refuse at least three times before accepting. It's very wearing on the host.)

Nuri laughed and said, "Yes, I will drink a beer."

"Good."

As I went to the kitchen, I remembered a story I had heard about a Turkish military pilot who had been sent to Texas for training and had been invited to his instructor's house for dinner the first night. He arrived with some other Turkish pilots who had been there some time, and the host said to him, "Would you like a drink?"

"No, thank you."

The other Turks all ordered martinis, gin-and-tonics, scotch-and-waters. When the host brought the drinks, the newcomer whispered in his friend's ear, "Where's my drink?"

"You said 'no!' In America if you want a drink you don't *nazlanmak!*"

I brought Nuri a Budweiser in a can and gave him a glass. (The Turks think the Americans are barbarians to drink out of a can or a bottle.) He poured the beer carefully into the glass.

"You don't *look* Turkish to me," I said.

"I'm not. I'm Yugoslavian."

"Oh, Yugoslavian! What are you doing here in Turkey?"

"I live here. I am a Turkish citizen now."

"Now?"

"We came from Yugoslavia when the Communists took over our country. My father is a strict Moslem. I am not, as you can see." He pointed to his beer, which he had hardly touched. "The Moslems are very anti-Communist, and all of them fled to other countries—some to Italy and France, and some here to Turkey. My father decided to come here because this is a Moslem country. The Turkish government had put out the word that Yugoslav Moslems were welcome here. They even set aside villages for them and gave them long-term loans at no interest to build houses." Nuri spoke slowly and thoughtfully. He took a sip of his beer.

"Do you like it here?"

He looked at me for such a long time before answering that I began to feel uncomfortable. I think he was trying to decide if he could trust me.

"No."

"Why not?"

"There are many reasons." He looked at his hands as if evaluating their worth. "I loved Yugoslavia. We had good schools—there were lots of sports, soccer, gymnastics, swimming. And activities like painting and woodworking, even dancing—and music—." He fell silent. Finally, he sighed and sipped his beer. "Then, we came here. We had to learn Turkish. We had to change our name. The Turks insisted. Our name was Dumovitch. I think in English it means 'son of Thomas.' The Turks changed it to Dumanoglu which means 'son of smoke.' My father didn't like it, but the Turks wouldn't give us identification papers unless we had Turkish-sounding names." He fell silent again. "My name was Yuri, but they said that wasn't a Moslem name, so they changed it to Nuri." He took a sip of his beer. "I think the cement is dry."

He went back to work, and I put some music on the phonograph—something soft—Chet Atkins's "Yellow Bird."

I still had my old Diyarbakir drapes. All my old furnishings fit perfectly in my new apartment. The walls were white (the landlord was horrified when I refused his offer to paint them blue or green or lilac—"That's only the first coat, Mister John!") and my orange-and-black corduroy drapes looked great when they came back from the cleaners. Surprisingly, they didn't fade—though they smelled to high heaven of 85-octane gasoline. I was afraid to light a match for days afterward.

Nuri finished before Chet Atkins did. We hung the drapes, and I didn't even hold my breath because I was so confident of the good work Nuri had done. They looked marvelous. Even the length was perfect—all Turkish ceilings must be four meters high. Nuri packed up his tools and started to leave.

"You haven't finished your beer, Nuri!"

"Oh."

"Sit down. I need another. Do you want another?"

"No, thank you, Mister John."

"Are you *nazlanmaking* again?"

"No, truly," he said, then laughed. "I still have half a can left."

"Well, I'm going to have a jumbo martini to celebrate the hanging of the drapes."

When I had fixed my drink, I started to change the records on the stereo, but Nuri said, "Please, Mister John, may I hear that record again?"

"Of course! Chet Atkins is one of my favorites."

"I play the guitar too," he said modestly.

"You do?"

"Not as well as this gentleman. But I love the guitar. It's the only thing I brought with me from Yugoslavia. My father was very angry." He lapsed into silence again.

Reluctantly, after he finished his beer, he said, "I must go now."

"How much do I owe you, Nuri?"

"Oh no, Mister John. Metin Bey will pay me. He told me not to take any money from you."

"Well, I certainly want to thank you, Nuri. You certainly did a beautiful job."

"You can call me Yuri."

Several weeks later I was sitting in the Londra Bar when a voice said, "May I sit down with you, Mister John?" I looked up. It was Nuri/Yuri!

"Yuri! Sit down! Let me buy you a beer."

"No, thank you. I already have one." He showed me his bottle, half full.

"How have you been, Yuri?"

"Fine."

"Do you come here often?"

"Yes."

"You do??"

"Nearly every night. I've seen you several times, but I didn't want to come over to your table."

"You should have."

He looked at the floor. "You had a girl with you."

"Oh, that doesn't mean anything. I can't sit down at a table without having a girl, or several of them, plop down with me and beg me to buy them a drink. Sometimes I do and sometimes I don't. They get fired if they can't get someone to buy them a drink. I often buy the ugly old girls a drink, just to tease the young pretty ones."

Yuri didn't seem to be listening to me.

"So, you come to the bars every night? You like them, eh?"

"I hate them," he said.

"But—"

"I only come to this bar for the music. They have the best orchestra, and they always play the latest American songs."

It certainly was true. I was always amazed at how current the songs were. And they sang them in a comic English that they obviously didn't understand. I guessed they had learned them by rote from the Armed Services Radio Network.

"I only buy one beer. It lasts me the whole evening. The manager doesn't like it, I know. But I never take up a table if it's crowded—I sit at the bar. And on Saturday nights, when all the GIs come, I just stand in a corner."

The male vocalist started singing "Volare," and Yuri fell

silent. When it was over, he said to me, "What does *volare* mean?"

"I think it means 'to fly' or 'let's fly away.' It's Italian. I don't know any Italian."

"I thought it was an American song. American music is the best." He sipped his warm beer.

"Don't you want a cold beer? Waiter!"

"No, no, really, Mister John!"

I realized he was serious, so I told the waiter to bring me another *kanyak*.

"I don't particularly like beer. My father thinks I'm a drunkard because I come here every night. He says I'm going to hell because drinking is forbidden by the Koran. But I only come to hear the music. I want to learn to play the guitar well and become a singer. Not famous, like Elvis Presley—just a singer and maybe make enough money to live on. Right now I'm a carpenter. I make 550 lira a month. I give my father 500 lira and I keep 50 for myself—for beer. My father is a shoemaker. In Belgrade, he owned a big department store, but the Communists confiscated everything. When we came here to Turkey, he had to start all over again, and the only thing he knew was shoemaking. That's how he got started in Belgrade as a boy. The Turks wanted to call us *Ayakkabicioglu*—'son of a shoemaker'—but my father said he couldn't even pronounce that word, so he agreed to *Dumanoglu*. My brother is a carpenter too—we both learned woodworking in Yugoslavia—but he's married, so he can't contribute very much to our family. My sister is a nurse. She gives all her money to my father. He adores her. She is a saint, I know, but I don't think she will ever marry—she is 28. My two younger sisters are still in school. I have a brother, two years old. He's very sweet, and I love him more than anybody in this world. But I keep wondering why my father keeps making babies when we're so poor."

Yuri was silent for a moment, then said imploringly, "But I only keep 50 lira for myself, Mister John."

When the evening was over, Yuri wouldn't let me pay for his beer—it was two lira.

"Come and visit me sometime, Yuri."
"I would like to. You have many records, Mister John."
"You'll always be welcome."
I thought to myself that he's certainly not going to get a kick out of Cole Porter or Ethel Merman (nearly all my records were Broadway musicals—the *only* guitar record I had was Chet Atkins), so I went to the PX and luckily found a record of Andrés Segovia.

Three weeks later the doorbell rang and there was a round table in the doorway, supported by two human hands and two human legs, completely obscuring the face of the caller. It was Yuri. He was bubbling with excitement as he brought the table in and placed it between my L-shaped sofas. It was black-lacquered and intended to be a match for my round coffee table, but the workmanship was so smooth and professional it put my Diyarbakir carpenters to shame. The top of the table was bare wood, and Yuri insisted we cover it with turquoise tiles to match my coffee table.

I gave him a beer, put a stack of records on the phonograph, and got out my tiles and Dupont cement. Yuri cut the tiles for the circular edge while I did the easy part, the center. He immediately grasped my idea of alternating blue and green in a haphazard fashion. Dave Brubeck entertained us with "Blue Rondo à la Turk" and Patti Page crooned her syrupy "Tennessee Waltz." Anthony Quinn stomped up a storm on "Zorba the Greek." I was saving the Andrés Segovia until last. Yuri asked to hear "Zorba" again.

"*Hi, hi!*" I said.

"American music is so wonderful, isn't it, Mister John?"

"That music happens to be Greek. And the composer, Mikis Theodorakis, happens to be a Communist."

Yuri immediately stiffened. I could have bit my tongue. Why do I always have to show off my knowledge? God will punish me some day for not putting it to better use. I quickly followed "Zorba" with Andrés Segovia. Yuri was enchanted and stopped working.

We had finished gluing the tiles. I let Yuri mix the grout—the white cement he had used on the wooden blocks for the curtain rods. The table was exquisite.

When Segovia had finished, Yuri said, "I must go now." He dashed to the door, fending off my attempts to pay him for the table, and started down the stairs.

"Yuri, stop! Wait!" I pulled the Segovia record off the turntable, put it in its jacket, and said, "This is for *you!*" He accepted it without *nazlanmaking*. "Come back again, Yuri. And bring your guitar! I want to hear you sing."

"Okay, Mister John. May I bring a friend?"

"Of course."

"Okay, next Sunday."

The following Sunday Yuri came with his guitar and his friend—a *beautiful* 18-year-old girl with olive skin, black hair, and green eyes. She was obviously a Turk. The green eyes, a recessive gene that now and then turns up in Turks, are much beloved. They even have a song called "*Yeshil Cozier,*" which means "Green Eyes."

"This is Sevil," said Yuri. (I knew her name meant "beloved.")

Then to Sevil, "This is Mister John."

I reached out to shake her hand, but she gave me only her fingertips. I asked them to sit down and went scurrying into the kitchen for a 7-Up and a beer. (Yuri had explained to her my objection to *nazlanmaking*.) I fixed myself a tall scotch-and-soda.

It was a delightful afternoon. Yuri sang three songs that were haunting and unnerving.

"Is that Serb or Croatian you're singing?" I asked, like a smart aleck.

"Slavic," he said, "I am Slovene."

Then he sang "Yellow Bird" in astonishingly good English, and finally, a Turkish song, *"Bir Mektup Yazdirdim Urfali Kizina."* Sevil clapped her hands in rhythm as he played and sang. The song title is: "I Had a Letter Written to an Urfa Girl." It means, I can't read or write, so I went to one of the public scribes in the city square and had him write a letter to my beloved in Urfa (a town in southeastern Turkey—notable as the birthplace of Abraham of the Bible). The song is full of regrets and longings for a clean, lost love.

"We must go now," said Yuri as he rose. The girl stood up and took his arm. As they strolled out the door, Yuri struck up a lively replica of Andrés Segovia's "Andalusia." Halfway down the stairs he looked back at me and shrugged his shoulders, meaning, "I haven't got it yet—I'm still working on it."

I hadn't thought of Yuri in weeks, when one Saturday evening the doorbell rang, and there was Yuri. His face was a blotch of red. He was swaying from side to side like a battered child ready to fall over. I reached out and grabbed him, and led him to the sofa.

"Yuri, what's the matter? What is it?"

He buried his face in the sofa and sobbed uncontrollably. Finally he lifted himself up and fell into my arms. "Mister John! Mister John! My father has disowned me! He threw me out of the house! He said I was no longer his son! He said he never wanted to see me again! He said I was worthless, a no-good, a drunkard, a hooligan, and he never wanted to see me again."

I was completely overwhelmed. I had never been in this position before—someone clinging to me for help.

After a while, he pulled himself together, dried his eyes with his knuckles, and began to speak very quietly in a dead voice. "This morning my father got a letter from the Yugoslavian government. They are going to compensate him for confiscating his department store. Full value plus interest. He is now a millionaire." Yuri fell silent.

I said nothing because I could think of nothing to say.

After a few minutes, Yuri spoke again. "When I got home tonight—it was payday—I gave my father my week's salary of 500 lira. He spit on it and threw it on the floor. He drove me out of the house yelling, 'I disown you! You are no longer my son!'"

Finally, Yuri stood up. "I must go now, Mister John."

"But where will you go? Do you want to stay here tonight?"

"No."

"Let me give you some money—for a hotel room."

"I have money. The money my father didn't want. Goodbye, Mister John."

"Yuri!"

But he was gone. I never saw him again.

Scotch and Holy Water

≈

I HATE TELEGRAMS. They always spell bad news.

ARRIVING IZMIR 10 SEPTEMBER FLIGHT TK 697.
DEPARTING 12 SEPTEMBER. ARRANGE HOTEL ROOM AT BUYUK EFES HOTEL, PREFERABLY ROOM 528, AND A TRIP TO MARY'S HOUSE.
MIKE AND MOLLY McCARTHY

Oh, how I dreaded their visit. He was a friend of one of the priests I knew when I was teaching at Notre Dame, and we all had dinner together one night. I was bored to death. Mike had spent the entire war in Washington, D.C. as a general's aide, arranging transportation to and from the airport, hotel accommodations, shopping tours, theater tickets, and dinner and nightclub reservations—always the best table (he knew the power of a $20 bill). He even bragged about bribing one of the Swiss guards at the Vatican to get a better seat at an "audience" with the Pope. So I knew he expected the red carpet treatment.

I understood the telegram:

—Mary's House was supposedly the final resting-place of the Blessed Virgin Mary in the hills above Ephesus, the famous ancient city about 40 miles from Izmir. Mike was always visiting shrines. He was one of those devout Irish Catholics who went to church every Sunday, said grace before meals even in restaurants, and loved to tell dirty jokes.

His wife Molly was no slouch at keeping up with him in all departments.

—Room 528 was probably a room occupied by some VIP that Mike had contacted when he was planning the trip. Mike was always soliciting (and accepting) the opinions of the great and the near-great.

I personally went to the Buyuk Efes Hotel (it *was* elegant) to make reservations. Naturally, the desk clerk thought I was mad to ask for Room 528.

"Sir, we cannot possibly guarantee *that* particular room."

"Is 528 on the sea side or the pool side?"

"The pool side."

"Then please try to reserve a room for the McCarthys on the pool side."

It figured. The pool was built above ground on the slope of a grassy mound behind the hotel. The entire wall of the lower side of the pool was made of glass. A bar faced it. The pool was the favorite watering spot of the Izmir elite, and watching the Turkish mermaids was the Americans' favorite spectator sport. I myself thought the waterfront side much better, with the view of the ferryboats plying the Bay of Izmir, especially in the evening when the sun was setting.

I had been in Izmir for a year and prided myself on being the best tour guide in the "Pearl of the Middle East." I never tired of showing people the birthplace of Homer and, of course, Ephesus. Archeologists had only uncovered about one-fifth of the city, and since they were working continuously, there was always something new to see each time I went. But I was *not* looking forward to squiring the McCarthys to Ephesus. Too many things could go wrong.

I met them at the airport and took them to the Buyuk Efes. Surprisingly, the hotel actually had a record of the reservation. (Mike always expected things to go *right* and would raise holy hell if they didn't; I always expected things to go *wrong* and would make the best of it if they did.) Room 522 turned out to be an entirely satisfactory substitute for Room 528. "Boy! Look at that swimming pool!" I said.

The next day I picked them up in our comfortable American company car and asked them if they minded if we took along with us Gustav Halving (my old Norwegian friend from Diyarbakir, who had recently been transferred to Izmir and had never seen Ephesus).

"Fine, fine, fine," said Mike, always glad to meet an underling.

Gustav was about 65, a regular Viking with a handsome head of blond-white hair, a ruddy complexion, a barrel chest, and a bottle of Johnnie Walker in his ditty bag, which he showed me surreptitiously when I picked him up.

"Keep that thing out of sight," I said, not wanting to upset this religious pilgrimage.

"I never go *anywhere* without my friend Chonnie Valker."

"Okay, okay, but keep it out of sight."

We stopped to take some pictures on the Kordon, the palm-lined street on the Izmir waterfront, then began the hour's drive to Ephesus. It was a glorious sunny day.

Suddenly, Mike started yelling from the back seat. I almost wrecked the car. "Where's the lens cover?" he shouted. "Where's the lens cover???"

"I don't know," said Molly.

"It's gone!"

I started to slow down but thought stopping really wasn't worth it.

"Maybe it's in your purse," he screamed. "Look in your purse!"

"It's not in my purse," she said, trying to be calm while rummaging frantically through her purse. "I didn't put it in my purse! I didn't have it. You had it! Maybe you left it on the wall when we took those pictures on the waterfront!"

"Look in the camera case! Maybe it's on the floor! Look in my coat pockets!"

This last order had to do with the fact that Mike's hands were paralyzed, and Molly had to do all the things his fingers couldn't do. He had had some sort of stroke years before that paralyzed his whole body. Eventually he recovered completely—except for the use of his hands. They were stiff, unbending, turned in like claws. It was unnerving to shake hands with him, as I had done at the airport, and to feel that stiff claw. He couldn't open his fingers at all, or even tighten them into a fist. So Molly had to be his fingers, buttoning his shirt, tying his tie. The lens cap wasn't in his pockets either.

The "discussion" continued for another 20 miles, and Gustav kept clucking in Norwegian about the noise in the back seat. I interrupted them to point out the Goat Castle we were then passing. It was on the top of a mountain overlooking three valleys. The castle was not impregnable, but it was certainly impossible to take it by surprise. I told them the story of the Seljuk Turks who stormed the castle one night with a handful of men and a herd of 1,000 goats. Each goat had a torch strapped to its head as they clambered up the mountain. The inhabitants of the castle, tired old Romans, surrendered without a struggle to this obviously overwhelming force. I didn't really believe the story. I personally think the local yokels called the fortress Goat Castle because only a goat could get to it. I had climbed it once—never again. The architecture of the castle, 4th century Byzantine, was dull and uninteresting to my poor eye. And climbing down turned out to be just as difficult as climbing up. The goats could have it.

Finally we arrived at Ephesus. We first toured St. John's Basilica. St. John had written his Apocalypse on the island of Patmos, just off the coast of Turkey, and had sent it to the Seven Churches of Asia. But he died in Ephesus and was buried here. The Basilica, now in ruins, was built in the 6th century over a 2nd century church that rested on the Apostle's tomb. It was being restored, according to a sign, by donations from a Protestant church in Lima, Ohio. Molly declared that standing on such hallowed ground made her the luckiest Catholic alive.

I next showed them a few marble blocks, all that was left of one of the Seven Wonders of the World, the Temple of Artemis. Most of it, including the glorious green marble pillars, had been carted off to Constantinople in 360 A.D. to build the famous St. Sophia Church, which the Ottoman

Turks turned into a mosque.

We then went to the ancient city of Ephesus. Molly pulled pamphlets, brochures, books, and maps out of her purse, and read aloud the details of each building as we came to it. I pointed out the brothel, but she said, "We'll skip that."

As we were climbing up the Marble Road, just above the Temple of Hadrian, Molly shouted, "Stop! Stop!" She started rummaging through her purse again (oh God, another crisis?) and this time pulled out a Bible. "This is where St. Paul gave one of his sermons to the Ephesians," she said, flicking madly through the New Testament. "Ah, here it is! Luke's Acts of the Apostles. Here, you read it," she said, handing it to me, "and we'll just stand here and drink it in. Oh, what extra meanings it will have, right here on the very spot. Go ahead, John, we're waiting."

Well, I wasn't about to make an ass of myself in front of all those tourists. I flatly refused.

"Oh, all right, I'll read it," she said. And in a voice loud and pure, she began: "'And Paul passed through the upper country and came to Ephesus. There he found some disciples. And he said to them, 'Did you receive the Holy Ghost when you believed?' And they said, 'No, we have never even heard that there is a Holy Ghost.'"

Her words went soaring out over the Temple of Hadrian, down the Marble Road to the Library of Celsius, over the Agora, the Theatre, the Baths, the Gymnasium, and down the Harbor Road to the Aegean Sea. Gustav appeared spellbound, but maybe it was shock. Mike was fidgeting. I was flushed. A group of Turkish schoolgirls in little blue smocks had gathered around us. They gaped and giggled. This only spurred Molly on.

"'And God did extraordinary miracles by the hands of Paul, so that handkerchiefs or aprons were carried away from his body to the sick, and diseases left them and the evil spirits came out of them.'" She went on and on. Finally, mercifully, she closed the book. She closed her eyes for a few seconds, then took a deep breath and exhaled luxuriously.

"Let's go!" she said, and charged up the Marble Road toward the Odeon. This was my cue to leave them, since I had made the tour so many times.

"You go on up to the Odeon," I said, "and I'll go back to the parking lot to get the car. I'll drive around the back road and meet you at the Odeon. Then we can drive up the mountain to Mary's House."

"Swell, swell!" said Mike. "Boy, you sure do know all the ropes, John. Whew! This hill is steep."

A few minutes later I met them at the Odeon and drove them up to Mary's House.

"Oh, this is lovely! Lovely!" cried Molly.

And it was—a series of curving terraces, lined with olive trees, just below the top of the mountain, and overlooking the Aegean Sea in the distance. We sat down at a picnic table and Molly said to me, "Now, John, tell us *all* about this place."

"Well, most people believe that Mary was buried in Jerusalem—there's a church there built over her tomb. But in 1823 a German nun named Catherine Emmerich had a dream. In it, she saw St. John taking Mary on a ship from Jerusalem to Ephesus. Then they climbed the mountain on donkeys to this very spot where John built her a home and where she spent the remainder of her earthly life. It became her final resting place. Catherine Emmerich had never been out of Germany, but she described the location and the house in precise detail. Her dream wasn't made public till long after her death. Then, in 1892 a German archeologist decided to test her "vision" and sure enough, right over there, he found the remains of a house that dates from the 1st century A.D., exactly where she had described it."

"Where do *you* think she was buried," asked Molly, "Jerusalem or here?"

"Oh, I don't know." (It was only a few years later that Pope John the 23rd, that sweet old man, resolved the dilemma by declaring *both* locations "a holy place.")

We walked around the house, which had been reconstructed of locally made red brick. A line was painted about three feet up from the ground showing the original foundation discovered in 1892. The old brick and the new brick were of identical composition.

Inside, the house consisted of a living room, a small bedroom, and a kitchen which was not much more than a fireplace. The building was now a church, with an altar, votive candles, and pews. We all knelt down and said a prayer, except Gustav, who had disappeared. Molly lit a candle.

"What on earth are all these rags tied to this candelabrum?" she whispered.

"Oh, the Turkish girls always do that when they visit a religious shrine. They tear off bits of their dresses, or scarves or handkerchiefs, and tie them to a tree outside the shrine. It's like a prayer or a wish."

"Do the Turks believe in the Virgin Mary?"

"Oh, yes. They're all Moslems, of course, and Mary is one of the three holy women of the Koran. But the girls make a wish at any shrine—it doesn't matter what religion."

"What do they wish for?"

"A handsome husband."

"You mean a good husband."

"No, a handsome man. Like a movie star."

We then strolled outside and took a path to a lower terrace, where there was a spring coming out of the rock, directly below Mary's House.

"This is holy water, isn't it?" Mike asked.

I was caught a little off guard and sputtered, "Well—I don't *know* if it's *holy* water—er—I always drink it when I come here. It's good—nice and cool." And I cupped my hands and took a swig.

Then Mike stepped up to the spring.

"Help me off with my jacket, Molly," he said. "And now, roll up my sleeves."

I suddenly realized what was happening. He was preparing to immerse his hands into the "holy" water. He was praying for a miracle. The clue was in the telegram. I started to get light-headed and dizzy. I felt sure if he *was* cured, I would simultaneously have a heart attack and fall over dead, right on the spot. Subconsciously, I suppose I was giving God a choice: a miracle and a death, or...

The spring had made a little pool below it, about waist-high. Slowly Mike lowered his hands into the water. I held my breath. My eyeballs were straining to get out of their sockets. My heart was pounding so loudly I thought it would burst my eardrums. He held his hands in the water for a long time—was it 10 seconds?—it seemed like an hour. Then slowly he raised them and held them in front of him. Another unbearable pause. Finally he spoke:

"Put my coat on, Molly."

I slowly let out my breath and began to relax, almost to the point of going to pieces. And then all hell broke loose!

"The canteen! The canteen!" he started screaming. "Where's the canteen?"

And she began screaming too. "What? Oh, the canteen! Didn't you bring it?"

"Didn't *you* bring it???"

"It must be at the hotel!"

"No! Oh my God! We bring a canteen all the way from America to get some holy water, and you leave it at the hotel!"

And on and on and on, each accusing the other. I tried to calm them down and told them I'd find a container. "Don't worry." I ran and found Gustav sitting under an olive tree, smoking his pipe. I shook him by the shoulders.

"Where's that bottle of scotch?" I screamed.

"It's right here in my ditty bag. I've yust been having a nip. I never go anywhere without my friend Chonnie—"

"Give it to me! Quick! I need the bottle! We'll pour the scotch out on the ground."

"Never!" he said, clutching the bag to his chest. "I die first."

And we started a tug-of-war. The old goat was much stronger than I expected. "I'll pay you for it!" I screamed. "I'll get you *two* bottles of scotch! *Ten* bottles!!!"

"Never!!!"

Suddenly I heard Molly behind me: "Scotch? Scotch? Did I hear someone say 'scotch'?"

"No, it's nothing, Molly. I mean, yes, he's got a bottle of scotch and won't give it to me. We can pour it out on the ground and then fill it with holy water."

"Oh, that would be a sin, John, wasting all that good scotch."

"That's what I said!" cried Gustav, still clutching his friend.

"Why don't we all have a little drink?" said Molly.

"Well, I—er—do you mean it?"

"Sure!" Then she turned and called, "Hey, Mike! Would you like to have some scotch?"

"Scotch!!!" He perked up immediately, apparently quite over his religious experience. "Great! Just what I need! Boy, John, you sure do think of everything!"

So we all sat down under an olive tree and got plastered.

"This is a great place!" said Mike.

"Heavenly!" said Molly.

"*Skol!*" said Gustav.

By the time the bottle was empty, we didn't even need it. We had explained our plight and pledged undying friendship to every Turkish man, woman, and child for miles around. They brought us pop bottles, beer bottles, vinegar bottles, baby bottles, and a mad assortment of jars and jugs. We were all on a first-name basis. One little tyke named Ziya even offered us his sand bucket. We filled up the whole trunk of the car with holy water. We could hardly get the lid down. Lazily and happily we weaved our way back to Izmir.

At the hotel I asked Mike to get his canteen so I could fill it up with holy water.

"Well, I've been thinking. We're already overweight, and we still have to buy some copper pots and brass trays, so why don't you just have your Packing and Crating Division send some of the water to me by mail?"

We parted on the best of terms. The pilgrimage had been a smashing success.

But since *I* was the "Packing and Crating Division" of our company, for the following week I fretted over how to mail a bottle of holy water to America without it getting broken. Finally, I went to the PX and found a large plastic bottle for 39¢. I filled it with holy water and packed it carefully in excelsior.[15] I took it to the Army Post Office and filled out the mandatory Customs Declaration tag. "One bottle of holy water," I wrote. Value? Well, I didn't want to declare the value as "nothing"—that seemed to be, if not sacrilegious, at least irreverent. I finally resolved my scruples by declaring "39¢" and sent it off.

I still had a whole trunkful of holy water and didn't know what to do with it—I couldn't just pour it into the gutter. So I carted it up to my apartment and served it to all my friends for months afterward. I felt very urbane saying, "Would you like a scotch and holy water? It's delicious!"

---

15. Excelsior: softwood shavings used for packing fragile goods.

The City Under the Sea

≈

I FIRST HEARD about the city under the sea at a cocktail party in Izmir. I was trying to make meaningful conversation to the hostess, who was quite drunk, and I told her I loved old ruins. There were so many in the environs of Izmir—Ephesus, Bergama, Sardis...

"And the city under the sea!" she said, crashing her martini glass against mine and swallowing the contents in one gulp.

"Where's that?" I said, intrigued.

"Oh, somewhere this way or that," she said, waving her free arm north and south (I took careful notice). "Roger knows. I never pay any attention when we go 'marbling.'"

"Marbling?"

"Oh, that's what I call it when Roger drags me out to all these dirty places to pick up these dirty marbles[16]—look at them!" She flung her arm out all around the room, which was crowded with a hundred guests—American and Turkish and Levantine. Behind a buttock or a curvature of the spine, I saw white marble statues and heads and chunks of rock sitting on tables and shelves.

"But where is the city under the sea?"

"Oh, God! Who knows? Only Roger! But he passed out in the bedroom before the party started. Who *are* all these people?"

I felt it was hardly my place to remind her that she was

---

16. Marble artifacts.

the hostess, the wife of the Political Attaché to the American Consulate in Izmir, and that we were all properly invited (my engraved card was in my jacket pocket, and I patted it in case she might ask for my credentials.)

The following week I quizzed all my friends about the city under the sea. None of them had ever heard of it. I checked all the guidebooks—no reference to it. I even asked the Turks, which I knew was hopeless. The Turks hated the archeological ruins since they were all Greek, and everyone knows how the Turks hate the Greeks. And they resented the Americans for preferring to photograph old ruins rather than their new modern hotels and factories.

I finally decided that my hostess was a little wacky, that she was probably referring to some pillars from the ancient city of Notium that had rolled down the hill into the sea and were quite visible under the crystal-clear water. It was fun snorkeling around them, but you could hardly call them a city under the sea. I didn't dismiss it from my mind—I just tucked it away and brought it out every time I was talking to old fishermen in villages along the sea.

One weekend I set out on my *motosiklet* to see the little village of Focha, just north of Izmir. Focha was founded in 3000 B.C., perhaps by the Hittites according to archeologists who found Hittite pottery there. Focha became prominent in the 8th century B.C. when it was colonized by the Ionians and renamed Phocaea. In 540 B.C. Phocaea was conquered by the Persians. Alexander the Great freed the city from the Persians in 334 B.C., but most of the inhabitants had already fled. The city never recovered.

From the highway, there was only a dirt road leading to Focha, an indication that it still hadn't recovered. At the edge of the plain, the road dropped straight down into the sea. I stopped to take a picture of the cozy little harbor, surrounded by high cliffs, and the village of Focha nestled in its bosom. I braked and even spragged[17] down the steep stony

---

17. Using the clutch in addition to the brakes to slow a motorcycle.

hill and coasted into the tiny cobblestone village square right on the water's edge.

Four or five beasties ran up to me and greeted me joyously, "*Hosh geldiniz!* (Welcome) *Hosh geldiniz!*" I could tell they weren't used to tourists. They jumped up and down, clapped their hands, and didn't ask for money or cigarettes.

"Are you the new school teacher?" asked one little girl.

"No."

"Are you the circumciser?" asked one little boy quite cheerfully.

"No." I laughed.

"Then who *are* you?"

"I am *turist*."

They obviously didn't understand that word, so I said I was a *fotografji*. They jumped up and down like bunnies and started getting in line to have their picture taken, standing rigidly with their arms at their sides and their chins buried in their necks.

"Later," I said. I didn't want to start a Polaroid panic the moment I arrived in town. I sat down at a table under an olive tree with two old men. We exchanged greetings, and they offered me tea.

After my insides got warmed up, I asked them about ruins. They said there were none. I noticed in the roughly constructed stone buildings around the square several pieces of marble in the middle of sandstone rocks. One doorstep was obviously the capital from an Ionic pillar. There were even pieces of fluted columns standing upright at the four corners of the tiny square. The beasties were playing leap-frog over one of them. No ruins, they said!

"Is there a city under the sea around here?" I knew they understood what I said and started a big confab that included the shopkeeper and two fishermen who were working on their nets. Finally, it was arranged that I should go out in a motorboat with one of the fishermen. One of the beasties tried to get into the boat with us, but he got a cuff on the ear. I persuaded the fisherman to let him come with us. He was a little charmer with big brown eyes and an angelic smile. The two old men also accompanied us.

We rode out into the tiny bay, and I kept looking for some sign of something under the water. The boat man drove us straight to a cave in the cliffs. We drifted in cautiously about 15 yards. The men pointed out scratchings on the walls that could have been made yesterday. I saw the initials A.G., but I doubted that they stood for Alexander the Great. They all wanted me to like the cave, so I said it was *"choke guzel"* (very beautiful). The beastie loved it, especially when the men showed him how to make an echo.

We cut back across the bay and I kept looking down and pointing, screaming in Turkish, "Old city?" They nodded. "Ruins? Marble? Columns?" They nodded. "Buildings? Ancient?" They nodded, and we entered another cave which was no different from the first. Had I been looking for caves and blue grottoes, I would have been enchanted. I finally persuaded them to turn back.

The boatman resolutely refused any money, so I took his picture and gave it to him. I could tell by the way his face lit up that it was better than money. I used up the last two pictures on the old men and the beasties. A fight broke out among them as I hopped on my *motosiklet* and went zigzagging up the hill.

One Sunday at Mass, my mind wandered during the sermon and I happened to find in the back of my Missal a delightful map of the Holy Land in the time of Christ. It included Turkey (Asia Minor) and showed the Seven Churches in Asia which St. John wrote to in the Apocalypse: Ephesus, Smyrna, Pergamum, Sardis, Laodicea, Thyatira, and Philadelphia. I thought of my friends Roy and Judy Stiles, who had persuaded me on many a trip to visit all seven churches since they were all within a 200-mile radius of Izmir. And then I noticed Cyme. Cyme? I didn't know that ancient city. When I got home, I got out my guidebooks and maps (I even had some U.S. Corps of Engineers maps of Turkey made during World War II for pilots who might be shot down. The maps showed every city, hamlet, ancient ruin, and even water well). Ah, there it was—spelled Kyme—just a few miles north of Focha. Hmm! The site was probably worth visiting since it was on such an ancient map.

So, the following Saturday, with Roy, Judy, their beastie Debbie, their dachshund Karl-Heinz, and a station wagon full of archeological equipment (bathing suits, an ice-cooler full of beer, Pepsi, hot dogs, boiled ham, marshmallows, Sterno), we started off to Kyme. We missed it and came to the little village of Aliaga, which the guidebook said was built entirely of marble stones scrounged from Kyme. The locals didn't have any idea what we were talking about. When we showed them the map, they kept turning it upside down, which didn't help at all.

We started back and came to a narrow dirt road that obviously led to the sea.

"This must be it," I said authoritatively.

"No," said Roy, "there's a barbed wire fence and a gate. It must be private property."

"And there's a stream across the road," said Judy, "just beyond the gate."

"And there's a bull!" said Debbie.

"Open the gate. We shall ford the stream, and I will personally fight the bull with my red sport shirt," I said.

We had no problem getting past all the barriers to the beach, which was strewn with pieces of marble columns lined up like slash marks diagonal to the shore.

"Eureka!" I shouted, wishing I knew the plural of that word so that I could include all of us, even Karl-Heinz, who had scared the bull away with his yapping.

We unloaded all the equipment, started a fire, donned bathing suits, swam, drank a beer, and then started out on our explorations. The land was level for about 200 yards inland from the beach. Then the ground rose steeply to a volcano-shaped mound, about 300 feet high, which to my eyes looked clearly man-made. Surely this was the acropolis mentioned in the guidebook. "Charge!" I yelled, and we streaked across some ploughed fields and assaulted the mountain.

On top there were potsherds everywhere and bits of iridescent glass. Soon we were all stooping and scooping. "I found a coin!" I shouted. They all gathered round, pronounced it genuine, but said it was puny. It *was* small—about the size of a shirt button—but it was *mine*. Judy soon found a coin the size of a quarter, and even Debbie found one. Debbie kept shouting every other second that she had found something, and we got tired of looking at her bits of glass and potsherds and even garden-variety pebbles. Roy, whom we humiliated as much as possible, finally topped us all by finding a red clay head of a woman, about one inch high. It was small but exquisite. He was sure it was a goddess. We hated him from then on.

Finally we descended the mound and found a Turkish farmer tilling the soil around and under the olive trees. His wife was leading (dragging) the old horse, and the farmer was struggling with a 2000-year-old wooden plow.

"This is the best place to look for goodies!" I shouted, "when the farmers are plowing their fields!" So we all dropped on our hands and knees, crawled madly behind the farmer, and sifted the dirt through our fingers. Naturally they knew we were foreigners, and naturally they thought we were mad—the wife was particularly unnerved—but they couldn't think of any real reason to object to what we were doing. We didn't find anything *really* exciting—bits of iridescent glass, ceramic tiles, and shards with black geometric designs—but it was fun. Clearly it was time for a weenie-and-marshmallow roast.

After our Olympian feast, we stretched out on the beach. When we were almost asleep, Debbie called our attention to a figure approaching from about a mile away. (The beach was almost three miles long, a simple, shallow curve.) As the figure approached, we saw it was a man, neatly dressed in a plum-colored suit—including a vest! As he got closer, we could see that he was about 25–27 years old. He stopped, and we exchanged all the flowery Turkish greetings. He was so enchanted with our Turkish that he sat down on one of the fluted pillars. We jibber-jabbered about a lot of nothings—who we were, Americans, names, John (he liked that because it meant "soul" in Turkish), Roy, Judy (he asked if she were Jewish—*Yahudi* in Turkish—she giggled and said no), and Debbie. He didn't get anything out of her name, but it soon became apparent that he had taken a shine to her. He gathered her into his arms. (Debbie was about four years old.) He started speaking sweet nothings into her face in Turkish, which she seemed to understand (American kids overseas pick up languages more easily than their parents). Judy and Roy began to tense up. I pulled myself together and became alert. He brushed Debbie's cheek with his hand, then reached into his pocket and drew out an object which he put into her little pink hands. It was a clay pig—about three inches long—and obviously ancient. Debbie squealed with delight.

We all relaxed and offered him a drink. He accepted a Pepsi. Debbie sat on his knee and kissed him many times. I learned that he lived on a farm next to the sea between Kyme and Focha. I took a flyer and said, "By the way, do you know anything about the city under the sea?"

He looked at me intently, trying to figure out if he understood my Turkish correctly. "The city under the sea?" he said questioningly.

"Yes," I said, pleased that he repeated my Turkish words.

He stood up, dumping Debbie onto the sand. Then he took off his shoes and socks and strolled up the beach a little way. He rolled up his pants legs and walked into the sea. He walked and walked, waving his hands in the air, farther and farther out to sea, and his cuffs were hardly wet. About 50 yards out, he stopped and threw his hands up into the air, clasping them together like a champion boxer.

We were astonished, speechless, mystified! We all rushed to the beach to follow in his footsteps. It was immediately apparent that there was a wall going out into the sea just below the surface of the water. We *all* trotted out. At the end of the wall, Majid—our new friend—pointed to the objects under the sea. We dived down and saw walls and buildings and parapets. Roy went back for snorkels. We took turns submerging and trying to guess what the buildings were. I insisted I had found an odeon, where they had poetry and music concerts. Judy insisted it was a council chamber, where the nobles came to decide what to do about the problems of the day—one of them being that they were sinking under the sea. We frolicked and took pictures of each of us walking on the water like Jesus.

Later, I took a Polaroid of Majid holding Debbie on one knee and Karl-Heinz on the other, and gave him the picture. We watched the sun sink into the Aegean, just like the city of Cyme/Kyme, and started home. It had been a lovely day.

Several months later, I ran into the Attaché's wife at a gala party at the American Pavilion the night before the International Fair opened. There were tables everywhere, loaded with dried-up hors d'oeuvres, but nobody minded because the whiskey was flowing like the Baths of Diana. At least 900 people were there—Americans, Turks, Yugoslavians, Russians, Pakistanis, you name it—and it was like a wrestling match just getting through them.

"Oh, hi!" I said to her. "We found the city under the sea!"

"Had you lost it?"

"No—I mean—er—you remember you told me about it several months ago. Well, we found it!"

"Well, bully for you. Now, you help me find Roger! He's under one of these tables somewhere. I last left him sitting cross-legged like an Indian guru spouting James Joyce. He must be finished by now." As she got down on her hands and knees and started crawling under all the tables, I chivalrously followed—feeling like a damned fool. It was so like our crawl through Kyme. But I didn't mind, because it was really Roger who had led us to the city under the sea.

Honeymoon in Didyma

≈

EARLY ONE MORNING, Tom Curington, our Site Manager, came into my office and announced that we were going to Didyma over the Thanksgiving holiday.
"We?"
"You, Kitty, and I." (Kitty was his bride of three weeks.) "For our honeymoon."
"But, Tom, I've already been to Didyma. I'd rather go to some place else. I'm thinking of going to Aphrodisias. It looks very interesting, according to the guidebook."
"We're going to Didyma! Kitty insists. She fell in love with your Polaroids when she saw them the other night."
"Fine! You and Kitty go to Didyma. I'll go to Aphrodisias."
"By God, I'm not going with Kitty alone!"
"But Tom, it's *your* honeymoon!"
"I don't care! Dammit, John, you've been there before—Priene, Miletus, and Didyma—and you're going to take us! Now, that's the end of that. We'll take the company Mercedes. I'll drive." And he lumbered out of my office.

I was exasperated. Tom was really a sweet guy, but let's face it, he *was* a little nutty. He had only taken a week off from work to fly to Alabama, marry Kitty, and fly back. And now, here I was going with him on his honeymoon! I couldn't say I didn't like honeymoons because I had never been on one, but I didn't like the shotgun way I had been railroaded into this one.

I had met Tom several years before in Diyarbakir. (He replaced Krogden as our Civil Engineer.) He was very civil and quiet, but we never socialized in those days. One day I had occasion to go to his room (he lived on the base), and I noticed a very neat stack of legal-size, blue Air Mail envelopes on his desk with letters inside.

"Who are those from?" I blurted out without thinking.

"Kitty, my fiancée."

"Oh, when are you going to get married?"

"One of these days."

"How long have you been engaged?"

"Eleven years."

"My God, isn't that rather a long time?"

"We want to be sure."

I was transferred to Izmir a year later. Tom too was transferred and made Site Manager—my boss! We soon learned we had a lot in common—whiskey, bars, cognac, nightclubs, girls, *raki*, beer, wine, a wide range, really—so we became nightly patrons at the *pavyons*.

But Tom never wanted to go to bed. One night I took him home in a taxi, and he begged me to come in to have one more cognac. His apartment was on the ground floor, just a few steps inside the wall from the street. He had decorated it himself, and it was a fright! I remember the first time he showed it to me. The walls were apple green, the draperies tomato red. One upholstered armchair had green arms and a red seat and back.

"Did you notice how it matches the walls and draperies?" he said proudly.

"I noticed."

The other chair was identical but had yellow arms and a blue seat and back.

"That's for contrast," he said slyly.

The rug was enormous—a gorgeous thick champagne-colored Isparta.

"John, do you think the rug is a mistake?"

I failed to assure him it wasn't.

"I'm building my own sofa. It's mosaic. See!"

My eyes popped out of my head. It was a 10-foot-long

plywood box, sitting on cinder blocks, half-covered with tiny black glass tiles. It looked like a coffin for Cleopatra.

"Won't it be rather hard?"

"Aha! I'm going to put a thick pad on it and cover it with goat skins!" (When Kitty arrived and took one look at the apartment, she rented a penthouse the next day, overlooking the fairgrounds.)

But in his single days, Tom was always trying to drag me into his "decorator" apartment for one final nightcap as he got out of the taxi.

"Come on in, John, just one little cognac."

"But Tom, it's almost three o'clock. We'll only get three hours' sleep as it is." I quickly ordered the taxi to drive on, leaving Tom looking rejected and dejected on the curb.

The next day he was quite bright and told me he had persuaded the *bekji* to have a drink with him. (A *bekji* is a watchman, employed by the government, who patrols the streets at night, blowing his whistle as he goes, meaning, "All is well." Robbery was rampant in Izmir, and we foreigners were bewildered by this practice because it let the burglars know exactly where the *bekji* was!) Tom said the *bekji* was interested in the *kanyak* but refused to come into his apartment. So Tom ran in, got the bottle, and they sat down behind the wall for a drink.

They passed the bottle back and forth toasting each other's honor until Tom said, "Don't you think it's time for you to blow your whistle?"

"Oh, Allah, Allah," said the *bekji*, with a pang of conscience and let out a blast.

"Bravo," said Tom, "have another drink." After a few more swigs back and forth, Tom said, "Er—do you think *I* might blow the whistle this time?"

"Hi, hi!" said the *bekji*, and magnanimously handed Tom the whistle.

Drinking and whistling went on till the sun came up and the bottle was empty. They parted bosom buddies and another chapter in Turkish-American relations was cemented.

Tom showered and shaved, went down to a waterfront cafe, had two bowls of tripe soup, heavily laced with garlic, and showed up at the office bright-eyed and bushy-tailed, except no one could stand to be near him.

One evening we went to a nightclub under the street near the Basmane Railroad Station, a raffish part of town. It was called the New York Pavyon so we were sure we would feel right at home. But as we descended the stairs, it was obvious that we were the first New Yorkers who had ever set foot in the place. The orchestra stopped and stared. The waiters carrying trays high over their heads paused in mid-delivery. And the girls all started licking their lips. But we had been to three bars earlier in the evening, so we were full of aplomb. We sat down at a table and before we could give the waiter our order, there were six girls fighting over us. The two who plopped themselves into our laps were the winners. They covered us with kisses and sent the waiter off for *shampanya*. It took some doing, but Tom and I finally got our *kanyaks*.

A little old lady from the railroad station came down the stairs carrying a basket of gardenias, camellias, and sweet peas. Tom called her over. I started looking them over to select the freshest bunch when Tom said, "All of them!" and dumped them on the table. The girls squealed and immediately started stuffing them into every available opening, even under their miniskirts.

"How much, Little Mother?" asked Tom, pulling out his wallet.

Little Mother was terrified and started making mad mental computations as to how much Tom was worth. "Er—40 lira!" ($4) she said nervously, but with a touch of defiance.

"Keep the change, Little Mother," said Tom, throwing a 50-lira note on the table. She snatched at it before Tom could sober up and scurried up the stairs. "John, I believe you have a magic marker in your pocket—I saw you using it today. Let me have it."

I gave it to him. He lifted up the miniskirt of the girl who was sitting on his lap, lowered her panties delicately, and started writing the name of our company across her belly. He looked up at me and said, "Ah, John, your brother would be proud of us tonight!"

After several months of leading me astray in the wicked dens and smoky haunts of Izmir nightlife, Tom abdicated and announced his decision to go home to marry Kitty. "Thirteen years is long enough," he said.

"So you're finally sure!"

"John, there comes a time in every man's life when he realizes there are certain things he *has* to do. And marrying Kitty is one of them. I'm 33, time to start settling down and raising a family. The bar girls are all yours, John, you lucky dog!"

Every evening after work Tom always sat in the garden and drank *raki* with a Turkish doctor who lived in the same apartment building. Even though the doctor's English was limited and Tom's Turkish was fractured, they managed to discuss all the important things in life—girls!

"Well, Doctor, I finally decided I'm going to get married."

"Fevkaladde! Wonderful!" said the doctor. "A Turkish girl?"

"No, no, no!" said Tom. "An American girl."

"Gechmish olsun!" (May this catastrophe pass!)

As Tom was leaving for Alabama, he gave me some instructions: "Kitty and I will be back next Sunday night on Flight 622 at 6 p.m. Do not meet us at the airport. We'll take a taxi. Do not expect to meet Kitty until Wednesday or Thursday—maybe later. Kitty will decide. She's tough as nails. We can all stop worrying about the Russians now—they wouldn't dare start another war against Turkey while Kitty is here."

I wasn't the least bit surprised by his instructions. I had long since given up trying to understand Tom Curington.

The following Sunday about 8 p.m. the doorbell rang. It was Tom, puffing on a pipe with a female on his arm.

"Tom!" I cried, and then, "Er—er—Kitty?"

"Yes. Hi, John," she said, holding out her pale hand with delicate long fingers. "May we come in?"

"Of course, of course! *Hosh geldiniz!* Welcome!"

I scurried to the kitchen and sloshed up a jar of martinis. I still couldn't believe my eyes—Tom had told me everything about Kitty except how old she was.

"Why, you're just a child! A baby!"

"I'm 19!" she said regally.

"Tom told me you've been engaged for 13 years."

"We have. He was 20 years old when he first walked into our house on my sixth birthday. He was very handsome in those days, and slim. I told him then I was going to marry him one day. That one day was last Thursday. Cheers!"

"Er—Cheers."

Kitty turned out to be an absolute lamb. She was full of quiet excitement about being in Turkey and wanted to see everything. *"Everything!"* she said. "The archeological sites, the bazaars, the Turkish baths, the beaches—even the *pavyons*. Tom says they're dreary but I don't believe him." Tom puffed on his pipe and stared at the ceiling.

She went through all my Polaroid pictures while Tom and I went through the martinis and made another pitcher.

"Where's this? Where's this? Oh, I must see *that!* And *that!*"

So, the day before Thanksgiving, Tom and Kitty picked me up in the Mercedes, and we were off to Didyma on our honeymoon.

Oh, how I loathed that vehicle. It was an old black diesel that had been driven as a taxi for 14 years before our company leased it. I drove it to and from work for several weeks. Every morning it took me 20 minutes and a lot of swearing just to get the steering wheel unlocked. Then I had to push a button to warm up the diesel oil or some such madness. Then it started, coughed, choked, and died, and I had to start all over again. When I finally did get it going, all four doors would often fly open while I was barreling down the street late for work. Since the doors opened backward (hinged at the rear), it was a traumatic experience—all that air rushing in as if my eyes, ears, nose, throat, and fly were open at the same time. I was always afraid of scooping up pedestrians or a bicycle or two. I soon learned you could close the doors by jamming on the brakes violently, but that was no way to begin a day at the office. When Tom arrived in Izmir, I turned it over to him and took to my red *motosiklet*, blithely ignoring the stares of the natives as I went putt-putting by in my business suit with my briefcase under my arm.

Our trip to Soke, the overnight stop, was uneventful except for the storks following in the wake of a farmer's plow, snatching up the worms. "Tom, I *must* get a picture," said Kitty. He was very patient with her and inched the car along behind her as she ran along the road trying to keep up with the farmer and the storks.

We checked into the Erol Palas, a three-story concrete building with a concrete lobby, a concrete restaurant, concrete hallways, and concrete cubicles for rooms, presumably designed by the owner of a cement factory or a prison architect. But Kitty loved it.

At dinner Kitty tried everything, and Tom finished everything, patting his ample belly with satisfaction. It was cold that night when I went back to my concrete cubicle. I called the desk (yes, telephones, very modern) and asked if they had electric heaters. A few minutes later the manager, who knew me from my previous trip, brought me a kerosene heater. It was belching clouds of black smoke, but I thanked him and tried to adjust it after he was gone. Just before asphyxiation set in, I turned it off and threw open the windows. I tried to shoo out the smoke with a blanket, feeling like an Indian smoke-signaler. The room by then was colder than ever, so I shut the windows and jumped into bed with all my clothes on.

A few minutes later there was a knock at the door. It was Tom. He was carrying a quilt and looking a little sheepish. "Kitty and I are going to sleep in one cot tonight. She thought you might like this." He threw it over me and ducked out. I was very grateful and slept like a bug.

The next morning we had tea, bread, and goat cheese in the concrete restaurant, then went upstairs to pack. We came down at nine and Tom said, "Now take us to a good restaurant so we can have breakfast."

"But we already had breakfast!"

"John, you don't call that breakfast. We need something to stick to the ribs."

I took them to the Deniz restaurant where Tom had an omelet, Albanian liver, stuffed grape leaves, ground lamb burgers, cheese, black olives, bread, butter made from water buffalo milk, honey, tea, and coffee. "Let's have a little *raki* to wash it all down," he said.

"Don't you think we ought to get going?"

"Plenty of time. Got to settle the stomach." And he lit up his pipe, his favorite occupation.

We checked out of Errol Flynn's palace[18] at 11:00 and were finally on our way.

"Stop!" shouted Kitty. All the doors flew open. "We have to have *mandalinas*." She had fallen in love with Turkish tangerines the night before, so back we went to Soke while I gave a lecture on the origin of the *mandalina*.

"From the Chinese *mandarin*. Both 'r' and 'l' are interchangeable in all languages. The English thought tangerines came from Tangiers. The Turks are much closer to the truth since the fruit came originally from China. Shall I tell you about the origin of our word "turkey," which is a bird native to North America?"

"No," said Tom. "We don't have time."

In addition to the *mandalinas*, Kitty bought peanuts, pumpkin seeds, walnuts, grape taffy, and Turkish Delight.

"Now, John, tell *me* why a turkey is called a turkey," said Kitty when we were back on the road.

"Well, it's a long story."

"Allah! Allah!" said Tom.

---

18. A joke; "erol" and "errol" are near homonyms.

"Hush your mouth, Tom Curington! Go on, John."

I rattled off: "The Sultan of Turkey sent Queen Elizabeth a brace of guinea fowl, which she promptly named turkey-cocks and turkey-hens. When Captain John Smith arrived in America and saw our strange wild fowl, he wrote to Queen Elizabeth about our much larger "turkeys," and the name stuck. End of story."

"Allah be praised!" said Tom, as we arrived at our first archeological site, Priene.

We parked the miserable Mercedes at the foot of the mountain and climbed up to the ancient city. The *bekji* remembered me.

"Oh, Mister John! Mister John!" He kissed my hand, thus ensuring a good tip.

Kitty and Tom, each with their own cameras, clambered over the rocks and ruins while I sat with the old *bekji* and learned that he had three children and five daughters. When you ask a village Turk how many children he has, he only tells you the number of sons.

"Let's go, John, time's a-fleetin'."

Back on the road, I said, "Miletus is the next stop, a very famous Ionian city. St. Paul came to Miletus several times and raised hell, as he did all over Turkey—before it was called Turkey."

"Time for lunch!" said Tom as we entered a mud village.

"But we just finished breakfast."

"It's twelve o'clock, John!" Tom slowed to a stop. "Ask that man standing in that doorway if there is an *iyi bir lokanta* (a good restaurant) in this town."

"I refuse to make a fool of myself. This is a mud village. There are obviously no *iyi bir lokantas* here!"

"Ah, John, why are you so unfriendly? Must be your New England upbringing."

"Please, John," said Kitty. I was sure she was not hungry, just the peacemaker.

"Okay, but *you* do the talking and I'll translate." Tom knew a lot of Turkish questions from the phrase book but could never understand the answers.

"Merhaba, Bey Efendi!" (Greetings, your Excellency), boomed Tom from the bottom of his diaphragm.

The old man quivered and mumbled something.

"Nasilsiniz?" (How are you?)

The old man mumbled.

"Iyimisiniz?" (Are you well?)

"Oh for God's sake, Tom, get on with it."

"Iyi bir lokanta varmi?"

The old man shook himself and spoke a bit louder.

"What did he say, John? Huh?"

I clenched my teeth. "He said there was a good restaurant just ahead in the town square."

"You see!" said Tom triumphantly.

The town square was round, about 30 yards in diameter and completely surrounded by mud houses. On the far side was a dusty old olive tree with a table and two chairs underneath it.

"There's your *iyi bir lokanta*," I said sarcastically as Tom pulled to a stop under the tree. The car doors flew open. We got out and looked. Behind the table was a shop, barely wide enough for a narrow door and a window, in which were hanging many brown sausages of varying lengths. We opened the door into what was essentially a tiny kitchen with an open grill in a chimney. The restaurateur was fast asleep in a chair. Tom boomed his Turkish greetings and the little guy jumped two feet, like a frog.

"Hosh geldin! Hosh geldin!" (Welcome, welcome) he shouted and scurried to seat us at the best table in the house—under the olive tree. Then he bowed with his hands folded at his chest to take our order.

"John, ask him to bring us the menu."

"Tom!" I said.

"Okay, okay, don't get huffy. Ask him what he's got to eat."

"Sosis!" (sausages) the restaurateur said, pointing to them, surprised that we should ask.

"Good!" said Tom. "We'll have sausages, won't we, Kitty?"

"Yes, Tom."

The old man was pleased and started to dash into the kitchen.

"*Bir daka!*" (Just a minute), I shouted. If I was being forced to eat again, one hour after we had had breakfast, I wasn't about to eat hot spicy Turkish sausages that would give me indigestion for three days, so I said, "I'll have two eggs lightly cooked."

"Oh sir, we don't have eggs. Only sausages."

"Don't tell me you don't have eggs. Look at that chicken scurrying across the square. Follow her!"

The restaurateur was getting very upset, so I pulled out a 5-lira note. He gave it to one of the beasties who had gathered around us and told him to bring back two eggs.

Tom wolfed down his sausages. Kitty nibbled at hers. My eggs were cooked to perfection—I fried them myself. Kitty gave one of the beasties a package of Chiclets, which started a riot, so we got out of there fast.

We arrived at Miletus at two o'clock. Miletus was once on the sea, at the mouth of the Meander River, but the river had silted up. Now there was only a stagnant inlet in front of the magnificent marble stairs leading up out of the green slime. It was easy to imagine the Emperor Hadrian arriving in his burnished barges, or St. Paul in a rowboat with Timothy pulling the oars.

Everything at Miletus was in shambles except for the theater. Unlike most ancient theaters which were built on the side of a hill, this one was free-standing, next to the sea, with its own special harbor where you could anchor your barge to see a play by Euripides or Aristophanes. For a theater that had had no reconstruction, it was in marvelous condition. There was a huge vaulted semi-circular tunnel underneath with inside stairways leading up to the highest tiers. The theater held 25,000 spectators.

The stage had collapsed, undoubtedly in an earthquake, but the marbles with lush carvings of rams, eagles, griffins, and lions were just waiting to be photographed by Kitty, Tom, and me. We had the whole place to ourselves! There wasn't even a *bekji*.

"Are we allowed to dig?" asked Kitty.

"No, but scratching is okay. Be on the lookout for coins. They're not shiny, just round. My brother keeps finding ancient coins on the Ankara golf course, and it infuriates me because he's only interested in his score."

I cursed myself for my addiction to coins because it got so that when I visited a new ruin, my eyes were glued to the ground when I should have been looking at the walls and pillars and temples against the ever-blue Turkish sky.

Kitty shrieked every time she found a potsherd or a mosaic or a bit of glass.

"Kitty, you must stop that! You'll give me a heart attack."

"But look at this red piece of pottery—it's got black markings on it and grooves!"

"That's nothing."

"Don't be so smug, John. This is my first dig."

The time was now four o'clock. I suggested to Tom that we ought to get on to Didyma, but we couldn't find Kitty. We called and called and were just beginning to become alarmed when we found her down in a hole on her hands and knees, digging away with a nail file.

"Why didn't you answer us?"

"Because I've found three pieces of a vase and I'm sure the whole thing is here."

Tom skidded down into the hole, scooped up his bride and handed her to me while he climbed out. Then he slung her over his shoulder like a caveman and carried her back to the car.

"Let me down, Tom Curington! John, help me!" He swatted her on the rump. "Oh, you brute! I hate you both!"

The sun was sinking fast as we drove along beside the Aegean Sea and caught our first glimpse of the temple on a promontory silhouetted against the sea and sky.

"Hurry, Tom," Kitty squealed.

We pulled up to the entrance, jumped out, and gazed down into the colossal ruins of the Temple of Apollo at Didyma. The temple took 600 years to build. Everything about it was gigantic: a forest of 103 marble pillars, some still standing their full height of 60 feet. The others, of varying heights, had been toppled by earthquakes. The toppled pillars lay in the courtyard like fallen stacks of mammoth poker chips.

"Oh, John, it's even more beautiful than I thought," said Kitty. "How awful we're too late to take pictures," she said as she clicked the Leica.

"Tomorrow there will be plenty of time. Save your film."

"I brought six rolls—36 exposures each."

"The columns were made of round blocks set one over another, then fluted after they were in place. Every conqueror from Alexander the Great to Hadrian worked on the temple, but nobody finished it. Tomorrow you'll see some of the pillars which aren't fluted. See that huge slab of marble in the middle? It's a single piece of stone that weighs 48 tons. That's where the oracle stood to make her pronouncements. This temple was as famous as the oracle at Delphi. In the center were sulfur springs that the oracle sniffed before making her predictions."

"I want to sniff."

"Sorry, the springs have dried up."

"What on earth does *Didyma* mean?"

"It's Greek for "twin." Apollo was the twin of Diana. But come on over here—I want to show you what *I* think is the most spectacular thing about Didyma. Close your eyes."

"You won't let me stumble?"

"Don't worry." I took her by the hand and led her through the gate, down to a grassy knoll. "Now, turn around and open your pretty brown eyes."

"Oooohhhhhh!" She stood there with her mouth wide open.

It was a block of marble 6 feet high, 6 feet wide, and 6 feet deep, carved in the shape of the head of Medusa, deeply incised with a dimpled chin, sensual mouth, classic nose, glowering eyes, and a head of writhing snakes.

"Oh, John, it's the most beautiful thing I've ever seen!"

"And look, that's not all. See, all around the courtyard, up against the wall, there are *80* heads! Just like this one! They all used to sit above the columns on a frieze running all around the temple."

"I want one for myself. Surely they can spare *one!*"

The *bekji* shooed us out—time to close.

Outside the gate, we stood and watched the temple disappear as the sun was sinking into the Aegean Sea.

"Kitty, do you see that column over there standing all alone?"

"Yes, of course." It was 60 feet high.

"The last time I was here, I met the mayor, a scruffy, charming old man. He told me that his daughter used to mount her horse from that pillar."

"John, you're pulling my leg."

"No. He said 30 years ago that pillar was the only thing visible of the Temple of Apollo and it was only five feet high—everything else was covered with dirt and grass. He said he built a little set of wooden steps so his daughter could climb to the pillar and jump on her horse and gallop away. Then in 1938 the Germans came and started digging, digging, digging. And every day the Germans told the villagers they had to move. The Germans built all those cinder block houses you see over there, but the Turks refused to move into them until the gendarmes came with a court order and bayonets. They hated their new houses until the tourists started coming and spending money—especially the rich Americans."

Just then Tom showed up with his mouth full, carrying a bag made out of newspaper. "Look, John, *simit!*" They were circular hard rolls covered with sesame seeds. Kitty and I both took one—it was about 7:30 and I had heard Kitty's stomach rumbling when I was telling her the story of the mayor's daughter. "Come on, I've found a *chay evi*." (teahouse)

It was made of cinder block, dark and dingy, lighted by two hanging kerosene lamps.

"This is so exciting," said Kitty, grabbing my arm as

Tom led the way.

The owner was delighted when we walked in, then flabbergasted when he saw Kitty with her long chestnut hair, white turtleneck sweater, and striped pants. He knocked several old men off their stools and gave us one of the three low tables in the room. All around the walls on a bench sat young, middle-aged, and old men sipping tea after a hard day in the fields—except they all stopped sipping when they saw Kitty.

Tom ordered tea in his loud booming voice as if ordering drinks for the house. One of the young men struck up a tune on the *saz,* a kind of primitive guitar shaped like a long-necked gourd. Then he started singing a mournful love song, in Kitty's honor, I'm sure. He kept sneaking glances at her.

"I love it," she whispered.

Our tea arrived, scalding hot and sickeningly sweet. I called the owner over and negotiated with him for some *raki.*

At the next table two old men were deeply engrossed in a game involving rectangular brass tiles which they slapped on the table like a crack of lightning.

"It's dominoes!" said Kitty, clapping her hands. "Oh, Tom, I want to play."

I looked, and sure enough it *was* dominoes. I was amazed Kitty could tell because all the black spots were worn off the tiles. Only the indentations remained.

"Mahmud!" We were on a first-name basis.

"Yes, Mister John?" he said as he filled my glass with *raki.*

"Madame wants to play *tavla.*"

"*Hi, hi!*" He rushed behind his counter and madly looked for another set.

"No, I want to play against one of those Turkish men," said Kitty coolly. "I *know* I could beat you or Tom."

"Mahmud! Come here." I explained Kitty's challenge, and he was delighted. He jibber-jabbered wildly to the two players, who kept stealing glances at Kitty. After an argument, one got up and Mahmud ushered Kitty to her seat opposite a fiercely mustachioed defender. I moved my stool behind Kitty's shoulder to be her translator in case of a misunderstanding.

The defender turned all the tiles upside down, though how he could tell I don't know. Kitty drew a six-five. The defender drew a four-two. The patrons all crowded around as Kitty drew her tiles like a Las Vegas thoroughbred. She placed a double-five on the table. The defending champion slapped down a five-three. Kitty slid in a double-three. The defender started clawing through the "kitty" pile looking for a three. He slapped his tiles on the table even louder and faster. Cool Kitty held her own. As the game got more tense, the sea of heads around us moved in closer, eyes bulging. Just as Kitty was about to make a crucial move, I heard a loud voice.

"Kitty! John! Come on, we're leaving!" Tom slapped a 50-lira note on the bar and stormed out. I grabbed Kitty by the arm and propelled her through a sea of faces.

When we got in the car, Tom already had the motor running and in gear. All the doors flew open as he started barreling down the road. He braked, the doors slammed shut, Kitty hit the windshield, and I almost flew into the front seat.

"What on earth is the matter with you?" I asked. "Why did we leave so abruptly?"

"Everyone was looking at Kitty," he said sulkily, like a little boy.

"Well, what did you expect? A teahouse full of Turks! They've never *seen* an American girl up close, let alone one playing dominoes in *their* clubhouse. They'll talk about this for years. Besides, they thought she was *my* wife."

"What fun," said Kitty.

"And furthermore, the teahouse was *your* idea! You knew it was full of Turks and yet you bring in this little slip of a girl—"

"Thank you, John," said Kitty, "but I'm five feet six. I towered over all of them."

"Where can we find an *iyi bir otel?*" said Tom sullenly.

"Don't start talking Turkish to me! There are *no* good hotels around here. There are *no hotels!* We'll have to go back to Soke to that god-awful Erol Palas!"

"Now, John, calm down." He let up on the accelerator and started looking happily from side to side. "We'll find one, you wait and see." On the left the Aegean Sea was lapping the road; on the right was a cliff. There wasn't a house within 50 miles, let alone a hotel. I slumped in the back seat and took to my bottle.

"Oh, look, here's a place to spend the night," said Tom, jamming on the brakes. "Look at all those tents beside the sea. It must be the Club Méditerranée![19] I've read about it in *Time* magazine." It was very dark, but the tents stood out clearly in the moonlight.

A man rushed up to the car. *"Buyurun?"* (Please, may I help you?)

"Kloob May-dee-ter-ran-nay?" boomed Tom in his best French.

"Efendim?" (Sir?)

"Tom, open your eyes! He's a Turkish soldier. This is an Army camp."

"Good! We can sleep here. I'm sure they have extra cots. Ask him, John."

"Are you out of your mind? Let's get out of here."

"John, where is your spirit of adventure?"

Another soldier came running up, buttoning his jacket. *"Ben Chavush Akbulut. Sizeh yardim edebilirmiyim?"*

"What did he say, John?"

"He said he was Sgt. White Cloud, and could he be of any help to us."

"There, you see! Now ask him if he's got any extra cots we can sleep in."

"You ask him. I'll translate."

"Ben Amerikali" said Tom, thumping his chest. *"Turista!*

---

19. Now known as Club Med, a private company specializing in all-inclusive holidays.

Otel yok! Yatak varmi?"
"Af edersiniz. Ingilizje bilmiyorum."
"What did he say, John? What did he say?"
"He says he is very sorry, but he doesn't speak English."
"John, tell the poor bastard I'm speaking Turkish!" Then he roared at the sergeant, *"Yatak!* Beds! Sleep!" He folded his hands and laid his head on them.

"Ah, yes," said the sergeant, pulling himself together as I translated madly for Tom. "You want beds. You wish to sleep here tonight. Yes, we have plenty of beds. The Captain isn't here right now. He'll be back very soon, I assure you, but I am confident that he will approve your sleeping here. Come, please, I will show you the beds. Follow me and please don't look at my faults!"

"You see," said Tom suavely as he got out of the car to follow the sergeant. "You always look on the dark side of the picture, John. Look on the bright side, like me."

I stuck my head out of the window and called, "To—om, you'd better tell your sergeant that we're not all of the same sex."

"Alasmaladik!" (Goodbye!) said Tom as he jumped back into the car and drove off in trailing clouds of blue exhaust. All the doors flew open.

"Well, after that ugly scene you made at the domino table tonight, I thought I'd better warn you. Would anybody like a drink?" I said, holding up my friend Johnnie Walker.

"No! Yes!" said Tom and Kitty simultaneously. I handed the bottle to Kitty.

"Should I wipe it off with my hand as they do in the movies?"

"Yes!" said Tom.

Kitty sipped sweetly, then Tom grabbed the bottle and guzzled down half a pint.

"Tom, dearest, would you please slow down a bit."

He did, and I settled down for the long bumpy ride back to the Erol Palas.

"Aha! Here's a good place to sleep!" Tom said as he careened off the road and came to an abrupt stop under a cypress tree at the edge of the sea.

"Where??"

"Right here! We'll sleep in the car. But dinner first! Come on, Kitty, I'll open the trunk, and you get out those sandwiches you made for us."

He fired up his pipe, which meant the matter was closed. It was a lovely night. The moon was high and pure white. The sea was beautiful. But it was nippy. Kitty spread a blanket and set the table, I built a fire, and Tom was the plantation owner watching his minions at work. We sang "On Top of Old Smokey"—the only song we could all agree on—then sat down to peanut butter sandwiches, dill pickles, hard-boiled eggs, pumpkin seeds, fresh walnuts, and *mandalinas*.

"This is the best Thanksgiving dinner I've ever had in my whole life," said Kitty.

"My God, it *is* Thanksgiving, isn't it?" I said. "I'd forgotten."

"Yes. Pour us another drop of whiskey, John dear."

It was getting very cold, so we had a big argument about sleeping arrangements in the miserable Mercedes. Tom insisted, with Kitty's support, that I take the back seat. I was too mellow to object. Tom sat at the steering wheel with Kitty cradled in his arms, while I curled up in the back seat with Johnnie Walker in mine.

I had just gotten to sleep when there was a rap on the window and a flashlight shining in our eyes. We all jumped out of our skins.

"John, wake up and translate!"

It was the Captain from the campsite. He was terribly polite and said his soldiers had told him about our plight and he was sorry that they weren't more hospitable and would we please come back to the camp? Madame needn't worry because he would give us the tent reserved for visiting inspectors and post two guards on duty all night.

It was an invitation no one could refuse, but Tom was adamant and insisted I translate every word like a faithful St. Bernard.

"No thank you, Captain, we'll be very happy here. Thank

you so much. You Turks are so kind. *You* are very kind. Your *soldiers* were very kind, and you must tell them I said so—"

"Slow down, Tom."

"My friend in the back seat speaks very poor Turkish but you must forgive him because he is a little bit *sarhosh*." (It literally means "happy-headed" but is a polite word for "drunk.") "John! Give the Captain that bottle of Johnnie Walker."

"Ehhh!"

Tom grabbed it from me and presented it to the Captain.

"Viski!" he said. *"Choke guzel!"*

The Captain reluctantly took his leave, but he seemed happy with my bottle of whiskey. I was miserable and cold and couldn't get back to sleep again. I shifted from one fetus position to another all night and vowed as long as I lived that I would never again complain about a lumpy mattress or sagging springs. *Anything* would be better than the back seat of that malicious Mercedes!

We spent all next day at Didyma—Kitty dashing around like a *Life* photographer, I creaking after her like a man with Hodgkin's disease, Tom sitting on a Corinthian capital smoking his pipe—and then we drove non-stop back to Izmir.

"It was the best honeymoon a girl could ever ask for," said Kitty as I stumbled out of the car. "Let's do it every year, John, on our anniversary!"

"I'm suing for divorce on Monday."

Crash MacKenzie

≈

MAJOR ALEC MACKENZIE didn't get his nickname for nothing. He was the Director of Materiel for the U.S. Air Force in Izmir, and everything to him was a crash program—whether it was getting a million-dollar fund appropriation for military supplies or just ordering lunch. He never asked anyone's opinion—he didn't need to because he knew exactly what he was doing, where he had been, and where he was going. He was determined and dynamic and actually looked like a bullet. He was also one of the monitors of our contract, so when he came crashing into my office one day, I cringed, thinking, "Dear God, what now?"

"John! You and I are going on an archeological expedition! This weekend! Priene, Miletus, Didyma! You're the only one I know who's been there and you're taking me! Now, don't open your mouth—I've seen your Polaroid pictures—Tom Curington showed them to me—and you and I are going together. I love old ruins, but I've never been able to get my wife to go *anywhere* since I've been in Izmir—except to the Commissary and the Officers Club! I married a ruin! Now, she's going back to the States for a month, and you and I are going to Didyma! Don't say a word! I'll pick you up Friday afternoon after work—bring a suitcase! It's a long weekend, and we won't be back till Monday night!" And he went crashing back to his office.

I hated the idea of going back to any place I had already seen. I usually had such a good time the first time that I was always afraid the second time would be anti-climactic. This trip would actually be my *third* to Didyma, but what could I do? When Crash MacKenzie made up his mind to do something, not even God would try to stop him. I made a note on my calendar pad to slit Tom Curington's throat.

On Friday afternoon I was standing in front of my apartment with my red plaid ditty-bag full of provisions for the four-day weekend: Polaroid camera, bathing suit, change of underwear, candy bars, and, of course, my friend Johnnie Walker. Crash roared to a screeching halt, his heavy 1953 Buick lumbering back and forth like a dark green dirigible settling into place. I jumped in, Crash made a U-turn, and we went roaring off in a cloud of blue exhaust. I gently reprimanded him for the U-turn, but he said, "There's only one rule, John—when in Turkey, drive like hell! It's the only way to survive!"

I needn't describe our trip to Soke—our first overnight stop—barreling around blind curves, gunning up hills, and careening down the other side. Crash talked all the way about hundreds of subjects and asked thousands of questions, most of which required no answers. "So, what would *you* say to the Base Commander in a situation like that? I just told him to go piss up a rope. Where did you and the Curingtons stay in Soke?"

"What? Oh, the Erol Palas."

"No good! Biff Bumbaugh says the Turist Otel is better!" (Capt. Bumbaugh was the Public Information Officer.) "You know he's got connections with the Minister of Tourism and all those cats."

Crash terrified the thin little desk clerk at the Turist Otel. He banged his fist on the counter as if he was in a bar and shouted: "A double! With twin beds! And no bedbugs! Make a note now to call us at six o'clock sharp in the morning. We need some bottled water! Have a bellboy bring us up some! *Shimdi!*" And he charged up the stairs. I translated hurriedly. *Shimdi* was almost the extent of Crash's Turkish vocabulary. It meant "right now!"

I sank down on my bed like a balloon running out of air. Crash unstrapped his battered, old-fashioned briefcase and pulled out a bottle of whiskey. "Do you drink?"

"Well—yes, I do."

"Bring me those glasses!" Crash held them up to the light to inspect them, then polished them with a clean handkerchief. He splashed a good amount of whiskey in each glass. "Where's that damn bellboy?" I took a big gulp without waiting. Crash opened a Pullman-size suitcase and started unloading shirts, trousers, pajamas, shaving equipment, and bugspray. He sprayed the room like a professional fumigator while I held my palm over my glass. The air was so thick we hardly noticed a tiny boy enter timidly with bottled water. He had apparently been warned by the desk clerk because he dropped the water on the table and ran like hell.

"Hmm!" said Crash. "Didn't even wait for a tip. Good! Do you snore?"

"Well—er—I don't know. I live alone, you know."

"Go down and get another room! I can't stand snoring! My wife does."

I was happy to comply.

"Get it?"

"Yes, it's right across the hall."

"Good! Let's eat! Biff says the Deniz Restaurant is the best."

"Why didn't you come here with Biff?"

"Because he's a horse's ass, that's why. He doesn't know anything about ruins. He hates Turkey. He's never been anywhere. He only reads all the books because he has to—that's his job."

We left the hotel and walked to the restaurant.

"Ah! Here it is. You order, John! But no goat meat!"

Crash ate like a goat—everything the waiter put on the table. Usually they present a lot of hors d'oeuvres on the table and the customer decides which ones he wants. But Crash tried all of them and said, "Bring on the main course!" I ate an olive or two and pushed the food around my

plate. But the *raki* picked up my spirits so much that I didn't mind Crash's constant flow of chatter. Nor did I listen to him much. "I don't know how you can drink that stuff, John. Tastes like cough medicine to me."
"It's lion's milk," I said dreamily.
Back in his room Crash said, "Like a nightcap?"
"Don't mind if I do."
He poured with such a heavy hand I lifted my glass to stop him. "Don't worry, John, lots more where that came from. Damn!" He swatted his arm. "Mosquitos! It's those damn toilets!" He grabbed his bug bomb and I escaped to my room. I collapsed on my bed and slept like a baby lamb.
The next morning I was shaken awake by Crash. "John! John! Wake up! It's five after six! They didn't call us—I knew they wouldn't! The mosquitos didn't bother you, did they? I looked in on you three times last night! You were snoring like a drunken sailor! I could hear you all the way across the hall. I didn't sleep a wink! Why don't you lock your door? Come on, time for breakfast! Can't waste time!"
After a hearty breakfast for Crash and black coffee for me, we started off to Priene, our first archeological site. The road was dirt, graded, but with lots of potholes. That didn't slow Crash down a bit. We barreled along, kicking up clouds of dust. After I hit my head on the roof twice, I suggested to Crash that he might break an axle.
"Naw, this is a good car, John. Buicks are tough. Besides, I'm going to sell it next year when I leave. I'll get twice what I paid for it. These poor bastards will pay anything for an American car. Tell me about these cities I'm going to see. I know you read all the books on the archeological ruins here in Turkey. Wish I could. I never have time!"
Surprisingly, he shut up, as if waiting for an answer, so I started reading from the *Blue Guide*: "Priene was probably founded in the 11th century B.C. by the Carians,[20] but the city didn't reach its greatness until the arrival of the Ionians

---

20. Ancient inhabitants of southwest Anatolia.

in the 8th century B.C.—"

"No, no, don't read all that crap! Just give me the highlights."

I shut the book and thought about the things that had struck me about Priene. "It was the first place in the world that permitted free speech."

"That's more like it! How do they know?"

"A proclamation by the ruler Aepytus was reported by the great geographer Strabo."

"Boy, are you brainy!"

"In the theater, it was the first time they built dressing rooms for the actors, under the stage."

"Good. What else?"

"Well, Priene used to be right on the sea. It even had two harbors—the east harbor and the west harbor. Now it is 10 miles from the sea."

"What happened?"

"Most writers say that the Meander River—that's it right over there to your left—silted up and finally blocked Priene from the sea, but I—"

"Yes?"

"Well, I think a more likely explanation was that it was caused by an earthquake. You know this is a very earthquake-prone area."

"Do I not! Wasn't that a dilly we had last month! What else?"

"Well, the Ionians had the idea that the maximum livable size of any city was 30,000 people. Once it achieved that population, they sent their best men, with wives and children, to found a new city."

"Neat! You and I would be the first to go, John."

"The Ionians founded Istanbul—Byzantium in those days—and Sinop, Samsun, and Trabzon on the Black Sea."

"Hey! Those are all our bases now! That's pretty cool!"

This seemed to spur him on, and I suddenly realized we were going to barrel right past Priene. "Crash! Crash! Slow down!"

"What for?"

"We're going to miss Priene, that's what for! Ah, we just passed it!"

"Where, where?" said Crash, hitting the brakes and throwing the Buick in reverse. "I didn't see a thing!"

"We just passed it again—backward."

Crash jerked the gear shift again, and we shot forward with only a slight case of whiplash.

"Now, there it is. Just ahead. See that road that turns off to the right? Well, that goes up the mountain to the city. We'll have to stop right here and walk up. This is actually the east harbor. Crash, stop! We can't go up this road! It's not really a road. It's a path!"

Crash simply jerked the automatic transmission into low, and we went charging up, skidding from side to side, spitting rocks and stones. The path was only about five feet wide with a gully down the middle. I'm sure it was the main entrance to the city, and paved, in ancient times, but now it was only fit for goats and donkeys and good walking shoes. Crash was yelping like a berserk barbarian—I closed my eyes. "What's the matter, John?"

Suddenly the ground leveled to a patch about 15 feet square. Crash wrenched the steering wheel to the left to avoid hitting a high wall, and came to a screeching halt about two feet from a sheer cliff overlooking the Meander River Valley below.

"There!" said Crash, as he pulled on the emergency brake. "John, you have no faith."

We got out and Crash started unloading his photographic equipment. My legs were wobbly. "Here, take this, John!" he said, handing me a tripod the size of a telephone pole. "And this!" He gave me a leather-encased telephoto lens the size of a sewer pipe. "Can you take this?" He added a leather bag the size of a bread box. "It's got all my film in it! I'll carry the Hasselblad, the Mamiya, and the Canon."

We went through a marble arch and climbed a grand staircase into the city square, covered with lush green grass, in front of the Agora (marketplace). My old friend, Hamit the *bekji*, came running over to us, delighted to see me again because there was no one else there and he was bored. He welcomed us with a flood of flowery Turkish and tried to kiss Crash's hand.

"Yeah, yeah," said Crash, brushing him off and unpacking his equipment. "Same to you, Pop!"

Hamit was about 60, bare headed, unshaven and tiny. He was still wearing a heavy army overcoat that reached to his shoes (his son's? his grandson's?), making him look like a walking tent. He was terribly impressed with all of Crash's equipment and probably thought that Hollywood had come to Priene.

It was a glorious day, and the view from this vantage point was magnificent. We were about 500 feet above the river, which meandered through the lush valley planted with vegetables, alfalfa, cotton, and wheat. On the slopes of the hills were Sultana grapes. Here and there a wood fire or a cottage chimney sent wisps of smoke into the flawless blue sky. In the distance you could see the Aegean Sea shimmering.

Crash barely noticed. He was too busy snapping pictures, switching lenses, or changing cameras. "John, will you get that madman out of the picture!"

The *bekji* was posing like Napoleon in front of a pillar. I led him off to the side and tried to explain to him that Crash didn't want any humans in his pictures. The poor old thing was hurt and bewildered because all the other tourists loved taking his picture.

Crash kept calling for bits and pieces of equipment: "Filters! Lens shade! Press release!" I felt like an attendant at surgery. As we moved from site to site, the setting up of equipment was like a Cecil B. De Mille epic, so I had some time to give Crash tidbits from the *Blue Guide*.

"This is the theater, the best-preserved building in the city. These five throne-like seats in the front row were reserved for high dignitaries."

"Sit in one, John. Oh, God! There's that old coot again!"

"Oh, Crash, let him stay." The *bekji* posed like a tiny Roman emperor. I felt sure that Hadrian, who built these seats in the 2nd century A.D., would have been amused and delighted.

"This is the altar dedicated to Dionysius. Those are the dressing rooms under the stage."

"Hand me the Mamiya!"

We trudged higher up the mountain, all of us lugging equipment like sherpas. "What's this?" asked Crash.

"This is the temple of Demeter, also known as Ceres, the goddess of the harvest. Here's an interesting story: 'Demeter had a daughter by Zeus named Persephone, goddess of spring. One day when Persephone was picking flowers in the fields, she was kidnapped by her uncle Hades (Pluto), who took her down to his underworld kingdom and made her his queen. Demeter looked everywhere for her daughter and finally, in despair, forbade all the trees to bear fruit and all the grasses to grow grain. A compromise was hastily patched together whereby Persephone returned to her mother for nine months every year and descended to Hades for the winter. Today, the temple is a pile of rubble, except for the marble ditch to drain the blood of animal sacrifices.'"

"Where's that ditch? Ah, there it is! I wonder if we could get some blood somewhere?"

"Crash, *please!*"

"Oh, all right, John. You're just too sensitive. Hand me that red filter!"

We moved down to the west side of the city. "This is the Temple of Athena. Alexander the Great liberated the city from the Persians and donated a statue of Athena 22 feet high, according to an inscription on an altar stone in the British Museum. Most of the statues from this city were taken by archeologists in the 19th century—Germans, British, French. Not Americans! We didn't have any archeologists in those days. We were too busy killing Indians. But that was before the Turks passed a law forbidding the exportation of archeological treasures. It was quite normal in those days for archeologists to take what they found—it was their reward. And all of it went to museums for preservation. Besides, the Sultan didn't care. None of the stuff was Turkish, and most of it was a reminder of his hated enemy, the Greeks."

"Film! 35 millimeter! Ektachrome!" said Crash, looking through a lens and holding out his hand.

We pulled up stakes and went down the mountain to the gymnasium near the west harbor. "Look," I said to Crash, "you can still see the graffiti on the walls. And look at these marble basins where the athletes used to wash. There were spouts right above them where water flowed from lions' mouths."

"Will you get that idiot out of here, John!" The little *bekji* had positioned himself behind a basin, leaning over with his mouth open and his tongue stuck out as if to demonstrate the story I had just read from the *Blue Guide*. I thought it would have made a charming picture, but Crash was Crash, so I eased the little old troll over to another basin and took his picture with my Polaroid camera. He was so pleased that he reached up and kissed me on both cheeks.

"Okay, John! That's enough! Finished! *Tamam!* Let's go! On to the next city!" And Crash led the safari up to the Agora on the way back to the car. When we reached that lovely grassy spot in front of the Agora and the *bekji* realized we were leaving, he got hysterical. He pleaded with me to stay, pulling me back. I told him my leader said we must go. He ran up and grabbed Crash and dragged him back to a half-pillar in the marketplace, pinning his arms behind it. Crash looked like a white man ready to be burned at the stake by the wild-eyed *bekji*. Crash was caught in his own web of strangling straps and tripod legs and couldn't extricate himself from his captor or paraphernalia.

"John! Get this guy off me! He's strong as an ox!!!"

The *bekji* was looking at me, pleading with me to make Crash stand still, to stay there and not move! I said to Crash, "Take it easy. Don't move! I don't understand what he is doing, but relax, keep calm." Reluctantly, Crash did. The *bekji* suddenly let go and ran behind a wall, emerging a few seconds later breathlessly carrying the head of a stone lion. He intercepted Crash in his flight and shoved the lion's head up into Crash's face. I gasped. It was obviously one of the lion's heads from the gymnasium. It was a pearly white marble, about 12 inches wide, 16 inches high, 5 inches deep—a cutout, with the lion's tongue sticking out in a long, low, voluptuous curve.

"Oh! Yes! Heh, heh! Beautiful!" said Crash. "Let's take a picture of that! John, you stand beside that pillar! Hold it up! Yes, let Pop get into the picture too, John. Just tell him not to stick out his tongue." Snap. "Good! Now, hold it just a minute, I'll take another one with the Mamiya." Snap! "That's great! Fine! John, give him a tip! That's too much!"

When we got into the car, Crash released the emergency brake, and the Buick rolled forward. Clunk! The right front wheel had eased over the cliff and the car rested on the axle. Crash shifted to reverse and spun the back wheels, but the car didn't budge. Crash got out and surveyed the situation in a glance.

"We're stuck, John! Get out!"

I looked out my window at the river below and decided to get out the driver's side, very gingerly.

"Hmm. John, go down to the village and get a tractor to pull us out!"

I wanted to say it was all his damned fault, that I told him not to come up this hill, but he was such a pig-headed maniac that it served him right! Instead, I said, "Yes, sir." I stumbled down the hill with the *bekji* following hot on my heels. I kept muttering to myself, "Where am I going to get a tractor? The Turks hardly even use tractors! Too modern! Too expensive! I'll probably have to go back to Soke—maybe Izmir—to get a tow truck."

At the bottom of the hill was a teahouse. If I hadn't been in such a foul mood, I would have found it quite charming. It was square, made of wood, quite weather-beaten, with a little square cupola on top to let the light in, all nestled under the branches of an enormous old sycamore tree. And lo and behold! Sitting beside the teahouse was a brand-new gleaming green John Deere tractor! Either Crash was psychic, or Allah was having pity on me. I charged into the teahouse, like Crash, and started shouting in loud clear Turkish, *Traktor kiminki?"* (Whose tractor is that?) The teahouse keeper was shocked, as were the four or five men sitting at tables drinking tea and playing dominoes. "That tractor outside! Who does it belong to?? I need a tractor! Now, dammit, whose is it?"

A young man at one of the tables raised his hand, halfway, like a schoolboy who was not sure of the answer. I glommed onto him. "Our car is stuck on the top of the hill—up near the old ruins. You get onto your tractor! Come up the hill and pull out our car! We are Americans!" I felt like a damn fool, but I had to be firm and use every wile I could think of.

The young man threw up his hands in terror and started backing away from me. *"Ben ajemi! Ajemi!"*

"Okay, Ajemi, if that's your name, let's go!"

Then everybody started screaming that he was *ajemi*, that he was not a real driver, and I suddenly realized the word meant "learner."

"My master would kill me if I took his tractor up on the mountain and had an accident or destroyed it! Please spare me!" He was practically on his knees.

The *bekji* started pulling me out of the teahouse. "Never mind, Mister John! Let's go back up the mountain—*we* can pull your friend out!" Several beasties had gathered in front of the teahouse, attracted by my shouting. The *bekji* immediately drafted a 14-year-old and swore at the others to go away. "Let's go, Mister John!"

I noticed a camel coming up the road, tended by a scruffy keeper. "Hamit! Hamit!" I cried to the *bekji*. "Let's engage this camel!" I was sure the camel was stronger than the three of us put together, but Hamit didn't even stop to listen.

He and the beastie were charging up the hill like mountain goats. I gave up and let them get far ahead. The whole situation was getting out of hand—certainly out of my hands. I stumbled up the hill, panting and wheezing, and fell on the ground at the top.

Crash was there beaming—his Buick had been rescued. He turned the car around and headed down the mountain. "John! Where have you been??" he called out the window, stopping the car.

The *bekji* and the beastie were also beaming and standing stiffly at attention as if waiting for me to pin a medal on them. I learned that with the *bekji* and the beastie lifting the right front wheel, and Crash gunning the Buick's back wheels, the car had popped out in a second. "Come on, John! Get up! Everyone in the car! Yes, them too, make them get into the back seat! Down we go!"

And down we went—bump, bang, pow, clang, clunkety-clunk! At the teahouse Crash started issuing orders like General Patton. "Tea for everybody! Yes, you too!" he said to the proprietor. "It's on me! John, take a picture of the *bekji!*" Crash posed him. "Good! Give him the picture! See, Polaroid! Take one of this stalwart lad! Great! Give it to him! And one for this old man—this tea is great! Here's an *iki buchuk* (25¢)—keep the change! Come on, John, let's go!"

As we roared down the road, Crash said smugly, "Well, I got the lion!"

"What?"

"I got the lion—you know, the one the old guy showed us. It's in the trunk!"

"Oh, no!!! Oh my God! Oh, Jesus!"

"What's the matter, John? I got it for you. It's yours! You like that kind of stuff!"

"Stop the car! Crash, stop! We've got to go back!"

"Are you crazy? I got it for *you!* I thought you liked collecting all this ancient crap. My wife won't let me have it around the house."

I tried not to panic. I pulled myself together and, as

quickly as I could, told Crash about my horrible episode with the police over a little stone I had found in Van.

"Oh, balls," said Crash.

"Crash, please! The *bekji* will know we took it. We were the only ones there. He'll know the car—how could he forget it? Maybe even the license plate. The Turkish police know everything! Their communications are better than ours! My brother in Ankara is probably getting a call this very minute!"

"Oh, calm down. This is only a little piece of stone. You said yourself the British got a statue of Athena 22 feet high!"

"That was different. Let's go back. We can slip it back in place without the *bekji* knowing."

"I'm not going back," said Crash as we roared across the Meander Valley toward Miletus.

The rest of the trip was painful for me. Crash noticed that I had grown glum and mercifully he didn't badger me about it.

The day after we got back to Izmir, Crash burst into my office about 9:00 in the morning and plunked down a Coca-Cola carton in the middle of my desk. "There it is, John!" and he stormed out. I looked inside. It was the lion! Blood started rushing to my head and my ears started ringing. Fortunately, there was no one in my office at the time. I stashed it under my desk and dialed Crash's extension.

"Look! You get this Coca-Cola box out of my office by noon or I'm going to call the Minister of Education and Antiquities!"

"Oh, John, you're over-reacting."

"By noon! Do you understand?" I slammed down the phone.

Curington came into my office and I jumped about two feet.

"What's the matter, John?"

"It's all your fault!"

"What is?" he said laughing.

I decided I'd better not tell him. "Nothing! Go away!" I

couldn't work. I couldn't think. I dreaded the thought of going to the Minister of Education and Antiquities. How could I ever explain how I had come into possession of this glorious object?

At five minutes to twelve Crash roared in like a snarling cyclone. "Well! Where is it???"

I lifted it gently from under my desk. He grabbed it and roared out.

It was three weeks before I could bring myself to ask Crash what happened to the Coca-Cola box. I met him at one of those "required-presence" cocktail parties at the Officers Club. Crash was carrying six drinks in his bare hands when I stopped him and lowered my voice to ask him about the final disposition of the Coca-Cola box.

"The Coca-Cola box? Oh, *that* box! Yeah! Oh, I gave it to Biff Bumbaugh."

"Good! And he turned it over to the Turkish authorities?"

"Yeah, sure! Great trip, John, great!!! We must do it again sometime!"

The Russians

≈

"YOUR BROTHER is calling you from Ankara. Hurry!"
"On the telephone or the radio?"
"The radio."
"Yuck!"
"He sounds a little violent."
"Doesn't he always?"

I went to the radio room, sat down, and pressed the one-way button on the microphone. "This is John, go ahead, over."

"Have you been running around with some Russians??? Over."

"What did you say? Over." I actually had heard what he said, but I was trying to compose an answer. I hated radio communications. There was no privacy. Anyone could listen in—even the Russians!

"You heard what I said! Have you been running around with some Russians??? The Turkish police came to see me! They said they had a report that *I* was seen in restaurants and nightclubs with some Russians. I told them it must be my goddamned brother in Izmir! Over!"

"Well, as a matter of fact, I did meet some Russians. I was introduced to them by the manager of the American Pavilion at the International Fair. We had dinner together and went to a nightclub. But they've gone now. The fair is over." I decided not to say any more, so I said, "Over."

"Well, you'd better send me a full report—everything—you understand? Over!"

"Yes sir, over." I mentally saluted.
"Jeez, as if I don't have enough problems! Over and out!"
Well, I had no intention of telling him *everything*. I had no desire to tell him anything. I decided to wait a few days to see if the whole thing would blow over.

I had indeed met the Russians through the manager of the American Pavilion. It was the last night of the fair, and I had gone with my friends Tom and Kitty Curington. The Izmir International Fair was held every year from August 20 to September 20, the most delightful time of the year. The nights were warm and balmy with never the remotest possibility of rain. We always went on the opening night and the closing night, and many times in between. It was mostly an industrial fair—lots of tractors and dentists' chairs with electric drills, but the smaller pavilions, like Pakistan and Ceylon, had stunning collections of fabrics, jewelry, and gemstones. A charming gaiety surrounded the fair. The fairground itself was gorgeous, with palm trees and magnolias and flowers everywhere. Pools and lakes featured arched bridges and fountains shot high into the air and sparkled from colored lights. There were even two nightclubs in the park. The walls were living palm trees, and the ceiling was the open sky. There were always stars, and when the moon came up no one watched the floor show.

The main competition each year was between the American and the Russian Pavilions. And each year we lost, according to the reviews in the Turkish newspapers. The Turks were very pro-American and fiercely anti-Soviet. Being Moslems, the Turks detested the atheistic Soviets. Besides, the Russians were traditional enemies, hated almost as much as the Greeks. "We've fought 105 wars against the Russkys, and we haven't lost one yet!" said one of the Turks to me. Still, each year the Turks conceded that the Russians had outdone the Americans once again. This particular year (1963), the Americans were determined to win! So they had bathing beauties gracing every display, and rock musicians in every corner banging out ear-piercing music. The Russians, on the other hand, had an enormous mock-up of a nuclear submarine, which *we*—not they—had recently launched and were trying to keep secret.

"Very bad, Mister John," said one of the Turks to me, as if I were personally responsible.

"But the Russians haven't even invented a nuclear submarine!" I said hotly.

"That's not important. We Turks are not taken in by naked girls and hippie musicians."

"Another fiasco," said Roland Greene, the manager of the American Pavilion, when we found him on the last night of the fair. "The State Department never listens to us. By the way, would you like to meet the manager of the Russian Pavilion?"

"Yes," said Kitty, bubbling with excitement.

Roland led us to the Russian Pavilion, which was adjacent to the American, and introduced us to Vladimir. He was very nice-looking, about 38 years old, slim, blond, and well-dressed. He was very gracious and gave us a tour of the pavilion, which we had seen many times, explaining each display in excellent bookish English, lingering the longest over the nuclear submarine. I bit my tongue.

When we were finished, it was almost nine o'clock, closing time. Roland had deserted us, and I impulsively said, "Vladimir, would you like to go out to dinner with us tonight?"

"I fear that is impossible. It would be unwise for me to be seen with Americans in a public place. Thank you so very much."

"But I know a place where no one will see us! Believe me, I *know* Izmir!"

Vladimir glanced around, then said, "Are you quite sure?"

"Positive."

"Please come," said Kitty.

"All right. I will meet you at the Alsanjak Ferryboat

landing in one half hour."

"Fine! And bring anyone you want with you—other Russians. Maybe you'll feel more comfortable," I said.

"It cannot be."

The lights started going out on the 19th International Fair as Kitty, Tom, and I headed for our car.

"Isn't this exciting?" said Kitty. "A real Russian! Where will you take us for dinner?"

"You'll see," I said cryptically.

We arrived at the ferryboat landing, parked, turned off the headlights, but left the parking lights on.

"Just like a spy movie," said Kitty.

"Maybe he won't come," said Tom.

We waited 30 minutes. Many taxis came up to the landing and discharged passengers, but none of them was Vladimir. Just as we were about to leave, there was a rap on the back window. It was Vladimir, who had appeared out of nowhere. Tom and Vladimir got into the back seat, and I zoomed off in the dark. We all talked at once.

"Vladimir, happy you came!" said Tom, slapping him on the back.

"Happy to be here."

"Where are we going, John?" asked Kitty.

"You wait and see."

"Vladimir, we must call John 'Ivan,' isn't that right?" asked Kitty.

"Yes. Ivan Ivanovitch."

"No," I said. "I'm John, son of James!"

"Oh, then 'Ivan Yakovlevitch,'" Vladimir said.[21]

"Er—ok," said Kitty.

We were all merry and excited. I took them to an outdoor restaurant across the bay from Izmir where my one-time girlfriend had sucked out my eyes. Kitty was enchanted with the spot, and Vladimir relaxed. It turned out to be a marvelous evening because we were almost alone—there

---

21. *Ivan* is the Russian equivalent of *John*. *-vitch* means *son of*. *Yakov* is *Jacob*, of which James is a variation. Tumpane's father was named James.

was only a fat old man staring into the eyes of a young girl who was obviously not his daughter. The broiled sea bass was delicious, and we felt we had snared a dangerous Russian defector.

At the end of the meal Kitty started making detailed plans, with a sketch on a paper napkin, for Vladimir to come to dinner the next night at the Curingtons' apartment, which overlooked the International Fairgrounds. "You can *see* our apartment from your pavilion!" she said, as if that settled it.

"I don't know if I *can* come," said Vladimir uncertainly—but he was wavering.

"You don't have to work tomorrow—the Fair is over."

"Oh, we have much work to do tomorrow—packing and crating and—"

"But not in the evening! Please come! I'll make you a typical Southern dinner!"

"God help us," I said. "Poke salad and chitlins."

"Hush your mouth, Ivan! You are a damn Yankee who was raised on New England boiled dinners."

"Yes, well, I *would* very much like to visit Americans in their homes," Vladimir said, "but—"

"Good!" said Kitty. "Bring a friend! Or two or three! It doesn't matter. We'll expect you at six!"

I dropped Kitty and Tom off at their apartment and drove Vladimir back to his hotel—an inexpensive but reputable one near the Railroad Station.

"Let me off here," said Vladimir.

"But the hotel is up the street two blocks."

"*Here!*" he commanded. I jammed on the brakes, and he got out. "Good night. *Dosvidanya!*"

Just like in a spy movie, I made a U-turn and drove off in the darkness to my apartment.

The next evening I went to the Curingtons', sure that Vladimir wouldn't show. But he was already there—sipping a martini! And with a friend—a young man about 25 years old, fair skin, pink cheeks, a flawless complexion, and a shock of blond hair.

"This is Nikolai," said Vladimir, "but since you Americans are so fond of nicknames you can call him Nicky."

"Hi, Nicky. I'm Ivan Yakovitch," I said.

"Yakovlevitch," corrected Vladimir.

"I can't pronounce that," I said.

"Then we'll call you Vanya. We Russians have many, many nicknames, too."

"Uncle Vanya!"[22] said Kitty, clapping her hands with delight.

We drank, we ate (the food was delicious—thank God Kitty couldn't find pokeweed on the local market!), and we expounded. Whether we realized it or not, we were trying to seduce Vladimir and his friend to our rich Western way of life—*Time* magazine, Duke Ellington, popcorn, jigsaw puzzles, Polaroid cameras. (Vladimir blithely pocketed each Polaroid picture I took.) Just as Vladimir was slipping into our clutches, he would pull back and make what sounded like a prepared speech: "We have freedom in our country, too! The People's Party makes all the decisions, so it is a government 'of the people, by the people, and for the people,' just like yours!" He preened as he quoted Abraham Lincoln.

"Can you travel anywhere you like?" asked Tom.

"Of course! Last year I visited my parents in Astrakhan on the Caspian Sea. It is a very important city for shipbuilding and caviar."

"Can I write to you?" asked Kitty.

"Naturally! We are a free country! I have received many letters from Western friends who I met at the Izmir International Fair. Good letters. I have them all in a special box." He sipped on his after-dinner drink, then leaned forward. "But I have my own special code—if I answer in red ink, it means 'don't write me again.'" Then he sat back in his chair and said airily, "Don't worry. Nikolai doesn't understand a word of English." Nikolai was trying to complete a jigsaw puzzle by pounding a spare puzzle piece into a gap

---

22. A reference to the play by Chekhov.

with his fist.

"When will you be leaving?" I asked.

"Next week. Most of our comrades will leave this week, but Nikolai and I have to stay until everything is loaded on the boat. Next Monday, or Tuesday at the latest. They get very upset if we linger too long." No one asked who "they" was.

"Are you free on Sunday?" I asked. "I could take you sightseeing. I'm the world's greatest living authority on historical places around Izmir—Ephesus! Bergama! Sardis!"

"Oh no, we cannot possibly be seen in such places."

"Why not?" asked Tom.

Vladimir spread his hands.

"I thought *you* were in charge of your delegation here," said Tom, leaning forward to pin Vladimir down.

"I am, but—"

"But what?"

"It is difficult."

"John told us he had to leave you off two blocks from your hotel last night."

"Yes."

"Why?"

"Nikolai, we must depart now."

"No, wait a minute!" I shouted. "I know thousands of places where there's no one! Colophon! Teos! Kyme! Claros! Yes, Claros! Even *I* could hardly find it. It's right near the sea—we can take a picnic and swim. I *promise* you there will be no one there but us!"

Tom and Kitty both urged Vladimir to accept. He agreed reluctantly. We arranged to meet at noon, in front of the Archeological Museum. I then drove Vladimir and Nicky back to their hotel, or at least the proximity thereof. Vladimir insisted we approach the hotel in the opposite direction from the first time, and drop them off three blocks away!

Later that week Tom told me that he and Kitty couldn't come with us to Claros. They had a previous engagement they had forgotten, which they couldn't get out of.

Impulsively, I invited a Turk and a German—both good friends of mine—to join us. They readily agreed, apparently as interested in fraternizing with the "enemy" as I was. I was a little apprehensive about Vladimir's reaction to these new elements that I had thrown into the melting pot.

On Sunday I picked up the Turk and the German first, then drove to the Archeological Museum. Vladimir and Nicky were nowhere in sight. We drove around the park once—no sign of them. We drove around a second time, and they popped out from behind some bushes. I introduced them briefly, "Vladimir! Nikolai! Kaya! Heinz!" and waited until we got out of town before making fuller explanations.

"Kaya is a musician. He works at the Londra Bar. He plays the trumpet. He's actually the orchestra leader! Kaya's name means 'rock' in Turkish, so we call him 'Rocky.' You can, too."

Rocky, who didn't speak a word of English, somehow seemed to understand what I was saying. He reached over the front seat and shook Vladimir's hand comradely.

"Heinz works for our company. He's our Supply Supervisor. And he's very good! He and I almost started the Third World War one night in my apartment when he claimed, 'You Americans only won the war because of your Federal Stock Numbering system!' Naturally I challenged him because I felt we had won because we had superior airplanes and guns and bombs and we were fighting for democracy! But Heinz said no! When they needed a part to repair a tank, they would send messages to Berlin giving the name of the tank, model number, year of manufacture, description of the part—and invariably the part they received wouldn't fit!"

Heinz picked up from where I had left off, leaning over the front seat to convince Vladimir. "It's true! The Americans simply sent a message (which we intercepted) saying, 'send two each 7390-181-9964.' Well! What were we Germans to make of *that* secret message? I know now since I am working for this American company that the first number means military equipment, the second number vehicle, the third number a tank, the fourth—"

"Enough! Enough!" I shouted to Heinz, even though Vladimir was fascinated. "I am *determined* we are not going to fight the Third World War today! Incidentally, we call Heinz 'Pickles' because he's one of the 57 varieties."[23] Vladimir was bewildered.

"*Nereye gidioryuz?*" (where are we going?) asked Rocky as we plunged down the abominable road into the valley toward Claros.

"*Sabir! Sabir!*" (patience, patience), I said.

Vladimir hadn't translated a word of our conversation to Nicky, but I heard Nicky say "*Turki*" and "*Alman*"[24] several times, and Vladimir said "*Da. Da!*"

Once we got to the glorious ruins of Claros, all inhibitions seemed to break down, as if the classical Greek marbles were bringing us all together in a common background. Vladimir took lots of pictures with his Japanese camera, which he had bought at the fair. Heinz took pictures with his Rollei and tried to start a fight with Vladimir over cameras. I saved the day with my Polaroid pictures.

Then we drove to the beach, scarcely a mile away. I opened the beer cooler, Vladimir produced a bottle of Russian vodka, Rocky brought out his Turkish cigarettes, and before long everyone was slapping everyone else on the back. Vladimir confiscated all my Polaroid pictures, like a true Russian annexing pieces and parcels here and there—Lithuania, Latvia, and Estonia. But I didn't mind since I managed to hide three of them for myself, but I was furious that I felt like a spy—hiding my own pictures!

We stayed long after dark, with a fire burning on the shore, each of us singing our national songs. I sang "You Are My Sunshine" and felt like an ass. But they loved it.

Finally, Rocky said we must be going so that he could

---

23. "Heinz 57" was an advertising slogan of the H. J. Heinz Company of Pittsburgh, Pennsylvania, which produced foodstuffs including pickles.
24. Turkish for "German."

get to his nightclub on time. Nicky insisted on jumping into the sea again. I sent two little Turkish beasties, who had joined us around the campfire, into the sea to fetch Nicky.

We dropped Rocky off at the Londra Bar and I drove straight to The Chateau, the best restaurant in Izmir.

"What's this?" asked Vladimir, somewhat alarmed.

"Let's have dinner here." The restaurant was perched on stilts on the side of the mountain overlooking the lights around the bay below. It was an irresistible sight, and when Nicky found out we were talking about food, he started slapping his flat stomach, and Vladimir capitulated.

"Oh, Mister John, welcome!" said the headwaiter as we entered.

In deference to Vladimir, I had the headwaiter show us to a secluded table at the far end of the open balcony with nothing but candles to light our table. I did the ordering, selecting all the exotic appetizers, hors d'oeuvres, and specialties the Turks were famous for. Nicky wolfed down everything in sight and pronounced them all Russian dishes. I didn't argue, especially when it came to the delicious Chicken Kievsky.

Right in the middle of the meal, Nicky jumped up and made a speech in Russian! He talked excitedly with his eyes fixed intently on mine, then reached across the table, shook my hand violently, and sat down.

I was amazed.

"What on earth was that all about?" I asked.

Vladimir patted me on the arm and said, "It's all right. Let me translate for you. Nikolai said he was only eight years old during the siege of Stalingrad, and he and his mother were starving. His father had been killed early in the war. When the siege was broken, the Americans sent in food and supplies by way of Persia. He remembers a Studebaker Army truck which stopped in the middle of the street in front of the apartment where he and his mother were hiding. The truck was loaded with Spam, and the soldiers distributed it to anyone who came to them. Nicky filled his shirt with

Spam and carried as much as he could in his arms back to his mother's apartment. Spam saved his life. Ever since that day in 1943 he has wanted to meet an American so that he could thank him."

Nicky had watched me intently during the translation. When it was finished, he bobbed his head several times meaning, "Did you understand?"

I nodded. I had a lump in my throat. I even felt guilty about all the nasty things *I* had said about Spam during the war. I looked at Nicky and said in my best Russian, *"Da! Da!"*

Nicky smiled, raised his vodka, and belted it down straight. Naturally I had to do the same. I was afraid he was going to smash his glass on the terrazzo floor, but he just filled it up again—and mine. For the rest of the meal, I would catch his eye from time to time, and down the hatch went the vodka again. I was pretty well schwacked by the time the bill came, but the rich Turkish food helped to absorb most of the vodka before my bloodstream did.

I was so keyed up on the way home that I suggested we stop at the Londra Bar to hear Rocky play the trumpet.

"Da! Da!" said Nicky, bouncing on the back seat. *"Trompetta!!!"* He even played a trumpet tune through his fists. Vladimir, who had also had his share of vodka, agreed.

The nightclub was dark and smoky with lots of red and blue lights everywhere. Rocky was playing as we entered. We had to cross right in front of the stage as the waiter led us to a table. Rocky nodded with his trumpet and I could see he was pleased that we had come.

Vladimir and I ordered *kanyak* but Nicky was sticking to vodka. At the end of the number, Rocky rushed over to our table, welcomed us excitedly, and said he'd come back to sit with us during the break. Nicky was all eyes—especially for the girls. I asked him if he wanted to dance since they were all bar girls and it was perfectly permissible. Vladimir refused to translate. Rocky played several solos especially for our benefit—"A Sleepy Lagoon," "Three Coins in the

Fountain," "Ya Mustapha." He really outdid himself and Nicky applauded wildly.

A little while later I noticed that the band was on a break and the club had switched to canned music. I looked around for Rocky, but he was nowhere to be seen. Soon afterward, the band started up again. I thought it very strange that Rocky hadn't come over to the table, but soon dismissed the thought. Suddenly Rocky was standing beside me whispering in my ear in Turkish.

He said, "The Turkish police are following your friends," and then went quickly to the bandstand.

"We must go," I said briskly, calling for the waiter. Vladimir seemed to understand immediately. He took Nicky under the arm and raised him to his feet. Nicky was a little groggy but waved to Rocky as we left.

I drove them straight to their hotel—that is, two blocks away. We all said *"Dosvidanya,"* and I drove slowly home with a jumble of mixed feelings.

It was three days later that I got the irate radio call from my brother. I didn't write him "a full report." I didn't write him anything. Instead, I went to the Commissary and bought a can of Spam. I was surprised how good it tasted.

The Circumcision Party

≈

Dear Mister John,
   You are cordially invited to attend a party in honor of the circumcision of my son Burhan.
   Kapris Gazino
   816 Maltepe Caddesi, Ankara
   8:00 p.m. 16 May 1964
   Kemal Shimshek

I THOUGHT I knew *all* about circumcision in Turkey. Of course, circumcision is a must because 98% of Turks are Moslem. In the villages the little boys wear dresses until they are circumcised. It's easy to distinguish little boys from little girls because the dresses are so short and village children seldom wear underclothes. Once the boy is circumcised, usually at the age of three or four, he graduates into short pants. The circumcision is a family affair.

But a party! I had never heard of a circumcision party!

I had just been transferred from Izmir to Ankara and I decided I'd better learn about big city life—and quick! I dialed on the inter-office phone for Sedat, our Customs man. He handled customs on imports of goods and supplies for our work, but he also was the one we turned to when we were baffled by the other kind of customs, the mores of the Turkish people.

"Sedat, can you come up to my office, please."

"At your service."

Sedat was a semi-celebrity—his brother was featured

prominently in Laurence Durrell's book about Cyprus, *Bitter Lemons.*

"Sir!" said Sedat, coming to attention in front of my desk. He loved to play this aide-de-camp role, and I often wondered why he didn't salute.

"Look at this invitation!"

He glanced at it briefly. "Yes, sir, I know about it."

"It's for tonight!"

"Yes sir. There was a slight mix-up at the printer's, and Kemal didn't get the invitations until this morning."

"Are other people besides me invited?"

"Oh yes, sir! The whole office."

"The whole office? You mean men *and* women?"

"Yes, sir. And all the wives, too."

"Wives? Are we actually going to *witness* the circumcision?" I was thinking that if I were still in the wilds of Diyarbakir, I could probably endure it—and even enjoy it after the blood stopped flowing—but here, in civilized Ankara, with American wives tittering and giggling—

"Oh no, sir. The circumcision will take place at Kemal's home in the afternoon. The party is at night at the Kapris Gazino."

"But that's a regular nightclub, open to the public." I had been there only a few nights before. I enjoyed going to the Kapris once in a while. It was typically Turkish: a four-hour show of belly dancers, acrobats, magicians, comedians, and fat Turkish ladies who sang sad love songs, each of which would last almost an hour. Nobody paid any attention until the lady finished. Then the audience would clap, stomp, and whistle, as if trying to make up for their bad manners during the song. I silently prayed for deliverance and a new act, but invariably the singer would return, launch into another mournful song, and the customers would go back to talking madly among themselves—probably politics—while I ordered "another *kanyak, doubleh!*" But it was interesting once in a while—an ethnic endurance test—and also there were never any Americans there. They didn't have any *Konsumasyon.* "Are we going to mix with the regular customers?"

"Oh no, sir, Kemal has engaged the entire nightclub for the evening—*and* the entire floorshow."

"Oh God."

"Sir?"

"Nothing. Should we bring a gift?"

Sedat lowered his head and looked at the rug. "Yes, sir."

"Okay, fine. How old is the beastie? Three? Four?

"Oh no sir, he's 13."

"Thirteen! Why, in Diyarbakir they snip them off at three or four years old."

"Yes sir, I know. But they're very backward there. Here in Ankara and Istanbul, we do it when the boy is old enough to know what's happening to him—when he's a man!"

"What kind of present should I give him?"

"Books, sir."

"Turkish or English?"

"Well—" Sedat hesitated. "I know it is illegal to give the Turks anything that comes from the PX, but you Americans have such wonderful comic books—educational books, really, and even I enjoy them—and Kemal's son speaks and reads English better than his father."

"Thank you, Sedat."

"I am always at your service, sir." He bowed deeply and left the room.

After I cleared out my IN box, I wandered into John Hicks's office. Hicks was our Comptroller and Kemal was his Chief Turkish Accountant. We had to keep a complete set of accounting books in Turkish.

"Did you get an invitation to Kemal's circumcision party?" I asked.

"Yeah! Isn't that great? Sedat said we're not going to see any skin game, but we should bring the poor sonofabitch a book. I called Betty Lou and she's all excited about going. She wanted to know what kind of a dress one is supposed to wear to a circumcision party. I told her to wear her old nurse's uniform and bring plenty of sutures."

I wandered into Fred Jensen's office. "Did you get an invitation to Kemal's circumcision party?"

"Yeah! Sounds very interesting. Sedat says I should bring a comic book. I thought a box of Band Aids would be more appropriate, but Sedat didn't think that was very funny. I called Jan and she went into hysterics. She loathes company parties, but she said she wouldn't miss this one for the world."

I went back to my office. My IN box was full again—requests, problems, reports. I tended to each item, but my mind was on a good present for the poor sacrificial lamb. Sedat apparently told everyone to bring him books, so I was determined not to. They get enough of that stuff in school. Finally I had an idea—a whim that didn't make any sense. I called for my driver.

"Mehmet, here's 100 lira. I want you to go downtown and buy the biggest, largest, longest, gaudiest flashlight they have on the Turkish market, complete with batteries. Test it before you leave the shop, understand?"

"Flashlight? But we have one in the car."

"Go! Buy one! It's not for me, it's a present. *Git!*"

I was pleased with my idea for Burhan's present, and suddenly it occurred to me why I had thought of it: when we were kids we *loved* to play with the family flashlight—forbidden!

I went to the party with John and Betty Lou Hicks. Mehmet deposited us in front of the Kapris Gazino, and we got into a long line of invitees.

"My God, how many people did Kemal invite?" said Hicks.

"What did you get Burhan?" asked Betty Lou.

"It's a secret."

"I got him all the classics I could find at the PX—*Robin Hood, Gulliver's Travels, Alice in Wonderland*—all comics, of course. I know he'll like them. His English is wonderful. Every time Kemal comes to visit us, Burhan has to be the interpreter. Kemal doesn't speak a word of English."

"He knows 'credit' and 'debit,' by God," said Hicks.

When we got into the casino, it was almost full. All the upper levels and tiers were filled with people at tables. Even the dance floor was covered with tables. We, in line, were directed to the back of the room where, on the highest tier, we saw a wide bed covered with white sheets. On it sat Burhan. He was wearing a white nightgown and a gold paper crown on his head. He certainly looked like a little king with his courtiers around him—Kemal and his wife beaming, two older sisters sitting prettily at the foot of the bed, and all of his subjects filling the hall below. He had a perfect view of the whole panoply and the stage at the opposite end of the hall. Kemal and his wife shook our hands limply. The boy eagerly grabbed the presents we brought, but his sisters snatched them away from him and arranged them artistically around his feet. He looked like a little Christmas tree.

I was a bit crestfallen that the presents were not going to be opened there. But this was typical of the Turks—they never open a gift in your presence. I often thought we should adopt the custom so you don't have to *ooh!* and *aah!* over some stupid thing you have absolutely no use for.

We shook the little king's hand and passed on to an excited waiter, who seated us at a table with our company's lawyer, Erdogan, and his wife, Sevil. Almost immediately we were served hors d'oeuvres, then soup, then a full meal of baby lamb chops and pilaf. I looked around the room—surely there were 500 people, half of them our employees, the others presumably friends of Kemal. How could he possibly afford to hire a nightclub, with floorshow, and feed 500 people a full meal? I was beginning to think we must be paying him too much when Erdogan explained that the Turks will go into bankruptcy to outdo their friends and neighbors when giving a party—circumcision, wedding, or whatever. "It's our damnable pride," he said.

Erdogan pointed out a large table of burly men punching and grabbing each other by the head in hammerlocks. They were the famous Fennerbahce soccer team. Kemal was their accountant on the side, a job that surely supplemented his income. Plus, perhaps, he made some judicious wagers on the side.

Suddenly the lights went dim, the curtains opened, and the *attraksiyon* began. The American men wildly applauded the belly dancer, while their wives tried to calm them. It was the same show I had seen before. The Americans loved the magician and the acrobats, but the Turkish Bob Hope was a complete mystery. The Turks howled at his jokes and Erdogan and Sevil tried desperately to translate them for us, but it was all rather hopeless. (Sample: A farmer went to the doctor complaining of kidney trouble. The doctor told him to bring a urine specimen. The man put a jar outside his door and used it during the night. Unknown to him, so did his wife. When the doctor analyzed the specimen, he said, "Nothing to worry about, you're going to have a baby.") Finally the fat chanteuse came on wearing a purple dress. She looked like an eggplant turned upside down. Everyone started talking.

I was bored to death when suddenly I was distracted by a faint spot of light moving around the proscenium arch. It appeared, then disappeared, then started moving along the side wall. I turned and looked back—it was the little king playing with his flashlight. He'd shine it on the performer, but the stage spotlights would drown it out. He'd shine it on people in the audience, but they all had their heads turned away from him, so it had no effect. Every once in a while he would lift the sheet and shine it down on the reason we were all there that night.

My evening was made. I cheered up considerably watching the antics of the little king.

When the eggplant lady was finished, the Americans heaved a sigh of relief, but the Turks brought her back for more. It was after midnight, so one by one the Americans stood up, bent over, and sneaked out like Indians in the night. We too beat a retreat. When we got in the car, Betty

Lou said, "Did you notice Burhan playing with a flashlight? I wonder who gave him that dumb thing."

I just smiled to myself.

A week later John Hicks burst into my office and said, "Kemal's dead."

"What??"

"Heart attack. Yesterday. At the soccer game."

"Oh my God! He was a young man."

"Thirty-eight! But oh, was he smart! A trained accountant to the end! He turned to Burhan, who was sitting with him, and said, 'I have 39,000 lira in my pocket—it belongs to the team'—and fell over dead."

Kemal's last name, Shimshek, means "lightning." I often wondered why his family chose it. Kemal himself was as slow as Moses, but he went out like a bolt of lightning. Burhan, poor waif, was now the head of the family. He adored his father, but he was very brave during the funeral. He held his head high and didn't shed a tear. He was a man!

Bert Organizing the Olive-Pickers of Nicea

≈

IT WAS EARLY 1965. We had just completed our first negotiation with a Turkish labor union, and we were elated. It wasn't very easy because American labor leaders had trained the Turkish union chiefs to ask for the moon and the stars—in addition to money, meal allowances, work clothing, transportation allowances, sick benefits, and work shoes. We granted half of everything they wanted except for the moon and stars and shoes. During the negotiations I had visions of myself sitting on a little stool in front of one of our workers saying, "Now, how does that feel, Mehmet Ali? Too tight?"

It was 3:00 p.m. as we left Karamursel Air Station on the Marmara Sea and began our drive back to Ankara, four hours away. Bert Crane, our company negotiator, talked a mile a minute before, during, and after the negotiations. He was an old Washington lawyer who talked so fast *nobody* could understand him; thus he could never be held responsible for what he said. I don't think it was intentional—I think it was simple hypertension. "Great negotiation! Great! First labor contract signed in Turkey, and we made out like a bandit stealing candy from a baby! You were great, Yuksel! A great interpreter, isn't he, John? A fine boy. You're going to make a great lawyer someday! Did you notice how I nailed them on that children allowance, John? 'Do you want

Bert Organizing the Olive-Pickers of Nicea / 297

us to pay you for f--king???' Did you translate that exactly, Yuksel?"

"I modified it a bit, sir."

"That's all right, ol' buddy-buddy," said Bert, whacking him on the back so hard it knocked the wind out of him. Yuksel was a very fragile little Turk, highly intelligent and so high-strung he gulped air and stammered as he translated Bert's machine-gun sallies and circumlocutions.

I interrupted Bert long enough to ask if he'd mind if we made a detour past Lake Iznik on the way back to Ankara.

"Lake Iznik? Iznik? What's that? Never heard of it."

"Oh, sir," said Yuksel, "it's very famous. That's where in ancient times they made all those famous turquoise tiles. The tiles for the Blue Mosque in Istanbul were made in Iznik. Alas, they don't make them anymore—the city has declined."

"Tiles, well yes," said Bert, "but I don't think I'm very interested in tiles. How far out of the way is it? You're surely not thinking of going swimming at this time of year! I was hoping we'd get home in time for dinner. I didn't eat a thing for lunch."

I remembered that he had wolfed down a hot roast beef sandwich with the "extra mashed potatoes, please," plus a bowl of soup with his package of crackers *and* mine plus a salad and a piece of pineapple upside-down cake, "a la mode, please." But I said, "It's only about 10 miles off the highway, and we'll join the main highway again a few miles on the other side of Iznik."

I had already instructed Mehmet on the detour while Bert was being photographed shaking hands with the union leaders. Mehmet had dutifully turned off the highway onto the dirt road which led straight to a ridge surrounding Lake Iznik. It was a glorious sight—the near side was treeless, covered with lush green grass and hundreds of head of cattle grazing the hillside right down to the lake. The far side was covered with trees. Our road took us around three-quarters of the lake, which was shaped like a bathtub 20 miles long.

Bert had a few thousand words to say about our having already turned off on the detour without waiting for a decision in the case, and he hinted at a conspiracy between Mehmet and me. Mehmet, of course, couldn't understand a word of what Bert was saying but giggled when he heard his name mentioned and leaned back over the front seat to pat Bert on the shoulder. "Mister Bert, *choke guzel*." (Very beautiful.)

"*Choke guzel*, yes, I'm very beautiful, and you are *choke fenah*, very bad!" Mehmet giggled, flattered at the attention.

"Iznik is the Turkish equivalent of *Nicea!*" I said to Bert.

"So?" said Bert in his shortest utterance ever.

"Surely you remember your Bible: Nicea? The Nicene Creed?"

"That's one book I always meant to read, but I've been too busy—reading law journals all my life."

"Well, in 323 A.D. Constantine the Great called a meeting of the elders of the Christian church from all over the known world (the Mediterranean) and made them sit down on the shore of this lake to decide once and for all what they believed in. I can just picture them saying, 'I believe in one God, the Father almighty, maker of heaven and earth, and of all things visible and invisible.' I can imagine the arguing and bickering, just as we did in negotiations these past few days—and the poor, beleaguered interpreters, since I don't believe any of the delegates spoke the same language—and the poor scribe taking all this down on parchment and crossing out words as they changed their minds. 'And in one Lord Jesus Christ, the only begotten Son of God—'"

"Sir! Sir! Sir! Let me interrupt!" said Yuksel. "Please forgive me. We Moslems respect Jesus as a great prophet, but the Koran points out repeatedly that Jesus never said he was the Son of God! If you will read the New Testament carefully, as I have in English, Turkish, Arabic, and—forgive me—German, you will see that Jesus never said he was the Son of God. Everyone else did!"

"What are all those people doing up in those trees?" interrupted Bert as we were zipping eastward on the south side of the lake.

"Those are olive trees!" I shouted. "How Biblical can you get? They must be picking olives! Are they, Yuksel?"

"Oh no sir, not in February, surely?"

"Well, I don't know. I'm from upstate New York, and we've never *seen* an olive tree there, let alone seen when it ripens. What do you think, Bert?"

"Don't ask me. I've never read the Bible."

"Stop the car, Mehmet!" I shouted.

He did. We all hit the windshield.

We got out and entered the olive grove that rose from the lake. The grove was so thick it was almost a jungle.

"Merhabalar!" (Greetings) shouted Bert, almost exhausting his supply of Turkish. "Ask them what they're doing up there, Yuksel. They look like monkeys, don't they, John? You don't have to translate that, Yuksel. Look at them: black hair, dirty faces, dark shirts, dark pants, black shoes. Look, there are five of them in that tree over there. *Merhabalar!* What did they say, Yuksel, what did they say?"

Yuksel said that they were indeed harvesting olives and added that olives have a one-year gestation period.

"What kind of period? Oh, never mind." Bert started marching among the trees, firing questions at the bewildered monkeys and shaking his fists. "How much money do you make? Are you organized? Do you have a union? How many olives can you pick in an hour? Do you work piece-rate or by the hour? Do you work eight to five? It's almost five o'clock—quitting time! What did they say, Yuksel?"

Poor Yuksel! He was flitting after Bert trying madly to translate, knowing full well the answers but trying desperately to be conscientious about his job. I heard them ask Yuksel who this madman was, and he very sensibly told them he was an American.

"Ah, *Amerikali!* Welcome! Welcome to our country," the olive-pickers said in Turkish.

Yuksel dutifully translated for Bert.

"Never mind that baloney," Bert said. "Tell them I've been here three years and I know all about labor conditions in Turkey and I want some straight answers so they can cut out all the bullshit. Tell 'em!"

"Oh sir, I couldn't translate *that!*"

I ran to the car and got my camera and snapped several pictures of Bert organizing the olive-pickers of Nicea. They slithered down the trees to see the Polaroids, and I got a good one of Bert shaking hands with one of them who looked like the ringleader. Yuksel explained that they were all fathers and sons and brothers and cousins and uncles, and they had no union but simply shared the profits.

Bert grabbed the ringleader and shook his finger in the man's face. "Look! These boys don't even have socks! In the middle of winter! If I had been negotiating with you today, I would have at least granted socks! Come on, John, let's get going! My stomach's growling. Are these olives good to eat?" he asked, popping one in his mouth.

"Oh my God, no!" said Yuksel, forcing him to spit it out as we got back into the car. "They're poisonous raw." And Yuksel, who was a bottomless mine of information, described the entire process of pickling olives as we drove through a gate in the outer wall surrounding Nicea. The outer wall was almost three miles in circumference, 16 to 23 feet thick, and 33 to 43 feet high. The inner wall, almost two miles in circumference, had towers 55 feet high.

Just inside the inner wall, we came to the remains of the Church of St. Sophia, built by Constantine VI in the 7th century. I shouted for Mehmet to stop. "I hear something."

"What? What? What is it? I don't hear a thing!" said Bert, looking in all directions.

"I think we have a flat tire."

We got out and kicked the tires. Bert pronounced *them* sound and *me* unsound.

"Must have been these Roman cobblestones. Oh look," I said, surprised, "this must be the Church of St. Sophia. This is where they held the second Council of Nicea in 787. The first one had been a fiasco, splitting the Christian world into those who believed that Jesus was the Son of God and those who believed he was just a man." I had to keep talking so Bert would keep following and not think about his allegedly growling stomach. "The Byzantine Emperors kept escaping from Constantinople to here every time one of the Crusades sacked the city. Then the Ottomans captured Nicea in 1326 and the famous Turkish architect Sinan turned this church into a mosque."

"Oh sir, Sinan was a great man," said Yuksel, grabbing my sleeve. "He designed over 300 buildings in Istanbul and they say that one of his students designed the Taj Mahal in India."

Just then we came to a wire fence blocking our further entrance into the courtyard of the church. "Oh, damn! This gate is locked," I said.

"Good," said Bert, "I'm hungry."

Just then a portly old man wearing a frayed black overcoat and a dilapidated derby came huffing up. He was shaking a huge iron ring with six-inch iron keys dangling from it. He welcomed us to Nicea with a flowery speech, bowed to each of us individually, and opened the gate. He was the Mayor of Iznik! Bert slumped, dejected because he knew we were trapped. I was delighted because I knew we were trapped.

The mayor led us into a courtyard in front of the entrance to the church. He looked like an enormous Charlie Chaplin, but he was full of facts about the church which he recited slowly in a sing-song fashion—surely learned by rote. Yuksel was in Seventh Heaven translating.

"Mehmet the Conqueror made Iznik his headquarters while he was planning the siege of Constantinople. He loved this city, and when he captured the infidels, he brought all the artisans and tile workers of Iznik to Constantinople. Look at that beautiful tile! Look at this one!"

I noticed that Yuksel didn't translate "infidels," but he gave me an apologetic look.

The mayor then led us to a circular mosaic on the ground directly in front of the doors to the church. "That," said the mayor, pointing to a large figure in the center, "is *Jesu!*"

"Jesus," translated Yuksel. It was exquisite workmanship. "Do you see the lamb? I know you understand the significance of that, Mister John, because you're very religious." I cringed. "The lamb of God who takes away the sins of the world," said Yuksel dreamily.

Around the central figure of Jesus were 12 smaller circles. "And this is *Buyuk Yakub!*" said the mayor, pointing to the figure at his feet.

"Big Jacob," said Yuksel.

"Well—Jacob is James, and we say 'James the Elder.'"

"Oh, thank you sir, thank you."

"And this is Kuchuk Yakub.*"*

"James the Younger," said Yuksel. Oh, he was sharp!

"Well—we call him James the Lesser—*please* don't ask me why!"

"And this is Luke, Matthew, Mark, and John," said Yuksel, pointing in four directions.

"And *this* is Judas!" said the Mayor, stomping his foot just outside the circle of the perfidious one. We were all very careful not to step on any of the apostles.

"Aha!" said Bert, suddenly interested.

"Look, Mister Bert, look, Mister John, you can see that Judas is the most beautiful of all the mosaics! This is just as it is in your Bible. Judas was the most beautiful of all the Apostles, it says."

"Where? Where?" Bert asked, searching madly among the circles in front of his feet. "Where's Judas?"

"Here!" said Yuksel.

"Well, that's not so different from all the others."

"Oh yes it is! Isn't it, Mister John? Judas is the most beautiful mosaic here and the most beautiful of all the apostles that Jesus loved, isn't it? That's why I wrote a letter to your Pope in Rome telling him he must declare Judas a saint!"

"*You* wrote a letter to the Pope???" I asked incredulously.
"Yes, of course!"
"When?"
"October 14, 1958."
"To Pope Pius the Twelfth?"
"Yes, of course."
"And he answered?"
"No, he died."
"Poor Pius! As if he didn't have enough trouble."

"No, Mister John, you don't understand. It was necessary for Judas to betray Jesus so that Jesus could be put to death and be crucified on a cross as it said in the Old Testament so many times about the Messiah! So then he could rise again and have Doubting Thomas put his hand into his side, and then ascend into heaven. Your Biblical story is so beautiful, like a detective story except for one thing—someone has to turn Jesus over to the authorities so they can kill him, and Judas did it. That's why he should be a saint."

I couldn't speak. Yuksel was so pleased with himself.

Fortunately, Bert took over and started cross-examining the mayor: "How much money do you make per month? Is your job as mayor full-time? Do you get any kickbacks from the olive-pickers?"

I got my camera from the car and discovered that I had only one more picture. It *had* to be a winner. I climbed a wall so I could shoot down on Jesus and his 12 apostles and still get the mayor and Bert in the picture. They were now throwing their arms around each other's necks. I focused carefully. Snap!

When the picture had developed (it was a beauty), the mayor deftly snatched it out of my hand. He pulled me across the street to his tiny office and ordered tea for all of us, as Bert gloomily followed us into City Hall. The mayor sat down behind his desk and motioned us into chairs around it. Bert was the picture of agony.

"You *must* give me this picture, Mister John," said the mayor, clutching it to his bosom. "We want to attract tourists to Iznik, but my government won't give me any pictures. Look! Only Ataturk."[25]

"Yuksel," I said menacingly, without moving my lips, "you *must* get that picture back from him. Tell him I will send him a copy. I promise. I'll have to send it back to America, so it will take some time, but I promise I'll get him a copy. Just give me his name and address *and* the picture!"

Yuksel lowered his voice and shamed the poor old mayor into giving it back to me. Yuksel got his vital statistics and grandly handed the mayor his business card. Tea arrived, and Bert scalded his throat trying to gulp it down. He had a coughing jag which propelled him out of City Hall as he motioned wildly to us to follow.

Bert sulked all the way back to Ankara (perhaps he was snoozing) as Yuksel expanded on his theory of St. Judas.

Colored Polaroid film had just come on the market, so I thought a blow-up of the original would be especially impressive. I ordered an 8 x 10 of the "Mayor and his Mosaics" for the mayor and an 8 x 10 of "Bert Organizing the Olive-Pickers of Nicea" for Bert.

It was weeks before they came back, but they were beauties. Each of the blow-ups was in an 11 x 14 white cardboard folder designed to look like white leather. Oh! The mayor will adore this picture, I thought as I sat down to write him a letter (in Turkish—without any help from anyone).

I told him he couldn't realize how much my visit to Nicea meant to me, because ever since I was a seven-year-old altar boy I had been saying the Nicene Creed and never knew where Nicea was and never dreamed that one day I would be standing on the very shores of the lake where the first Christians gathered to put down on parchment what they really believed. Oh, it was unashamedly drippy and sentimental, and full of errors I'm sure, but I knew he would like it because I had made an attempt to write it in his language.

I slipped the letter and the photograph in a large enve-

---

25. The mayor may be referring to official Turkish tourism pictures that feature Kemal Attaturk.

lope, added thick cardboard stiffeners so the PTT (post office) couldn't mangle it, and took it to the post office, feeling very pleased with myself.

A week later I stopped by Bert's house to give him his own surprise. He and his wife were just finishing dessert and asked me to sit down with them to have a cup of coffee. Then I grandly handed him a large envelope.

He pulled the photograph out, opened the cover, and said, "Oh, yes. Very nice. Good picture. Look, Paula. That's Iznik, where John made us stop that time coming back from our negotiations at Karamursel. That's why I was so late that night. That's some kind of an old church, isn't it, John?"

My heart stopped dead. Eight quarts of blood rushed to my temples. I grabbed the picture out of Bert's hands.

Oh my God! I had sent the mayor the picture of Bert organizing the olive-pickers! Oh my God! And with that stupid letter about me being an altar boy and how much the picture would mean to me for the rest of my life! Oh my God!

"I must go! Excuse me! Oh my God!"

I rushed out of the house. I'm sure they thought I was having an epileptic seizure or an onslaught of diarrhea, which I almost did.

I slapped the photograph into an envelope and fired it off to the mayor without so much as an "Enclosed please find—."

When the eight quarts of blood finally distributed themselves equally throughout my body, I began to relax and even enjoyed the mental image of the mayor's wall with Ataturk flanked on one side by Jesus and all his Apostles, and on the other by Bert organizing the olive-pickers of Nicea.

Oh yes, I did later get a blow-up of Bert for him. He fell unabashedly in love with the picture. "Ah, yes! The olive-pickers! Iznik! Look, Paula, that's me! Oh, that was a great time! Look at that monkey up in the tree! Great camera, John! See, Paula, they got no socks!"

That Midnight Ride

≈

"GOOD EVENING, Mister John," said the waiter. "What would you like to drink?"

"How do you know my name?"

"You were here last Saturday. Sureyya sends her best wishes, but she's busy now."

"Aha!" said Loren, slapping his wife Barbara on the back.

"Stop that!"

"Er—I'll have a scotch and soda," I said. "Barbara, what would you like?"

"Scotch and water. Not soda! Not *gazoz!* Water, just plain water."

"Diane?"

"Can they make a Jack Rose?"

"Honey, *please—!*" said her husband Lucien in agony. "We'll both have a scotch and water."

"George?"

"What?" He was busy looking all around the nightclub, casing the girls and licking his lips.

"What will you have to drink?"

"Oh, anything, I don't care. Scotch and water."

"Francie?"

"Ayna, ayna." She loved to show off her Turkish.

"Same, same," said Roy, translating for his wife.

"Loren?"

"Oh, hell, just bring a whole bottle and we'll all make our own drinks."

"*Hi, hi!*" said the waiter brightly and looked at me for permission.

I was stunned. My God! I wondered how much a bottle of scotch costs in a Turkish nightclub. But since this little "nightcap" was my idea, I put on a good front and said, "Fine, fine!" We had all been to the Friday night Happy Hour at the American Officers Club and had been thrown out at 1:00 a.m. when O'Leary closed the bar. I was the one who suggested a nightcap at a Turkish nightclub, so I could hardly be niggardly at this point. "Make it Johnnie Walker, please."

"Yes, Mister John."

"I want a *portakal*," said Francie.

The waiter was terribly impressed that one of us ugly Americans knew a Turkish word and departed in high spirits. Surely a good tip was in store for him, he thought.

"What's a *portakal?*" asked Diane.

"Orange," said Francie.

"A corruption of the word 'Portugal,'" I said.

"Oh, you're so smart," said Barbara. "Who's got a cigarette? I'm all out. I'll die if we have to buy Turkish cigarettes."

George went off to find a girl; Loren went off to the men's room; Roy and Lucien exchanged wives and went off to dance; Barbara and I were left by ourselves.

"John, this was a marvelous idea! That Officers Club drives me up the wall! Imagine closing at one o'clock on a Friday night! Next time we have a wives' meeting, I'm going to complain. But this is much nicer. I've never been to this nightclub before. I thought you had taken us to absolutely *all* the nightclubs in Ankara. What's the name of this one?"

"Aksaray. It means 'white palace' or 'White House,' as in Washington, D.C." Actually, the nightclub was under the street.

"It doesn't look like a palace to me. I wish they'd turn down those goddamned bright lights. Oh! Here come our drinks."

The waiter was carrying the bottle of Johnnie Walker

high on a tray as he weaved his way between other tables so all the other patrons could see what *real* spenders were like. He was followed by a caravan of busboys bearing glasses, soda, bottled water, Pepsi, *gazoz*, nuts, grapes, bananas, and a mountain of *portakals*.

Loren returned refreshed and started pouring the drinks. The dancers converged on the table, thirsty. George, 6 feet 4, brought back a sweet little blonde, 5 feet 2, with black roots.

"She doesn't speak a *word* of English," said George, blissfully feeding her an orange wedge.

"Isminiz nedir?" I asked. (What is your name?)

"Aynur." She blushed.

"Ah, Aynur. Very sweet."

"You know her?" Loren asked. "You old rascal!"

"No, I don't know her."

"You said: 'I knew 'er.'"

"That's her name—Aynur. A-y-n-u-r. That's the way it's pronounced in Turkish."

"Oh, I thought you said 'I knew 'er'—ha, ha, ha!" He slapped Barbara smartly on the rump.

"Stop that, you old goat!"

"Aynur's name means 'moonlight,'" I said. She beamed at all of us.

When Loren finished pouring his heavy-handed drinks, the bottle was three-quarters empty. I was fearful that Loren might call for another bottle, but everyone was quite well-oiled from the Officers Club, so they all went off dancing again. Barbara started a litany of complaints about life in Turkey. "That dressmaker tried to charge me 110 lira ($10) for a *very* simple sheath—imagine! So I said to her..."

The club began thinning out. I looked at my watch—it was quarter to three. Sureyya sashayed by, running her finger over the back of my shoulders and saying, "How are you, my sugar?" I tried to maintain decorum, but Barbara didn't even notice. The orchestra had stopped and packed up their instruments. The management turned up the lights.

Barbara said, "My God! More lights! It looks like a sports arena!" The dancers returned and guzzled down their drinks. The waiter brought the bill and ceremoniously presented it to me. I blanched. It was 1250 lira—about $125—well, $139 to be exact!

"How much is it, John? We'll all pitch in," said Lucien.

"Where are you going?" pleaded George, as Aynur slipped out of his arms and ran across the room. "John! Help me get her back!" He took off in hot pursuit.

"I have to pee-pee," said Fran.

"So do I," said Diane.

"Me, too," said Barbara, "but *hold* your water!"

"Why?"

"Have you ever *been* to a Turkish john???"

"What's the damage, John?" asked Loren, rummaging through his wallet. "I don't have very much Turkish money, but I've got plenty of dollars."

"Never mind," I said, "I'll take care of the bill, and you can all pay me later." I dashed up to the cashier. "Where's the manager?"

"In his office—there!"

I barged in.

"Efendim?" he said. He was so fat that he could only raise himself an inch off his armchair as a gesture of politeness.

I let loose with a flood of Turkish. "Look at this bill! One thousand two hundred and fifty lira! For *one* bottle of scotch which costs *you* 90 lira on the local market!"

The waiter, who was at my elbow, quickly explained about the *portakals*.

The manager took the bill, grandly crossed out the 1250 lira, and wrote: T.L. 1100.

"Voila, monsieur!" He said, beaming at his own French.

I still didn't have that kind of money—Turkish or American. I quickly decided we had to get out of there *fast*— all of us. We were too drunk and I knew the others would start a fight. I'd come back in the morning with an interpreter and settle the bill.

"*Teshekkur ederiz,*" I said bowing to the manager. "We thank you."

He hoisted himself an inch off the chair again and said, "You velcome."

I moved swiftly but smoothly back to the table. Fortunately, the waiter didn't follow me. "Now, listen to me *carefully,*" I said, with a clenched jaw, scarcely moving my lips, "I want you *all* to *leave!* Quickly, casually, climb the stairs and go out to the street. Get into your cars and go! My driver, Mehmet, can take some of you. George, you take the rest. Go to my house. I'll meet you there. I'll take a taxi."

"But, what is it, John?" "What happened?" "What about the bill?"

"Go! Just go! Don't look back!" (Or you'll turn into a pillar of salt, I felt like saying to instill fear in their hearts.)

They all nervously sobered up and collected their handbags, cigarettes, and lighters. Francie grabbed a *portakal.* Loren drained the infamous bottle of Johnnie Walker. "Can't waste this," he said.

I gave them as much of a head start as I dared, then casually followed them. At the bottom of the stairs, the waiter intercepted me.

"Mister John, the bill?"

I paused till the others had reached the street. They all turned and looked down at me as if I were in hell. I made a furious face at them, baring my teeth, and they disappeared. I started up the steps, casually but with determination. "I'm sorry, but I don't have enough money with me. I'll come back in the morning and pay you. I promise."

"But you can just sign the check, Mister John. We'll trust you."

I kept climbing and the waiter kept pace with me step by step, but I was impervious to his entreaties. At the sidewalk, I saw immediately that my friends were still there (dammit) across the wide boulevard—Mehmet in the white Oldsmobile with Americans hanging out the windows watching me, and behind him George in his Volkswagen with Francie and Lucien. Fortunately, there was a taxi at the curb in front of the nightclub. I jumped into the back seat and shouted "Chankaya!" (the district where I lived). The waiter stuck his head in the front window and let loose with a barrage of angry Turkish. I didn't understand all of it, but I figured they were in cahoots and this scene had happened many times before with other deadbeats. The taxi driver got out and joined the waiter on the sidewalk with his arms crossed. They were soon joined by two other waiters, who also crossed their arms.

The blood started rushing to my head. I began to panic. It was like jumping on a train that wouldn't move. I looked across the street and saw all these white arms reaching out of car windows wildly gesticulating for me to come. I hadn't wanted to involve them, but I also knew when I had met my match. I looked carefully front and back to see that I wouldn't be mowed down by some mad Turkish driver, then leaped out into the street and streaked across like a hysterical chicken losing feathers all the way. I piled into the front seat on top of Barbara and screamed, "Go, Mehmet, go!"

Since the motor was running, we shot off like a white bullet, with everyone screaming like cowboys. George followed in his Bug. We looked back and saw the waiters pile into the taxi, which made a screeching U-turn in hot pursuit.

"Step on it, Mehmet! Faster, faster!" Mehmet giggled because I was always telling him to go slower—trying to break his inbred Turkish compulsion to be king of the road. I cuffed him on the ear and shouted, "Turn right! Go, go, go!"

We shot up Ataturk Boulevard (toward the Officers Club, where all this trouble had its roots). My street was halfway up the hill, but I looked back and saw the taxi. Even though it was quite far behind, I knew they would see the white bullet make a turn, and that would be fatal because my street was a dead-end. "Don't turn, Mehmet! Go straight up!" I stomped my foot on his foot. He shifted into a lower gear and we zoomed up the hill like a rocket. The taxi was an old stick-shift Chevrolet, so we gained ground. At the top of the hill we roared past the Officers Club, crossed the ridge, and descended into the city again. Ankara sits in a bowl surrounded by seven hills. Ataturk Boulevard is like a horseshoe, up and around and down. At the bottom near the winery, I shouted, "Turn right! Up to Ondort Mayis!" (another district). Cheers went up because Loren and Barbara lived in Ondort Mayis, as well as Diane and Lucien.

"John!" shouted Barbara, "this is our house! Can't we stop for a drink? Dammit, we just passed it! I wonder if Brian is asleep. I see a light in his room." (Brian was her devilish beastie.)

Mehmet was giggling again. "I love Brian," he said. He looked in the back seat at everyone hanging out the windows, looking for the pursuers and issuing bulletins, and said, "I love the Americans. We Turks never do anything like this."

I gave him a smack and told him to turn right, down the hill again. At the Tennis Club, I shouted, "Slow! Left here! Good!" We had cut into the middle of the horseshoe. "Now, left! Right! Left! Right!" The rear guard reported in—we had lost not only the taxi but also George. "Good!" We crossed the horseshoe and into my dead-end street. I breathed a sigh of relief when we saw George's Bug in front of my apartment but no taxi.

We had a happy reunion, everyone embracing as we climbed to my apartment on the third floor. Loren went to the kitchen and started mixing drinks. The women went to the "john"—an expression I have never really resented. My living room jutted out over the building with windows on three sides, and a balcony with a glorious view of the twinkling lights of the city of Ankara below. It was a perfect outpost—there was no sign of the taxi—but not necessarily a fortress. Still, everything was peaceful below.

Barbara demanded music and started fingering "What Kind of Fool Am I" on my brand-new piano. I got the point and put on Anthony Newley, Patti Page, Petula Clark, and

Roy Acuff's classic "Wreck on the Highway." Everyone started singing:

"Who did you say it was, brother?
Who was it fell by the way?
Where whiskey and blood run together,
But I didn't hear nobody pray.

I didn't hear nobody pray, dear brother,
I didn't hear nobody pray.
I heard the crash on the highway,
But I didn't hear nobody pray."

Diane and Lucien gravitated toward my white jigsaw puzzle—completely white, no picture, and round.
"John, what *is* this puzzle?"
"It's *Snow White Without the Dwarfs,* and if you find a piece that fits you are allowed to put your initials on it."
"Francie, why are you limping?"
"I lost a shoe!"
"Where?"
"Well, you know I had to pee-pee at the nightclub."
"Oh, oh!"
"Aaaaaauiughhh!"
"Don't mention that place!"
"Well, when we got here, I went in John's bushes," said Diane.
"Yeah, and she lost her shoe," said George.
"And she made us go and look for it!" said Lucien. "Yuck!"
"They didn't find it!" said Francie happily, "so I might as well take off my other shoe." And she leaned back on the sofa and flipped it in the air.
"I'd better wash my hands," said Lucien.
"Me, too," said George.
Patti Page started asking, "How much is that doggie in the window?" It was Mehmet's favorite song.
"John! How much *was* the bill?" asked Loren, who was our chief accountant.

"Twelve hundred and fifty lira."
"What???"
"Oh my God!"
"Jesus!"
"Now, wait a minute," I said. "The manager cut it down to 1100 lira." I fished the bill out of my pocket and flourished it high in the air.

Everyone started grabbing at it, shouting, "Robbers!" "Gangsters!" "Devils!" "Blackmail!" "Extortion!" "Wicked Turks!" "God-damned Turks!"

I slipped it back into my jacket pocket and said I'd go down the next day and pay it.

"Never!"

The party broke up at sunrise. Everyone was very jolly and solicitous as they left. I slept like an innocent babe.

The next morning I woke up about 10:00 a.m., quite happy. Then I remembered! I put on my bathrobe and went slowly into the living room. Inch by inch, I crept toward the balcony. Yikes!!! There was a taxi sitting below—surely the same taxi from last night—with three black-suited men pacing outside it. I ducked back into the living room, hoping they hadn't seen me. I took another peek and one of them spotted me. His arm flew up, pointing at me accusingly. They all started shouting, "Mister John! Mister John!" and raised their arms, imploring me to come down. Well, I wasn't about to walk into that trap! I had planned to go to the office to get some lira and an interpreter, but I quickly scotched that plan. Clearly the only thing to do was to fix myself a stiff Bloody Mary.

Barbara called. "Did I leave my earrings on your coffee table?"

"Wait a minute—yes."

"Oh, good! I thought I might have left them at that nasty nightclub. I'll have Loren stop over and pick them up."

"Have him bring me some milk, I'm in a state of siege." I explained my pitiful situation to her.

"Oh, God! You poor lamb. I'll come with Loren. Need anything else? Eggs, bread, butter?"

"Yes."

"We'll be over as soon as possible. Hold the fort, John! Toodle-oo!"

I hung up and tiptoed to the window again. I was getting irrational—as if they could hear my footsteps. The Turkish mafia was still there, pacing about smoking cigarettes.

The phone rang. It was Colonel Jurnegan, who lived on the first floor of my building.

"G'moanin' John. Did y'all order a taxi?"

"No!"

"Wail, they's one right out front, and it shore looks t' me like they's a-waitin' fer yew, old buddy-buddy."

"Tell them to go away!"

A few seconds later I heard him in his dreadful drawl yelling, "Looky here, they's nobuddy in this yere buildin's done ordered a taxi, so *git! Git!* Ya heah me!"

Git is the Turkish word for "go," but it didn't faze the mafia one bit. They just crossed their arms and circled the car like vultures waiting for the carrion to fall.

Diane called. "Did I leave my glasses on your jigsaw puzzle?"

"Wait a minute—yes."

"Oh, good! I thought I might have left them at that charming nightclub last night. I'll have Lucien stop over and pick them up."

"Have him bring me some whiskey, too. I'm on my last bottle of vodka. I'm in a state of siege." I explained my problem to Diane.

"How simply marvelous. I'll come, too!"

George called, "Did you pay that bill?"

"No."

"You're not going to, either! I've got it!"

"What do you mean?"

"I took it out of your jacket pocket last night when you weren't looking. I have it right here in front of me. Boy!

Eleven hundred lira for one bottle of scotch! Do those Turks think we're extinct dodo birds or something?"

"Yes! Hang onto the bill because I'm in a state of siege." I explained again. "I'll let you know what to do with it."

"Roger! I'll bolt my front door and wait for further instructions! Oh, by the way, I found Francie's shoe. It was in my car all the time, under the front seat."

I was secretly pleased that George had taken the bill, because that meant that "Exhibit A" was no longer in my possession. I peeked out the window again—the vultures were still there. But I headed for the vodka bottle feeling a little perked-up, because my troops were rallying round me! I was already out of tomato juice, but I didn't care.

There was a knock at the door. I stiffened. I tiptoed to the door and silently slid the chain-lock into the slot. Then I opened the door a crack. It was our puny little unshaven janitor. He said there was a taxi waiting for me outside. I terrified him by screaming and yelling in Turkish that I hadn't ordered a taxi, and if they didn't go away I was going to call the police! *"Polis! Polis!"* I screamed.

He took to his heels and scurried down the steps. I ran to the window and watched him gesticulating wildly at the mafia, but they just lit up more cigarettes. It started to rain. Good!

Diane and Lucien arrived first. I heard Lucien yelling, "No *konishmak* Turkish" as they ran into the building, each carrying brown paper bags. They were bubbling with excitement.

"Isn't this fun!" said Diane.

"No."

"Oh, John, you just need a drink. Lucien, fix him a martini!"

"Right! John, where's your sense of humor?"

"I lost it at the Aksaray."

"Here, try this as a restorative. Cheers!"

"Well, how's *your* sense of humor? George found Francie's shoe. It was in his car all the time—not in the bushes."

"Yuck! I think I'll wash my hands again."

"If only we had a fourth person, we could play bridge," said Diane brightly. "Guess I'll work on the puzzle."

Loren and Barbara arrived, also loaded down with brown bags. I could hear Barbara's piercing voice saying, "Don't you *dare* come near me, or I'll bop you one!" If anyone could, it was Barbara—she weighed about 200 pounds, all muscle.

"Hi, all you lovely people! Isn't this fun! John, have you had your breakfast? I brought bacon and eggs. Loren! Fix me a Bloody Mary. Let's play bridge!"

"Great!" said Diane. "Barbara, you and I will take on the men."

"There's no more tomato juice," I said.

"Oh, Loren, just fix me a martini—it's almost noon. John, where are your cards?"

"Hey, men! Let's cut to see who's out," said Lucien.

"You all play," I said. "I'm not in the mood."

"Then put some mood music on," said Barbara, shuffling and dealing the cards. "Anthony New—"

"I know, I know: 'What Kind of Fool Am I,'" I said, emphasizing the "I." I placed the stack of records from last night upside-down on the spindle.

"This is my idea of a *perfect* way to spend Saturday afternoon," said Barbara. "Loren was going to go to his office to work this afternoon, but this is a lot more fun, isn't it, honey?"

"Four spades," said Loren.[26]

"Four spades?" challenged Barbara. "Are you *opening* with four spades?"

"Why not?"

"If there's anything I can't stand," said Barbara, "it's a

---

26. The men's team begins with an extremely ambitious bid, and the women's team "doubles" the stakes, asserting skepticism. The men's team "redoubles" the stakes, asserting confidence. After the hand has been played, the men have come nowhere near their goal ("down three"), so the women get a lot of points.

smart-ass. Double!!!"

"Redouble!!!" said Loren.

I was looking out the window when Mehmet arrived. As he came up the hill, I saw him stop and hesitate when he saw the taxi, but he pulled the white Oldsmobile right up beside them. The mafia jumped out of the taxi and converged on him, flailing their arms in the air.

When I let him in the apartment, I asked him what they were saying, but he insisted on saying *"Merhaba"* to all my guests and greeting them with maddening Turkish politeness.

"Never mind all that, Mehmet. What did they say?"

"They just want to talk to you, Mister John. Only you."

"In a pig's eye," said Barbara. "Diane, it's your lead."

The phone rang. It was Roy. "George just called me and told me about your predicament. Why don't you bring those guys over to my house. I can handle them."

Although I knew Roy *could* handle them (he had connections with the OSI,[27] the FBI, and the CIA), I said, "I'm not going anywhere *near* them!"

"Then, have Mehmet bring them over to my place. He knows where I live."

"Well, okay," I said reluctantly, but glad for a chance to get rid of them. I instructed Mehmet carefully in babyish Turkish, and we all ran out onto the balcony to see if he was successful. There was a lot of yelling and screaming and pointing up to my balcony (I was hiding behind Barbara). They finally appeared to capitulate. Our waiter got into the Oldsmobile with Mehmet, and the taxi followed. Barbara shouted, *"Güle, güle!"* (goodbye, keep smiling) as they left. Everyone cheered except me.

"Now, let's see," said Barbara, "four spades, double and redoubled, down three, 2, 5, 800 points for us, Diane. We'll show these stupid men! Whose deal?"

I was persuaded to sit in on a couple of hands while

---

27. U.S. Air Force Office of Special Investigations

Barbara fixed a boatload of hors d'oeuvres, snacks, sandwiches, and relishes. Everyone ate lustily as more queens were finessed and more aces were trumped. Finally the phone rang. It was Roy.

"John, they *only* want the bill. They're not going to charge us anything if they get back the bill."

"I don't have it."

"Who does?"

"George."

"Where does George live?"

"Ondort Mayis. Mehmet knows."

"Well, here! You tell Mehmet to go to George's and get the bill." I did, carefully. Then Roy got back on the phone. "What's all that noise I hear?"

"Just some of our guests left over from last night."

"Sounds like a party! Francie and I will be over as soon as we can."

I told the gang the good news. They all cheered.

"Aha!" said Loren. "They knew we'd take the bill to the police, and the police would close the nightclub. That calls for another drink, eh Barbara?"

"Stop pinching me, you dirty old man! It's your bid!"

Again the phone rang. "This is George. Mehmet is here speaking a mixture of pidgin English and Turkish. I think he wants me to give him the bill."

"Yes, give it to him!"

"But, but—"

"Give it to him, dammit!!! Roy is going to take care of everything!!!"

"Okay, okay. You don't have to get so huffy. It's all right, though, because I've photographed the bill three times with my Minolta. Sounds like you're having a good time over there, John. What's going on?"

"It's an Irish wake."

"I'm Irish on one side—can I come?"

"Why not? The streets are clear. The mafia's gone."

Roy called. "They've gone now. They tore up the bill in

front of my eyes. We'll be right over!"

I relayed the good news to my loyal troops.

"Let's have a drink!" "Let's have champagne!" "Loren, it's your bid!"

George arrived. Roy and Francie arrived. Francie got back her shoe. Barbara got back her earrings. Diane got back her glasses. And I got back my *joie de vivre*.

"Oh, by the way," said Roy. "The manager has invited us all back to the Aksaray tonight. Drinks are on the house!"

"Bleeeaaaauugghh!!!"

Trauma in Termessos

≈

I COULD HAVE bit my tongue when I said to Julie, "I'm going to Termessos for the holidays."
We were sitting in the Ankara Officers Club one night after duplicate bridge, having a last drink.
"Oh, what's Termessos?"
"It's an ancient city in southern Turkey. It has the unique distinction of being the only city in Turkey which Alexander the Great *didn't* conquer!"
"How marvelous! Why not?"
I waxed poetic. "It was impregnable. Built on the top of a mountain with a commanding view in every direction of the plains of Pamphylia 2000 feet below, no enemy would *dare* storm it! So Alex just mopped up all the cities around the base of the mountain—Antalya, Perge, Aspendos—and moved on, leaving Termessos sitting high and dry. I'm dying to see it."
"Take me with you," said Julie, clapping her hands. "I'd love to go!"
"Well—er—sure! It's a long trip, just to Antalya, where we'll have to stay overnight. Eleven or twelve hours—"
"I don't care! I haven't seen anything since I've arrived in Turkey. Nothing but work, work, work!"
Julie was the new Assistant Superintendent of all the American Dependent Schools in Turkey. The *Sugar Bayram* was to start the next day—the holiday to celebrate the end of the month-long fasting of Ramadan. We had so many holidays in Turkey—not only the eight American holidays, but

17 Turkish holidays as well. I loved all of them and never failed to take advantage of them to see famous historical sites in Turkey. But I loathed traveling with anyone—especially Americans. They always wanted to have three meals a day, shop for souvenirs, and set aside time for sunbathing (which I loathed) or swimming (which I considered a waste of time unless you needed a bath).

"I've just *got* to get away for some rest and relaxation! *Please* take me with you."

"Well, okay. We leave tomorrow early! Is that all right with you?"

"Seven! Six! Five! I don't care!"

"Let's make it seven."

"I'll be waiting!"

And she was. When Mehmet and I pulled up in the white Oldsmobile, she was standing in front of her apartment building with an enormous blue suitcase and a matching make-up kit. Mehmet leaped out to relieve her of her bags. He was excited that she was going with us.

"Good morning, Mehmet," she said angelically.

"Good morning, Miss Julie," he said, blushing crimson as he put her bags in the trunk.

We arrived at Antalya exactly at 6 p.m. We checked into the Perge Palas, a charming hotel overlooking the Bay of Antalya. It looked like—or actually was—just a pretty two-story white house sheltered by pine trees in the midst of a garden of amaryllis. The hotel had exactly six rooms. The manager was neat and trim in a worn tuxedo and welcomed us warmly. The Turks have a real eye for beauty, and his eyes lit up when he saw Miss Julie. She looked like a young Joan Fontaine. I looked like a Jeff Chandler reject, and Mehmet looked like a handsome chauffeur right out of the movies with his powder blue covert-cloth suit which matched Miss Julie's luggage he was carrying.

The manager, who didn't speak a word of English, personally showed us the way to the rooms. The first bedroom was very large with polished white oak floors and snow-white sheepskins thrown here and there. The four-poster bed was covered with blue silk and so high you would have to climb up into it. There were fresh flowers on each table. The manager opened the casement windows which looked onto the sea, and the blue silk curtains billowed in the cool breeze. Next, he showed us the bathroom, which was quite modern. He pointed out the blue tiled floor and walls. He was particularly proud of the toilet, which had the tank right on the back—not the overhead type with the pull chain. He even demonstrated how to use it.

"We have just remodeled this hotel. It was an old house that belonged to a rich plantation owner. We only opened two days ago. You will be our first couple!"

Miss Julie didn't get it. Mehmet giggled.

The manager led us out of the room. "And down this little passageway is a room for Mehmet—isn't that your name?

He returned us to the big room with his arms outstretched. "Well, how do you like it?"

Suddenly Miss Julie did get it. "No, no, no, no, no!" she said, holding her ears and heading for the door. The manager was bewildered. Mehmet jabbed me slyly with his elbow and told the manager that he would prefer to have a room somewhere else in the hotel—farther away—because... He turned and winked at me brazenly.

"*Hi, hi!*" said the manager, delighted, and led us back to the lobby.

Everyone started babbling at once. Miss Julie kept saying, "Separate rooms, separate rooms!" I was shouting what I thought was the same thing in Turkish: "*Ayri oda, oda ayri!*" Finally, the manager threw up his hands, gave Mehmet and me each a key, then escorted Miss Julie up the stairs to another room. She followed like a haughty princess.

The next morning we started out at seven and conquered Termessos in one day. Of course, we had all kinds of modern machinery and equipment which Alexander the Great didn't have—235 mechanical horses (the white Oldsmobile), a magic machine to zap the enemy (the Polaroid camera), and excellent logistics and supplies (an ice chest full of Budweiser, Beefeaters, Pepsi, sandwiches, and fresh fruits—and a tankful of gas to feed the horses).

Halfway up the mountain the road suddenly ended in a grassy meadow surrounded on three sides by cliffs that went up 1000 feet. We parked the Olds under a huge old leafy fig tree and jumped out. Immediately the enemy charged us. He was the *bekji*, the only person in sight, and he surrendered with a big, broad smile.

"Welcome, welcome, welcome! My name is Mustafa."

We made the rest of the assault on foot. The mountain had two peaks with a saddle in between, and was completely overrun with pine, locust, birch, and bracken so thick we practically had to hack our way through. We couldn't see a single building until we were right on top. We followed the *bekji* like an Indian guide, single file, ducking branches and holding bracken back for Miss Julie to pass through. She was a good sport and mercifully was wearing slacks. It took us four hours to make the climb to the theater, which was right smack on the top of one of the peaks. We flopped to the ground exhausted, but the view was worth it. I couldn't help feeling that if a play by Aeschylus or Euripides was boring, the people of Termessos could always enjoy the glorious view: the Bay of Antalya with a necklace of sand stretching for miles and miles as far as the eye could see, completely uncluttered by a single building, house, or shack. Beyond the bay we saw the sparkling blue Mediterranean. No wonder it was called the Turkish Riviera.

"Miss Julie!" Even I had picked up Mehmet's expression. "Look at that snow-capped mountain over there! That's Mount Climax! Now that's what I call a classy name for a mountain."

But it was noon and Miss Julie was hungry. I could have used a dry martini and a canape or two, but we were four hours from our C-rations in the Oldsmobile below. Poor logistic planning, I thought. So we started down.

We stopped to marvel at five large cisterns which were

right in the middle of the saddle, each 36 feet in diameter and 24 feet deep. And there was a spring nearby, still bubbling up pure mountain water which once filled the five cisterns. No wonder Termessos could resist all invaders. Mehmet, Mustafa, and I drank from the spring. Miss Julie resolutely refused. I was sorry I couldn't convince her that she wouldn't die on the spot because I knew she must have been thirsty, but she was new in Turkey and was probably still boiling the tap water, brushing her teeth in 7-Up, and soaking her vegetables in Clorox.

The trip down was almost as arduous as going up because of the bracken, but we got back to the car at three o'clock and had a drunken, rollicking victory celebration on the grass. I should say I got drunk. I insisted on being addressed as Kuchuk Iskender (Alexander the Little). Mehmet got the giggles on two beers, climbed the fig tree like a monkey, then sat like a gargoyle on one of the branches and spat grape seeds. Miss Julie sipped gin and nibbled on a sandwich—a far cry, I thought, from Alexander's girlfriend, Thais, who persuaded him to burn down the palace of Darius the Great during a drunken victory brawl after conquering Persepolis.

"Drink up, drink up, everybody! More booze! More pictures! Mehmet! Come down out of that tree and take a picture of Thais and me! Give Mustafa a beer! All right, all right, so he's a Moslem—give him a Pepsi! *Sherefinize*, Mustafa!"

"What does that mean?" asked Miss Julie.

"To your honor!" I said, raising the gin bottle to her. "Come, give me a kiss, Thais!" She hit me in the eye with a fig. And then the fruit started flying and we chased each other around the fig tree until we collapsed on the grass. "What a glorious day!" I shouted. "Oh, Julie, we done did what Alexander the Great never did done!"

"It's time to go," said Miss Julie. "Mehmet, help Kuchuk Iskender to his feet." Then she started cleaning up the mess.

"No, no, no!" I shouted. "That's one of the sinful joys about traveling in Turkey. You can leave beer cans, bottles, napkins, paper bags, pretzel boxes—anything anywhere!

The poor peasants will clean them up. They'll cherish them!" Miss Julie tried to shut me up and Mehmet tried to tell her I was right. "They'll use those bottles for goat's milk," I said, "or vinegar. They turn the cans into drinking cups or flower pots or funnels—and the papers are for starting fires." Even the *bekji* was trying to shoo her away since he was lusting for the leftovers. Finally, her schoolmarm conscience wouldn't let her leave until she had made three neat little piles—one of cans, one of bottles, and one of papers. Just like a garbage separator, I thought.

The next morning I had a little difficulty pulling myself together. I didn't have a hangover—I rarely did, a fact that has never endeared me to my friends—but I was a little groggy. However, after a shower and a shave I felt great. I wrapped a towel around my middle, lit a cigarette, and decided I would enjoy in sobriety the pictures I had taken the day before in revelry. And then tragedy struck. Or at least the onslaught of trauma set in. I couldn't find them! I searched my ditty bag. Everything was there—the camera, one unopened box of film, the maps, the guidebook, the emergency candy bars, the cigarettes—everything *except the pictures*. By the time Mehmet knocked on my door I was in a state of Freudian frenzy.

"Mehmet, I can't find the pictures!"

He started rifling through my ditty bag. "No, I've already looked there!" He went through the pockets of my jacket, my shirt, and my pants. "I've already looked there!" He got down on his hands and knees and looked under the bed. "That's more like it," I said sarcastically. "Look under the mattress, too!"

"Maybe you left them in the Oldsmobile."

"Ah, yes! Quick, let's look!" I jumped into my clothes. We searched the glove compartment, the trunk, and under and between the seats. No pictures.

"Maybe Miss Julie has them?" suggested Mehmet.

"Ah, yes! She's so maddeningly organized. She's supposed to meet us on the terrace for breakfast at eight—what time is it?"

"Fifteen to eight."

"Come on! She's always early."

We dashed through the hotel and onto the terrace. There she was, sitting at a table, looking cool and crisp as the cantaloupe she was already eating.

"Good morning, good morning," she chirped. "Isn't this a heavenly spot? We're absolutely suspended in space. I don't dare look straight down—it makes me light-headed. And look at the view! Glorious! I can hardly bear to leave today. I could sit here forever if duty didn't call."

"Julie, listen to me—"

"Good morning, Mehmet. Did you sleep well?"

"Yes, Miss Julie."

"I did too, but my bones ache a little. I'm a bit creaky after all that climbing we did yesterday."

"Julie, *will* you listen to me?"

"Why don't you sit down, Baby Alexander, and have a cup of tea and some cantaloupe. It's delicious!"

"Do you have the pictures???"

"What pictures?"

"The pictures we took yesterday at Termessos."

"No, why should I? Don't you have them?"

"I can't find them," I said miserably.

"Well, if you hadn't been so inebriated yesterday, you wouldn't have misplaced them."

I ignored the barb. "Go, look in your room! See if they're in your purse!"

"I will *not* go look in my room because they are *not* there. And I will *not* look in my purse—which is right here beside me."

I grabbed for it.

"*Nor* will I let you look in it! A woman's purse is *very* personal." (She did, however, open it, take a quick look, and snap it shut—which I thought was rather sweet of her.) "Now, why don't we all have a nice breakfast and then be on our way back to Ankara. Ah, here's that dear man again."

The manager, still in his tuxedo, appeared and bowed, ready to take our order. I wondered, fleetingly, if he was the entire staff of the hotel.

"Mehmet, will you order for me, please? Two boiled eggs, toast, marmalade, and a cup of that delicious Turkish coffee. John, what will you have?"

My mind was whirling like a broken egg beater. I *couldn't* leave without the pictures. I was getting feverish. "Aha! I've got it! They must be up on the mountain! I remember putting them into one of the empty film boxes. We must have left them there with the rest of the trash."

"Well, if we had only cleaned up our mess, as I wanted to, we would have found them."

"Come on, Mehmet! We're going back to look for them!"

"John, are you completely out of your mind? We have to get back to Ankara today, and you know perfectly well it's an eleven-hour trip. I have school tomorrow! Now, maybe *you* take your duties toward the United States Air Force lightly, but *I* consider my responsibilities to the Armed Forces School System *sacred!* I must and will be back in Ankara tonight, even if I have to walk! I don't understand all this hysteria over a couple of pieces of Polaroid paper!"

"Julie, listen to me. It will only take us an hour to drive up and an hour back. You stay here and have your breakfast. We'll be back by ten o'clock—I promise—and leave immediately. We'll be in Ankara by nine tonight—ten o'clock at the latest!"

Before she could protest, I grabbed Mehmet and dragged him across the terrace toward the car. Mehmet was giggling so much (he loved abrupt changes in plans like in the movies) that I practically had to carry him. I looked back at Miss Julie, who was steaming like a little teapot.

I turned Mehmet loose with the 235 horses and delivered myself into the hands of Allah. I knew I was being a fool about "a couple of pieces of paper," as Julie had said, but I had become obsessed with Polaroid pictures ever since I had arrived in Turkey. The Polaroid was my passport. It got

Trauma in Termessos / 329

me into places no tourist—or Turk—could ever see. A handsome tip couldn't compare with a Polaroid picture. I'd rub my magic box and out would pop a picture of a guard, who would unlock gates marked *Yasak* (Forbidden), or a nightclub manager who would let me take pictures of the belly dancers, or an owner of a Turkish bath who would let me take pictures *inside* the bath. Sure, I would always have my memories, but without the Polaroid, I would be just another tourist. The Polaroid actually created the adventure.

As we started up the mountain, I grieved over the lost pictures—Mehmet at the Necropolis, stretched out in a granite sarcophagus which was decorated on all four sides with a beautifully carved face of the original occupant.

And the picture of Miss Julie and Mehmet peering out of the only window in a strange two-story black granite building as I stooped outside trying to get a shot of them through the trees and lowering my butt deeper and deeper into the scratchy bracken, telling them to say *"Peynir!"* (cheese).

And Miss Julie, flopped on the top row of the theater with the Mediterranean below and Mehmet standing behind her shading his eyes and gazing at snow-covered Mount Climax.

And the *bekji* who dragged me down into the orchestra pit, foraging through the trees and bracken to find a life-size crouching stone lion. (I made him crouch beside it because I always have to have a human in my pictures. I'm a snapshot-taker, not a photographer.)

And the picture of Miss Julie, Mehmet, and Mustafa—all lying on their bellies—peering down into one of the cisterns while I snapped their picture from below.

And the spring with Miss Julie standing with crossed arms and pursed lips while Mehmet drank from it with water dripping from his cupped hands.

And the sarcophagus carved into the living rock with a life-size horse and rider above the tomb, and the *bekji* standing at a basin pretending to cleanse his hands and face before praying over the dead.

And even that foolish picture of a little Star of Bethlehem

plant struggling out of the base of a marble column in the Agora.

Were these all lost to me—to say nothing of the pictures of our drunken victory celebration afterward?

Mehmet roared to a slippery stop under the fig tree. The *bekji* was nowhere to be seen. The trash was all gone. I saw not even a scrap of paper anywhere. It was as if no human had set foot on this grassy knoll in 2,000 years.

"Look in the sarcophagi, Mehmet!"

"What?"

"Turba! Turbalar!" There were 15 or 20 tombs within a stone's throw of our picnic spot and I thought maybe the *bekji* had used them as trash bins. They were all empty. I saw no remains of the present or the past.

We called for the *bekji*, "Mustafa! Mustafa!" but only got an echo from the resounding hills. I looked at my watch. It was 9:05.

"We must go now, Mehmet. Miss Julie is waiting."

As we started down the mountain, I saw a jeep coming up. "Slow down, Mehmet! Maybe the *bekji* is in it!" It was a covered jeep, and I saw two soldiers in the front seat, and then a glimpse of the *bekji* in the back. "Stop, Mehmet! Mustafa is in the back seat! Blow your horn! Back up!"

The *bekji* had seen us, too. He jumped out and came over to the car. Mehmet quickly explained our problem to him. He swore he hadn't found any pictures, holding one hand over his heart and the other up in the air.

Without moving my lips, I started firing questions to Mehmet in English (one of the few advantages of our language). "Ask him what he did with all the trash."

The Turkish word for trash is *chirp*. It was maddening to hear them saying *"chirp, chirp, chirp"* as if my problem were of no more importance than the twittering of birds.

"I took it all to my house—you said I could have everything." Mustafa began to get belligerent.

"And the photos?"

"There were no photos!" he screamed. "I swear I looked

through everything!"

"He's lying," said Mehmet in English.

"Mehmet! Don't get angry. Tell him if he finds the pictures and sends them to us, we'll send him 100 lira. Give him your address in Ankara."

Mehmet grumbled under his breath as he wrote out his address on a scrap of paper. He gave it to the *bekji* with menacing instructions as if he were a judge talking to a juvenile delinquent. "You understand?"

"Yes, yes!" said Mustafa, clutching the paper to his breast and backing away cautiously.

They commended each other to God, and we left.

"He's a liar!" said Mehmet angrily.

"Only Allah knows. Now, if you don't mind, let's not talk about it again."

Miss Julie was waiting outside the hotel with her suitcases at her feet and the manager in attendance as we drove up. She looked at her watch. It was exactly ten o'clock.

"Did you find them?"

"No."

"Two hours wasted! If you hadn't imbibed so deeply yesterday—shame on you!"

"Julie, please! If you love God, let's not talk about it anymore. Let's try to have a pleasant trip home."

"Of course, of course," she said as if soothing a baby. "It really *was* a marvelous weekend, and I shall never forget it. Do you want to play Twenty Questions?"

"Not particularly."

Julie chattered all the way to Ankara. Fortunately her conversation required no response, perhaps due to her occupation. We got back in good time—at eight o'clock, to be exact—and Miss Julie rewarded Mehmet and me with a kiss. On the cheek.

Eventually I forgot about Termessos and the pictures, until one day Mehmet arrived to pick me up for work, grinning from ear to ear.

"Well, what is it?"

He giggled.

"What's the matter with you?"

He teased me as long as he dared, then reached into his inside pocket and produced a letter. Inside were the pictures.

"Ah! Great! Bravo! Look at that beauty! Wonderful! Allah be praised!"

The letter was in Turkish. I had Sedat translate it as soon as I got to the office. It read:

2 May 1968

Dear Friend Mehmet,

I would like to say hello and shake your hands without hurting them. How are you my friend? I hope you are all right and I beg to God, The Creator, that you be well. If you ask your unlucky Mustafa how he is, I am existing and healthy from the first to the last line of this letter that I am writing to you. I hope you will be in the same way.

My friend, following a detailed inquiry and chasing, I found the lifeless pictures that you have lost at Termussus in the possession of a Nomad who is from Essenyurt village of Korkuteli. He found the pictures under a tree while he was looking after his sheep that he had lost the day we left that place and took these pictures to his residence and his children played with them a little. I don't know whether there are any missing ones. However, I am sending 17 that I could locate. I request that you let me know when you receive them. I am keeping my promise, and I request that you keep your promise too. Your friend promised me 100 liras. I send you, your lawyer friend, and his wife my deepest regards and say hello and shake your hands. Further, I request your letter and hope to see you in Antalya again.

THE END

Hellos.
My address is:
Mustafa Jivelik
Termussus Bekjisi
Orman Isletmesi Eliyle Yenije
Bolgesi

"What a sweet man," I said, kissing the Polaroid of Mustafa. I couldn't imagine how he got the idea that I was a lawyer. Perhaps Mehmet had thrown that in to intimidate him. "Mehmet, we must send Mustafa the money right away!"

"One hundred lira is too much. Send him 50!"

"Mehmet, shame on you! We gave our promise. Look what a good, honest man he is."

"Honest? He's a liar and a thief! *Oruspu!* You shouldn't send him anything!"

"If you keep talking, I'll send him 150 lira."

I sent him the money and a letter that I composed and wrote myself. In Turkish!

Dear Mustafa,
My wife and I thank you very much for sending the pictures.
We are enclosing 100 liras, as promised.

THE END

Mister John
The Lawyer

The Amphora

≈

I KNEW that Fortune was blind, but I never thought she would smile on *me,* especially when I was sitting at the bar in the Ankara Officers Club after a disastrous night of duplicate bridge. The Captain who was sitting next to me, a bridge acquaintance, said, "John, would you like to buy an amphora?"
"A what?"
"An amphora! Don't you know what they are???"
"Oh yes, of course, of course!" My God, the amphoras I had seen at the museums were gorgeous things—great huge clay pots that had been dredged up out of the depths of the Aegean Sea. Some were thousands of years old.
"Oh yes, I know that an amphora is—a wine jug. The ancient Greeks used them to transport wine in ships." He had caught me off-guard, so I decided to display my knowledge of Homer. "I know all about the wine-dark sea, and ancient Smyrna where Homer was born, and how the people there grew the best grapes in Asia Minor, and how they shipped the wine in clay jugs to Athens."
"I have an amphora I don't want. I'll sell it to you for 57 lira. Just what I paid for it. We're rotating back to the States next week and I don't want to take this one with me. I have to tell you, John, that it's got a chip out of the lip, but otherwise it's in good condition. I bought two of them from some guys in our outfit who had been here since 1952. We were the first American military group here after the war. They used to fly to Izmir all the time and pick up old stuff for a song in those days."

I thought about asking to see it first, but at that price I was afraid it would sound kind of chintzy.

"Well, yeah, sure, Captain, I'd like to buy it."

"Okay, I'll bring it over to your apartment Saturday morning."

I didn't tell any of my friends about it, but I began to have some doubts about the price as the week went by. Surely I had misunderstood him. Maybe he said 570 lira. Or 5700! Or maybe it was just a little thing. Or worse, maybe his idea of an amphora wasn't the same as my idea of an amphora. He didn't really strike me as the type who would be interested in archeological artifacts.

By Friday I was a wreck, but I decided to see it through. I was determined to pay any price so that there would be no embarrassment on either side. I went over to see John Hicks, our Comptroller, who was an archeological nut too, and my arch rival in collecting stuff. He was also our banker for exchanging money.

"I want to buy 6,000 lira." (That was about $600, surely enough.)

"My God, 6,000 lira! What in hell are you going to do with 6,000 lira???"

"Well, I have to pay my rent soon—"

"Ha! 900 lira. What are you going to do with the other 5,100?"

"And I have to pay my houseboy—"

"That's 450 lira."

"No, 500."

"When did you give him a raise, dammit? Now Aziza will want a raise as soon as she hears about it! So what else?"

"Look, Mister Moneybags, I don't have to explain to you or anyone else what I'm going to do with *my* lira! You should be happy enough that I'm buying it legally and not on the black market!"

He got me the money, and I signed for it.

"You sly dog, you've got some Turkish broad you're keeping on the side, haven't you?"

The next morning at 9:30 the doorbell rang. My heart started pounding. It was the Captain. He and his 14-year-old son lugged in the amphora—the Captain holding it by the handles and his son struggling along with the bottom. My eyes popped out of my head.

"Where shall we put it?" It was pointed on the bottom and couldn't stand on its own.

"Over here on the sofa!"

They laid it down gently and then started catching their breath. It must have weighed 50 pounds and they had carried it up three flights of stairs.

And it was sensational! About three feet long, classic in design, covered with fossilized barnacles and tiny snails—the most beautiful amphora I had ever seen! The chip on the lip, which probably happened when the ship hit bottom, only added to its beauty.

I tried to offer them a drink. I certainly needed one to recover from my surprise and to prepare myself for forking over the money.

"No thanks, John. We've got too much packing to do."

"Ah, yes." I pulled out my bulging wallet. "Now, how much did you say that was?"

"Fifty-seven lira." He acted surprised at my question. "Just like I said."

"Oh, yes." I quickly peeled off a 50 and a 5 and dug into my pocket for two 1-lira coins.

"Thanks a lot, John. Good luck at duplicate bridge."

I sat down and gazed at my newest possession. I was numb. Only 57 lira for this gorgeous hunk of ancient history! It was insane! 57 lira at that time was worth exactly $6.30!

I had to have a party—an amphora party! I called up all my archeological friends and invited them to a surprise party the following Saturday night.

"Who for?"

"You!"

I had a wrought-iron tripod made—a ring with three V-shaped legs—to set it into. Then I placed it by my fireplace and covered it with a sheet. When all the guests had arrived, we had the unveiling. Since they were all archeology buffs, I could see them visibly turning green as they stared at it in wonder.

"So *that's* what you wanted the 6,000 lira for!" said Hicks. "How much did you pay for that thing?"

"You'd better have another drink—a stiff one! And sit down, I don't want you to hit your head on the fireplace when you fall."

Naturally, none of them believed me when I told them the price—even when I offered to find my Bible to swear on.

"I'll never speak to you again!" said Kitty Curington, turning her back on me.

"Jeez," said Hicks, "I've *got* to learn how to play duplicate bridge!"

Fred Jensen got even with me by taking a trip to Bodrum (a city in southwestern Turkey) and buying one from a fisherman. *Bodrum* means "the cellar" in Turkish, and it was the site of the ancient city of Halicarnassus, where most of the amphoras have been found. But mine was more beautiful.

Miles Worth did us one better. He went deep-sea diving in Bodrum and found his own! It was indisputably ancient, but mine was more beautiful.

John Hicks finally acquired an amphora which he declared to be the most beautiful of all, but I think his opinion was colored by the circumstances surrounding its acquisition.

One fine Sunday morning we filled the trunk of the white Oldsmobile with booze, Cokes, and sandwiches, and started off on an archeological trip to Gordium, 35 miles west of Ankara. There were four of us—me, Hicks, and his two daughters. Gordium was the ancient capital of Phrygia, the home of King Midas, and the place where Alexander cut the famous Gordian knot. We had heard that archeologists from the University of Pennsylvania were digging there, and we wanted to see what they had dug up.

Marsha, 16, had been on trips with us before and was no trouble at all—she was genuinely interested in archeology. Chrysta, 14, was only interested in boys but, because she was trying to avoid one of them that morning, she declared she was coming with us. Hicks was pleased; I was not. I was sure she'd be bored after 10 minutes. She was—five minutes after we arrived at the site.

"What do you people see in all these stupid rocks?"

"Chrysta, shut up," said her father.

"When are we going to eat?"

I could hear him grinding his teeth.

We first toured the tomb of King Midas, which had been discovered only a few years before, in 1958. The Sakariya River Valley was quite flat and treeless, but covered with lush grass and wildflowers. All over the valley were mounds that were obviously man-made since they were so regular, and undoubtedly they were tombs. We learned later that the University of Pennsylvania had a grant to excavate them. There were 57 in all. They dug into 17 of them and found them completely empty. They had all been plundered—who knows when? Just as they were running out of money, they discovered the 18th one intact. They later pronounced it the tomb of King Midas.

They had drilled a small hole 150 feet down from the top of one mound and hit wood. Then they dug a tunnel at ground level straight into the center of the mound, where they found the burial chamber. It was a 25-foot cube completely enclosed in two-foot-thick timbers of cedar from Lebanon. They cut a doorway into the tomb and found the bones of Midas lying on a wooden bed surrounded by iron pots, bronze urns, brass goblets, shields, swords, and knives—but nothing was made of gold!

We were able to view all the treasures in a makeshift museum across the way. Everything was handsome—simple, but well-made. I remember coveting a bronze cauldron that was about three feet in diameter with four horned bulls' heads for handles, each three-dimensional and one-half life size. But my mind kept whizzing and whirring trying to reconcile all those stories I had been taught in childhood about everything Midas touched turning to gold. Now, the Alexander the Great story—I thought that was cheating when he "untied" the Gordian knot with a swipe of his sword. But Midas! Oh, I believed that golden touch! I finally decided that Midas was one of the first to use metal for knives and utensils and, as the story spread far and wide and down through the ages, the wondrous metal became gold.

"When are we going to eat?" moaned Chrysta.

Hicks blew. "*You* can go back to the car right now and eat anything you want, but *we're* not ready to eat yet! We're going now to visit the Old City, and if you don't want to come, good!"

"Can I have a beer?"

"No, dammit, no!"

She tagged along behind Hicks, perhaps to torment us.

The Old City was built on a man-made plateau in the middle of the valley at the edge of the river. We climbed up the hill and looked down into the excavations below. Nothing but broken-down walls. One of the American students volunteered to give us a tour. He showed us the palace, the council chamber, the shops, the houses, the bakery, the pottery kilns, and the foundry. But the whole city had caught fire and burned to the ground. It was delightful to see him so excited about his work and so interested in every room and niche. But to us amateurs, it was nothing but walls, each building like the other except for size. Still, we had learned from our travels in Turkey that the older the ruin, the more interesting to archeologists. We liked the gaudy newer Greek and Roman ruins with their temples and fluted columns, capitals and carvings, and broken statues—an arm here, a leg there.

"This is so boring," said Chrysta.

Later we ran into a pretty American girl in blue jeans on her hands and knees sorting potsherds. Hicks took an immediate shine to her. He liked girls almost as much as

Chrysta loved boys.

"Hi! What are you doing?" asked Hicks.

"Oh, I'm an archeology student. We're from the University of Pennsylvania. I work for Dr. Young."

"What's your name?"

"Cathy."

"Hi, Cathy," he said, offering his hand. She put out her grimy paw and let him shake it.

"There he goes again," muttered Chrysta.

"Now, you tell me exactly what you're doing," said Hicks.

"Well, this is Dr. Young's garden and—"

"Garden?"

"That's what he calls it. And every day the Turkish workers bring me these wooden boxes of things that the supervisors think Dr. Young might like to see. I have to tag them and catalog them. Of course, I don't know what they are, but I have to put down where they were found, what level, what area. See, here's my notebook."

Hicks gladly peered over her shoulder.

"Then Dr. Young comes around and decides what he wants to keep and takes them to the warehouse, way over there. See?"

"I see," said Hicks without looking.

"Then we throw away everything Dr. Young doesn't want."

"How old are you, Cathy?"

"Twenty. This is my second summer here."

"Do you like your work?"

"Well, it was fun at first, but now it's rather boring."

"When are we going to eat?" said Chrysta.

"Can we look through Dr. Young's garden?" I asked.

"Yes, but don't touch anything."

Dr. Young's garden was a patch about 30 feet square, subdivided into blocks about five feet square which were separated by ordinary stones. In each square were shards and tiles and bits of iron and glass, all marked with Cathy's mysterious numbers. We gingerly tiptoed through the potsherds but didn't really see anything interesting.

Outside the garden I noticed a number of rough, round, clay objects with a hole in the middle.

"What are these, Cathy?"

"Oh, we call those Phrygian doughnuts. We've found thousands and thousands of those. Dr. Young is sick of looking at them and swears every time we dig up another one."

"But what are they?"

"Nobody knows. They come in all sizes, from little doughnuts to big ones like those yummy glazed doughnuts we used to get back at school. Gee, I wish I had one of them right now."

"When are we going to eat?" wailed Chrysta.

Marsha smacked her.

"At first, Dr. Young thought they were bobbins for weaving machines. But they're too rough. Look!" She reached into the garden. "These are *real* bobbins. See how nicely they're fired and glazed, with a design on each side." She carefully put them back. "But these doughnuts—phew! One of our students came up with the only idea Dr. Young liked. He figured the women used to go down to the river, make thick mud pies, impale them on a stick, and carry them back to their houses to use in making pottery. If they dried out, they simply softened them with water when they were ready to make another pot. But when they had the big fire that burned down the whole city, these blobs of clay got fired just as if they were in a kiln."

"You're cute," said Hicks.

"Can we take one of them?" asked Marsha.

"Oh, yes! Anything outside the garden we don't want."

"It's martini time," said Hicks, "Why don't you join us, Cathy?"

"Oh, I couldn't. Dr. Young would kill me if I left his garden unattended."

"Well then, we'll see you later," said Hicks.

On the way to the booze, Marsha spotted a neat little pile of potsherds sitting alone in a patch of buttercups.

"Oh, look!"

We all stooped down to inspect them.

"I think they must be part of one pot," said Marsha. "See, they're all the same color."

"I think you're right," said Hicks. "Look, there's a handle."

"Do you all want me to die right here on the spot?" moaned Chrysta, flopping on her bottom.

"Oh Chrysta, you're such a selfish snot!" said Marsha. Then she turned to her father and said very sweetly, "Come on, Dad, I'm starved, too."

We carried the beer cooler down to the river bank. Hicks mixed the martinis in paper cups.

"Here's to King Midas!" said Hicks.

"And here's to Alexander the Great!" I said.

"And here's to Dr. Young!" said Marsha.

"I want a martini," said Chrysta.

"No!"

"Oh, you grown-ups have all the fun!" She flounced away and walked right into the river, eating a bologna sandwich.

The famous Sakariya River which had protected great armies in the past was now only a ghost of its former self—a pleasant, swift-flowing stream with muddy banks and cattails. It was easy to imagine the Phrygian women coming down here to gather their mud doughnuts.

"Come on in, John, the water's great!" She was in up to her waist. Then she dunked her head into the water and flung her hair high in the air, spraying water everywhere with her two-foot tresses. What a wicked child!

I took off my shoes to test the water. Chrysta dragged me in and crowned me with a slimy mass of bullrushes.

"Daddy, take a picture of him quick! A picture of King Midas!" He did. I was a mess but mighty proud that I hadn't spilled a single drop of juniper juice.

Chrysta rushed out of the water, took off her skirt, and laid it in the sun. What a shameless hussy! Her panties were darling. I dragged myself out and shook each leg like a dog.

My white duck pants didn't look nearly so bad as I thought they would, and I knew they'd dry quickly in the hot sun. The girls wandered away, and Hicks and I sat on the bank of the river swapping stories and myths like two old Phrygian philosophers.

"You know, there's a theory that Alexander didn't really cut the Gordian knot with his sword," I said.

"How'd he do it?"

"Well, to go back to the beginning of the story, you know that an oracle told the Phrygians that the first person to come through a certain gate—probably that big one at the south end near the towers—would become king, and he would put an end to all their troubles. Just then, Gordius, a poor peasant, happened to come through the gate in his oxcart. Let's drink to Gordius."

"Right!" Hicks threw an ice cube in my cup and filled it with gin.

"Where's the vermouth?"

"Never mind the vermouth!"

"Not even an olive?"

"Chrysta ate 'em all. Go on, let's hear this phony theory of yours."

"Oh, it's not mine. I just read it somewhere."

"Well, you go on!"

"Yes, well, where was I? Ah yes, so poor bewildered old Gordius was crowned king. And they promptly named the city after him. Wasn't that sweet?"

"Will you go on before I promptly crown *you* on the head with the Beefeater bottle?"

"Well, Gordius was so grateful that he dedicated his oxcart to Zeus!"

"Sheeit! What would Zeus want with an oxcart?"

"Now wait a minute, I haven't got to the good part yet. The pole of the cart was fastened to the yoke of the oxen with a very, very intricate knot made of bark."

"BARK?"

"Yes, bark. They didn't have rope in those days."

"They had clothes and blankets and rugs and weaving machines and bobbins, and you're trying to tell me they didn't have *rope?*" Hicks asked.

"Well, maybe they did have rope, but this knot was made of bark. And the oracle then said that anyone who untied the knot would become the ruler of all Asia! So there!"

"So what?"

"So Alexander the Great came marching through Phrygia—with his 10,000 Macedonians right behind him—or was it a 100,000?"

"Will you get on with this wretched story?" Hicks said.

"And they told Alex Baby that the only way to conquer Asia was to untie the knot. Well, now Alex was interested *only* in finding the end of the world—you know they thought the world was flat in those days, and Alex wanted to look over the edge—an amusing thought, isn't it? Okay, okay! So Alex knew he had to conquer Asia, and he had no time to waste with these foolish Phrygians so—"

"So he pulled out his sword and cut the goddamn Gordian knot with one swipe."

"Ah, ha, ha, no! He simply removed the kingpin between the pole and the yoke."[28]

I lay back on the ground with my hands clasped behind my head. Hicks was speechless for a moment.

"Well, if that isn't the stupidest story I ever heard!"

"I agree. I like the sword-swiping business much better. More dazzling! More Alexander-the-Greatish!"

"You're sick!" Hicks said.

"I really don't feel too well."

Hicks turned to Marsha, who had been listening quietly.

"Marsha, give me a hand with this cooler, and let's get the hell out of here before he tells another one of his stories. John, give me the keys. *I'll* drive!"

I surrendered them meekly and slumped in the back seat. Hicks turned the Oldsmobile around, grinding all

---

28. Joke unclear. (A kingpin is a vertical bolt that connects a yoke to a (tug)pole.)

my poor gears, and was ready to barrel off when Marsha screamed that Chrysta wasn't with us. Hicks got out and started bellowing like a wounded ox. "Chrysta! Chrysta!!!"

I got out too, to see if I could help. "Couldn't we just leave her here?"

Hicks cupped his hands to his mouth and bellowed louder. "CHRYSTAAAAAAA!" You could have heard it all over Phrygia. Just then Chrysta came wobbling madly down the hill holding her skirt over her belly.

"My God, she's got pregnant!" I said.

"Open the trunk, quick!" she screamed. "Open the trunk!"

Hicks did, without really knowing why. Chrysta lifted her skirt and unloaded the contents of her belly into the trunk. It was the pile of potsherds we had seen in the buttercups. "Now let's get the hell out of here!" she said as she jumped into the back seat and slid below the window level.

We drove home in silence though our consciences were screaming. Except Chrysta's. "Well, you all drooled over it so much, I figured you wanted it. Step on it, Daddy, I've got a date with Phil at 6:30 and I've got to take a bath. Phew! I stink."

Betty Lou Hicks had dinner waiting for us when we got home.

"Well, how was the trip?" she asked.

"Great!" said Marsha. "I'll get the Elmer's Glue."

"Great!" said Hicks, with a glint of greed in his eye.

"Great!" I said, "but I need a drink."

"*Boring!*" said Chrysta, flouncing off to her bath.

Marsha sat in the middle of the floor and started gluing the purloined potsherds together.

"What's that?" asked Betty Lou.

"We don't know yet."

"You know, the pieces really *were* outside Dr. Young's garden," said Hicks tentatively.

"Well, I think it's great!" said Marsha. "Isn't that Chrysta a pistol! She sure takes after you, Dad. Oh, look! Here's another piece that fits. This is much more fun than a jigsaw puzzle!"

A week later Hicks insisted I come for dinner. He had a Cheshire cat grin on his face when he let me in the door and led me into the living room. I spotted the pot immediately.
"My God! Is that the one—the one Chrysta—?"
"Yes."
"Isn't it beautiful?" said Betty Lou.
It wasn't exactly an amphora—it was more like a large water pot, about two feet wide, a gorgeous persimmon color and in excellent condition. It was exquisite!
"Only one goddamn piece missing," said Hicks. "Look! A three inch triangle on the back side! We've got to go back to Gordium next week to find it."
We didn't. But Hicks had his pot, which certainly rivaled my amphora in beauty.

When I finally returned to California after 20 years overseas, I was unpacking my goodies when my landlady wandered into my apartment with a lease to sign.
"My God! What's that?" she shouted, pointing.
"That's an amphora," I said proudly. "It may be 2,000 years old. The Greeks used these to transport wine in ancient times between islands and the mainland, and sometimes the ships would go down in a storm."
"Yuck! It looks like something that came out of the trash barrel!"

The Curse of Troy

≈

I KNEW we were tempting the gods when we ran oiled and naked around the tomb of Achilles, just as Alexander the Great had done in 334 B.C. We weren't exactly naked—we had stripped to the waist. And we weren't exactly oiled—we didn't even have suntan oil with us—so we smeared our bodies with Pepsi-Cola and started running around the tomb while Mehmet stood on the sidelines to take a Polaroid picture of us.

"Mehmet! Be sure to get all of us in the picture! On the front side of the tomb, not the back side! Tom! Hugh! Hurry up and catch up with me so Mehmet can take the picture!"

Hugh passed me on one lap, which didn't help matters at all. He was a thin, wiry Georgia mountain boy who normally moved as slow as blackstrap molasses, but he was inspired that day. Potbellied Tom threw himself into the ceremony with tits a-flapping and finally caught up to me as Hugh passed us again.

"Take it, Mehmet! Take it!" I screamed just before Hugh disappeared behind the tomb. (That boy certainly wasn't being very cooperative.) I veered off toward Mehmet to pull the picture through the camera. Tom collapsed on the side of the tomb. Hugh sprinted around five more times because the guidebook didn't say how many times Alexander had run around the tomb, and Hugh wanted to be sure. The picture came out fine, though you really couldn't tell who the naked runners were.

Alexander the Great was the first to pay homage at

the tomb of "the greatest warrior of all times." Then came Julius Caesar in 41 B.C. After him came the mad Emperor Caracalla in 211 A.D. Caracalla wasn't content with running around Achilles's tomb oiled and naked like Alexander—he wanted someone to grieve over, like Priam over his slain son Hector. So that night at dinner he poisoned his best friend and went into an orgy of grief.

Well, I wasn't content, either. I wasn't sure this really was the tomb of Achilles. It was just a mound of earth about 40 feet high. True, it was obviously man-made. And there was a hole near the top where robbers had undoubtedly plundered it long ago. But somehow the site didn't seem right to me. It wasn't grand enough. Actually, we were in a depression on the plains below the citadel of Troy, but there was a ridge between us and the Dardanelles. Surely Achilles would have been buried on the ridge, in a grand tomb restored by Alexander or Hadrian, overlooking the glorious battlefield, the Dardanelles, and the Aegean Sea.

I proposed my theory to Tom and Hugh who had gotten into the beer-cooler for Johnnie Walker and some ice to soothe their savage breasts and wash off the Pepsi-Cola. They shouted down my idea and said the sun was baking my brain.

"Well, let's just take a look."

"No, no, no, John. Our Troy trip is over. We've got to be on our way to Cotton Castle so we can get back to Ankara tomorrow. Here! Have a nip." Tom handed me Johnnie. "Mehmet Bey, do you want some *viski?*"

Mehmet giggled and said no. Then we started on our way.

A few yards down the road, I saw a dirt road leading up to the imposing ridge.

"Mehmet! Turn right!" I shouted. He turned before he knew what he was doing.

The road was bumpy and full of ruts, but well-used. Tom and Hugh bounced happily around in the back seat like boozy sailors. The road got rougher and steeper.

"Keep going, Mehmet, put 'er in low!"

We came to a round, rusty sign that said, *Yasak Bolge!* It meant "Forbidden Area!"

"Look at that!" said Mehmet, his eyes bulging.

"Never mind! Keep going! We can't read Turkish!"

The Oldsmobile spit rocks and stones as we spun our way to the top of the ridge. Suddenly two soldiers jumped out of a tiny guard shack and stuck their bayonetted rifles through the open windows on each side of the car. The soldier on Mehmet's side started screeching like a hysterical hyena.

"What are you doing up here? Who are you? Don't you know this is a forbidden area? Didn't you see that sign down there! This is a military installation! Guns! Cannon! Emplacements! Tanks! Who are you? Spies? Greeks? Are you Russians?!!"

"Is there some sort of a problem, John?" asked Hugh laconically.

"I could shoot you right now," screamed the hyena, "like the mad dogs you are, and I'd be within my rights, but I'll call my captain. Don't make a move!" He went into the shack and started ringing madly on his field telephone.

"Well, we're under arrest," said Mehmet coolly with a smug I-told-you-so tone.

Tom and Hugh started cheering. "Let's have another drink."

"Will you keep that g.d. bottle out of sight!" I muttered under my breath. "We must be respectful!"

"That's your problem, John, you treat these Turks too well," said Tom. "Ask that cat who's jabbing you in the ribs if he'd like a little libation."

Actually, the bayonet was at my throat, and the farther I edged away from it, the farther he pushed it in the window.

"Mehmet, please ask this guardian of the Turkish Republic to withdraw his bayonet. You may promise him we won't try to escape."

Mehmet spoke to him very gently and persuasively. The

soldier actually withdrew to the guard shack but kept two beady eyes on us and his weapon cocked.

The other soldier finally got through to his captain and screamed so loud there was hardly any need for Alexander the Bell's great invention. After cataloguing all our crimes, the soldier rang off and came over to the car without his gun. The other guard covered him.

"My captain is coming right over," he said to Mehmet.
"Ask him where his captain is."
"In his village, having lunch," translated Mehmet.
"Ask him how far away his captain's village is."
"Two hours," said Mehmet.
"My God, does he have to walk here???"
"No, he's got a jeep, but he has to finish his lunch."

Tom said it was just enough time for a little siesta and collapsed like a baby blimp in the back seat. Hugh curled up like a kudzu vine in the other corner.

While sitting in my Oldsmobile prison, I went back over the events which had brought us to this predicament. Everyone had told me not to go to Troy, and not because I'd get arrested. They said that there was nothing to see. "Just a pile of rocks." "Not worth the trip." "Very boring." So for 10 years I had avoided it. There always seemed to be too many other places to see first:

—Bergama (Pergamon), where parchment was invented
—Sardis, where King Croesus first coined money
—Zile, where Julius Caesar said, *"Veni, vidi, vici"*
—Tarsus, where St. Paul was born
—Cedra, where Cleopatra kept her rendezvous with Antony
—Sinop, where Diogenes was looking for an honest man
—Myra, where Santa Claus (St. Nicholas) was born

But I felt it was important to visit Troy. I didn't care if there was nothing to see. I just wanted to stand on the site of Troy so I could always say, "I've been there!"

And so in the spring of 1968 I decided to follow in

Alexander's footsteps and make a pilgrimage to Troy. It was *Kurban Bayram*, a five-day holiday celebrating the end of the month of *Hajj* with the sacrifice of a lamb. I planned all the logistics and got Tom Curington and Hugh Sneed to fly with me. I sent Mehmet ahead in the white Oldsmobile, the trunk loaded with the barest necessities: ice chest, beer, Johnnie Walker, Pall Mall cigarettes, candy bars, Ritz crackers, sardines, Pepsi-Cola, dill pickles, playing cards, and Polaroid film.

We flew from Ankara to Istanbul and then to Bandirma on the northwestern tip of the Dardanelles. As we circled the tiny airport in a DC-3, I saw the white Oldsmobile parked beside the grass runway. Mehmet greeted us like long-lost brothers. Tom and Hugh raided the Budweiser (well, I had one, too) and we started off for Troy.

"I've brought some books with me," said Hugh in the back seat, digging into his knapsack. I was amazed when he pulled out *The Dream of Troy; Troy and Its Remains; The Story of a Gold-Seeker; Troy and the Trojans; One Passion, Two Loves;* and *Memoirs of Heinrich Schliemann* (the discoverer of Troy in 1872). "I've been flipping through some of these books," said Hugh, "and I think it's interesting that the whole world thought Schliemann was crazy when he started digging for Troy in 1870. All the historians said Troy was imaginary and the Trojan War a myth invented by Homer in the 9th century B.C. But Schliemann was convinced that Homer was telling a true story, handed down by word of mouth for hundreds and hundreds of years before Homer lived. Schliemann's faith was bolstered by the fact that it was historically recorded that Alexander the Great, Julius Caesar, and the Emperor Caracalla visited Troy to pay homage to the great Greek warrior Achilles. Listen to this." And Hugh read us the story of running around Achilles's tomb, oiled and naked. "Here, Tom, you read some of this."

"I have to make water," said Tom. "Mehmet Bey, stop the car."

Tom watered the wildflowers of northwestern Turkey

and got us all another beer. He also chomped down a full jar of pickles.

We entered the tiny town of Chanakkale right on the Dardanelles, just across from the Gallipoli peninsula, site of the ignominious defeat of the Allies by Ataturk in World War I. My guidebook said the museum in an old Byzantine church was worth seeing, so we made it our first stop. It was small and poorly lighted, but the objects in it were sobering—gold! gold! gold! Scepters and goblets and maces and jewelry—all from the tomb of Dardanus, the first King of Troy, discovered intact in 1958. We made that tomb our next stop.

Dardanus's final resting place was halfway to Troy, a tumulus only 50 yards from the waterway that had been named after him. A recently constructed concrete tunnel ran inside the tomb to a chamber near the top of the tumulus. Tom kept bumping his head on the top of the tunnel, which was only about four feet high. When we told him to bend over, he said his belly kept getting in the way. The tomb was empty—everything had been taken to the museum at Chanakkale—but the bearded watchman told us the story of the discovery.

Adnan Menderes, the Prime Minister who was hanged just after the 1960 revolution, had tried to continue the modernization of his country that Ataturk had started in 1922. When he came into power in 1956, Menderes decreed that concrete was the wave of the future. So he ordered cement plants to be built all over Turkey—on the Black Sea in the north, on the Aegean Sea in the west, on the Mediterranean Sea in the south, on the Russian-Iranian-Syrian border in the east. The only trouble was the raw materials and the energy to run the plants weren't available in most of the sites Menderes had selected. Still, when they started clearing the site for a cement plant near Troy, they kept running into huge boulders, marble blocks, pillars, and lintels. Menderes rushed a team of archeologists to the site and they discovered the tomb of Dardanus in a tumulus overlooking the cement plant. What a lucky find!

Mehmet had gotten bored with all this jazz about the ancients and had slithered down the passageway before us to turn the car around. When we finally emerged, Mehmet had the Oldsmobile sunk to its axles in a lovely, green-carpeted swamp surrounding the Tomb of Dardanus. He was so embarrassed. He had wanted to please us by having the car ready to go!

We all gave him a piece of our mind, then stepped into the squish and pushed him out of the bog. Mehmet laughed and told us how beautiful we were.

"Yes, Mehmet, we know. Now will you please watch the road and take us to our motel."

The motel was charming, on the side of a hill surrounded by pine trees. We watched the sun go down between the trees and sink into the Dardanelles.

After we had showered and met in the dining hall where Tom ordered every Turkish dish he knew, we conjured up a bridge game. Tom wobbled over to a table where a beautiful blonde of perhaps 30 or 35 sat with a saturnine man of perhaps 50 or 55. He bowed all the way to the table to ask her if she would like to play bridge. Hugh and I were poised to protect Tom in case the dark man lashed out at him. But the woman said, *"Memnun oldum."*

"What did she say, John, what did she say?"

"She said she'd be happy to play bridge."

"Bravo! Bravo!"

"But not with you," I said. "I'd better be her partner. You and Hugh play together."

The Turkish lady and I kept skunking Tom and Hugh until her husband (perhaps) gently took her off to bed.

"We had bad cards," said Tom. "Waiter! More *kanyak!*"

The next day we drove up to the citadel of Troy and parked the Oldsmobile in the place allotted by the Turks for about 20 or 30 cars. We passed through a wicket where each person was to pay a fee of one lira (10¢). I paid before Tom created a scene.

As we entered Troy from the very top of the citadel, I saw a stretch of green grass dotted with hundreds of anemones, little flowers about four inches high with petals the color of fresh blood and deep blue centers.

"Look, Hugh! These anemones are the drops of blood of the Trojan warriors as they fell in battle."

Hugh gave me a pitying look. "Oh, John, you are so mixed up! Those were the poppies of Flanders fields."

"But these came first!"

"You really must see a doctor soon."

We first visited the remains of an ancient amphitheater on the side of the citadel. Nothing was left but a few mosaics on the orchestra floor and some clay pipes which indicated they had water spectacles there—perhaps for *The Frogs* by Aristophanes, in which the characters sit on lily pads in the water and croak.

Then we came upon a small Roman theater built by the Emperor Hadrian. It was in remarkable condition, with 10 semicircular rows of marble seats, highly decorated in typical Roman fashion. Lying on the ground around the orchestra were decorated marbles and bases of statues inscribed with the names of Roman emperors. (I thought immediately of all the creeps who had told me there was nothing to see at Troy.) It seemed to me that the tiny theater was an *odeon* where concerts and dances were given, but Hugh insisted it was a *bouleuterion*, where the senate held their meetings. He motioned us to take our seats (Tom preempted the emperor's place) and proceeded to tell us the story of the discovery of Troy in 1872.

"Heinrich Schliemann was a self-made German millionaire merchant. He was a shrewd businessman and made one fortune after another, first in Germany, then in Russia, and then in France. In 1850 he went to California for the Gold Rush and shrewdly made another fortune in banking—not in panning for gold. He managed to finagle an American citizenship without the five-year prerequisite and went back to Paris in 1852 with his gold. He was an indefatigable writer and signed his 12 books with 'Citizen of the United States.' During the American Civil War he made another killing by cornering the market in Egyptian cotton, all while sitting in Paris.

"All his life he had a passion for things Greek, and especially Homer. So he taught himself to read and write classical Greek in six weeks, just as he had previously taught himself Russian, French, and English. Then he decided to devote the rest of his life and fortune to finding Troy. He was 48.

"He wrote to a trusted business acquaintance in Athens and asked him to find a Greek girl to marry. (His Russian wife refused to leave St. Petersburg, so he divorced her.) His only specifications for a bride were that she be young, well-mannered, and know all of Homer by heart. The friend selected his 18-year-old cousin Sophia. Schliemann was delighted with her since she met all his specifications and was a beauty as well.

"Using only Homer as a guide, they set sail for Turkey in 1870. Homer had lived in Smyrna (now Izmir). The Scamander River and Mount Ida were less than 100 miles north of Izmir, on the Turkish coast of the Dardanelles. On horses, Schliemann and Sophia toured the area around the Scamander, looking for landmarks mentioned by Homer. Schliemann rejected a mound selected by earlier amateur archeologists because the springs nearby dried up in the summer. One day, in the shadow of Mount Ida, they came upon another mound, 80 feet high, with springs gushing out of its sides—just as it said in *The Iliad*."

Hugh looked up from his books and said, "You're supposed to ask me why Homer called his story *The Iliad* and not *The Troiad*."

"Okay, Brother Hugh," said Tom, "I'll ask why Homer called it *The Iliad* and not *The Troiad*."

"Thank you, Brother Tom. I'm glad you asked that question. Because one of Alexander the Great's commanders, who was left behind to rule Troy while Sandy[29] went on to conquer the rest of the world, renamed the city New Ilion after his home town in Macedonia."

"Well, I declare!"

Hugh continued the story.

"Henry and Sophie rode to the top of the mound and started digging with a pickaxe. Uncovering potsherds, bits of glass, and finally a marble block six feet thick, Schliemann immediately declared that he had found Troy. For the next two years he organized and financed a dig with Greek foremen and hundreds of Turkish workers. Every night the Turks carried home blocks of marble (which irritated Schliemann because the blocks were Roman) to build a mosque in their village nearby."

"And now," said Hugh closing his books, "we will proceed into the city. Follow me. Stay in line, Mehmet, and don't get lost."

Mehmet giggled.

We entered a trench which Schliemann had bulldozed (literally, with oxen) straight across the citadel. The Turks had put up signs showing the nine levels of Troy which Schliemann had uncovered, dating from 400 A.D. to 2750 B.C. Above us were Troy IX, Troy VIII, and Troy VII. We were on the Troy VI level, which turned out to be Homer's Troy. We inspected some huge amphoras, bigger than a man, which were sunk into the floor of the granary, or perhaps they were used for olive oil or wine. The side of the floor had been sliced away to show the size of the amphoras. I got a picture of Tom peering down into one sniffing for wine, while Mehmet embraced the amphora.

Then we started descending on simple dirt pathways through Troy V, IV, III, II, and I. At the bottom was a ramp of granite blocks that rose from the plain through the west gate of the city and into Troy VI. It was the very ramp upon which the Trojans had pulled the Greek gift horse into the

---

29. Diminutive of Alexander.

city. Since we didn't have a wooden horse, I took a picture of Tom chugging up the ramp and trying to look like a horse with Hugh on his back. Mehmet clapped.

Hugh then made us sit under a fig tree next to a hole in a wall in Troy III, where there was a sign with an arrow and the words "Priam's Treasure."

"Schliemann was sure that he had found Troy," said Hugh rummaging through his knapsack for his books, "but he had no proof. He had been hoping to find inscriptions and tablets, but not one word! Apparently the Trojans couldn't write. And then one day—" Hugh found a place he had marked and began to read.

Mehmet didn't understand one word, but he knew that Hugh was the *hodja*[30] and we were the pupils as we sat crosslegged at his feet. Mehmet giggled and waved to some tourists who took our picture and gathered around us.

"Ah, now, Mehmet you're not paying attention. Jumping Jupiter, I'll have to start all over. And *you* pay attention too, madam. Yes, *you* with all the Nikons around your neck." She cowered behind her ample husband. Hugh held the book at arm's length and read in true Homeric style, except for his dreadful drawl:

Troy, June 17, 1873

Early in the morning Schliemann and his wife Sophia routinely returned to the main dig. As they were descending to a depth of 28 feet, the sun at that precise moment sent a shaft of light ricocheting off the wall. For a fraction of a second, it blinded Schliemann. He stopped. Another ray of light rebounded into his eyes. Heinrich tugged at Sophia's arm, and her gaze followed his. They stood transfixed.

Two gangs of day laborers were working nearby.
"Go at once," he told his wife, "and shout *paidos*."
Paidos was a Greek word which had come into the Turkish language. It meant "feeding time" or "rest period."

---

30. A Muslim schoolmaster

Mehmet recognized the word immediately and got up shouting, *"Paidos! Paidos!"*

"No, no, not you, Mehmet!" said Hugh peevishly. "You're not supposed to shout *paidos*, Sophia is! Now sit down."

Mehmet giggled behind his hand like the class cut-up. Hugh composed himself and went on:

> "Go at once, Sophia, and shout *paidos*."
> If anything was likely to arouse the suspicions of the workers, it would be the cry of *paidos* only a few minutes after the start of the day's work. Why would this piaster-pinching, hard-nosed German merchant-turned-archaeologist give the workers an extra rest period? With the cunning of Ulysses, Schliemann's mind wrestled with the problem. Aha! He would cast himself in the role of the crazy foreigner.
> "Tell them today is my birthday, and that I just remembered it," he said. "Everyone will get his wages for the day without working. Tell them to go back to their villages. Tell the Greek foremen to go back to their barracks. Hurry, Sophia, hurry! Shout *paidos!* Tell them it's my birthday!"

"Happy birfday to you..." Mehmet began singing. It was the only song he knew in English. "Happy birfday to you..."

Hugh threw down his book and went into a blue funk. "Dadgummit John, what are we going to do with that child? He's a disruptive influence in this class. He's an anarchist! He's got to be punished!"

I whispered in Mehmet's ear to go back to the car and get us some cold beer. I gave him my ditty bag to carry it in.

"Please continue, dear professor," said Tom soothingly.

Hugh picked up the book, brushed it off and went on, a little less fervently than before:

> Sophia emerged from the dig, shouted *paidos,* and laughingly provided them with the phony reason. The workers were amused. The foreigners were indeed crazy. With Sophia leading the way, they abandoned the site. All except Schliemann.
> With only a knife, he loosened the object which turned out to be only a tarnished copper bowl, a foot in diameter, but behind

it gleamed a treasure trove of gold objects. He had found Priam's treasure.

Hugh stopped and pointed to the hole in the wall. "Right here," he said. "This is the very spot."

Then Hugh pulled out another book which he had marked. "And now, Brother Tom, would you pleasure us with a reading from Schliemann's *Memoirs* so we can hear his very own words about the discovery?"

"Gladly, Brother Hugh, gladly," said Tom, struggling to his feet. "Shall I do it in a German accent for you?"

"If you love God, no!" I said.

"Well, okay, but you don't know what you're missin'. I used to be a Thespian in my college days. Where do I start?"

Hugh pointed out the spot and Tom began to read in his booming voice, which stopped tourists in their tracks from Troy I to Troy IX:

> As stones and dust tumbled from above, I cut out the treasure with a stout knife, which it was impossible to do without the very greatest exertion and the most fearful risk of my life, for the great fortification-wall, beneath which I had to dig, threatened every moment to fall down upon me.

Tom glanced nervously up at the wall. So did we.

> But the sight of so many objects made me foolhardy, and I never thought of any danger. It would, however, have been impossible for me to have removed the treasure without the help of my dear wife, who was clever enough to return wearing a large red shawl. She stood by me all morning ready to pack the things which I had excavated into her shawl and to carry them up the hill to our house on the top of the citadel.

Hugh took the book out of Tom's hand and said, "Your turn, John," handing me my script.

"But I was just gettin' warmed up," said Tom as he squatted on the ground. The Nikon lady gave him a little burst of polite applause. "Thank you, ma'am, I can tell you're

a real lover of elocution."
"Hush, Tom! Go ahead, John."
I felt like an ass since Tom's elocution had attracted a great crowd, but I plunged in with both feet:

> Back at their wooden house, Schliemann announced to the foremen that Sophia had a touch of fever and that they did not want to be disturbed. "Nothing serious," he said. "She needs a rest and a cold water pack." Too bad; it had ruined his birthday.
> Locking the door behind them, they stood transfixed at the cache of gold and silver scattered on the floor: 8,772 objects running the gamut from gold diadems, necklaces, and rings; to silver goblets, breastplates, and arm bands; to bronze lanceheads, spears, and battle-axes. "Priam's Treasure," Schliemann murmured in a daze as he recalled the scene from *The Iliad* when Priam sought to ransom the body of his dead son, Hector, and offered Achilles, the victor, the booty of a king.
>
> "Weigh then the gold," Priam said, as he took 10 full talents of silver and two shining tripods and four cauldrons and also a most beautiful double goblet, a rich possession which the men of Thrace had presented to him when he went thither as ambassador: even this the old man did not spare now as he excessively desired to ransom his beloved son."
>
> Dramatically, Schliemann filled a double cup with wine, poured a libation from one spout to the gods and goddesses of Troy, and drank from the other spout. He passed the double cup to Sophia, who did the same. Then Schliemann placed the largest gold diadem on the head of his dark-haired 20-year-old Greek beauty and draped about her throat a necklace containing 4,190 individual pieces of hand-wrought gold. "Helen," he whispered with a catch in his voice, "Helen of Troy."

I looked up. Everyone was silent.
Then Mehmet arrived shouting *"Paidos! Paidos!"* and everybody started clapping wildly. He reached into the red ditty bag like a Turkish Santa Claus, preparing to pass out the beer. I snatched the bag away from him just in time to

prevent a riot.

We made our way to the temple of Athena, a short distance away. It was quite secluded from the rest of the city, and Mehmet passed out the Budweiser. Tom held his beer high in the air and poured it down his throat as if he were drinking from a Thracian rhyton. Then he let out an enormous belch which reverberated off the walls of Troy like a Jovian thunderbolt.

"You done saved my life, Mehmet, toss me another."

Hugh sat on the altar, legs crossed, thumbing through his Trojan bibles. "Here's an interesting sidelight," he said, looking like a Southern Baptist seminarian, which he once had been. "Unbeknownst to Schliemann, two Turkish workers had found a cache of gold jewelry two weeks earlier. They split it and kept it a secret. One Turk melted it down and saved it for a rainy day. The other Turk gave his portion of the jewelry to his wife. She was enchanted and couldn't wait till the next *bayram* to wear it in the streets and lord it over her neighbors. The police confiscated the jewelry and sent it to the Istanbul Museum. They sent her husband to jail."

"So what happened to the jewels that Schliemann found?" asked Tom.

"Schliemann smuggled them out of Turkey in a diplomatic pouch and had Sophia's relatives, who were numerous, bury them in their gardens all over Greece. Eventually, he gave them all to the Berlin Museum. Then the Russians stole them at the end of World War II and carted them off to the Kremlin. Oh, why did Eisenhower insist on letting the Russians take Berlin first? I don't like Ike."[31]

"Speaking of diplomatic pouches," I said, "I have a friend at the American Embassy in Ankara who told me that it was strongly rumored that the Russians were going to give the treasure back to the Turks this year...to woo them away from the American sphere of influence and sign a friendship treaty." (That was 1968, but the Russians still haven't given

---

31. A pun on the 1952 Eisenhower political ad "I Like Ike."

back Priam's treasure.)

Tom wolfed down a jumbo-size package of potato chips and said, "I'm hungry, let's eat!"

We drove down to the shores of the Dardanelles and had our very own Thanksgiving Sacrifice on the beach in honor of *Kurban Bayram*. Early that morning Mehmet had gone to the nearest village and bought two live chickens, a dozen eggs, tomatoes, cucumbers, green peppers, green onions, romaine lettuce, bread, fresh-churned water buffalo butter, salt, peanuts in the shell, tangerines, and pomegranates. Mercifully, he had had the chickens killed, plucked, disemboweled, and dissected. He built a fire on the sand as Tom, Hugh, and I tried to swim the Hellespont like Lord Byron. I gave up first. Tom floated back in later. We finally got Hugh to turn back by shouting to him that he was going the wrong way!

When Mehmet dished out the broiled chicken and baked eggs on pieces of Kleenex, I noticed that he had confiscated all the gizzards. I grabbed a liver, Tom grabbed a heart, and Hugh grabbed a kidney. Mehmet was surprised and laughed because he thought the Americans liked only the breast.

"John, does Mehmet know the story of the Trojan War?" asked Tom. "Did they teach him that in school?"

"I don't know, I'll ask him."

Mehmet had never heard of Troy and, like most Turks, had no interest in the foreign archeological sites—especially if they were Greek. But traveling with me, he had begun to take a tolerable interest in ruins. I think the turning point in his conversion took place at Alanya, a peninsula rising 800 feet out of the Mediterranean Sea with a castle-fortress on top. We threaded our way up the rocky road in the white Oldsmobile and got out to inspect the castle which had been built by the Greeks and rebuilt by the Romans, Byzantines, Arabs, Seljuks, Venetians, and Ottomans.

I was surprised when a wiry old lady popped out from behind a wall and spoke to me in charmingly wacky English.

"Good day, sir. I am a guide provided by our Turkish government for your pleasure." She was wearing a blue smock and pointed proudly to the insignia stitched on it which read "*Rehber*/Guide."

I was immediately enchanted with this Turkish Grandma Moses who started spouting mile-a-minute information until I realized it was straight out of my guidebook and learned by rote. I gave her the slip and she fell back on Mehmet, lapsing into Turkish. She hugged his arm and guided him all over the citadel. I could see that Mehmet was blushing but enraptured.

When we left, I knew Mehmet would tip her (his duty everywhere we went because he insisted I was spoiling the Turks). As we started down the mountain I asked him how much he had tipped her.

He blushed and said, "Ten lira."

"Ten lira!" Mehmet had given her a dollar!

"She used a kilo of butter on me," he said, covering his eyes in happy shame. It took me a few seconds to realize he was saying, "She buttered me up."

So Tom said, "Well, let me tell Mehmet the story of the Trojan War. You translate, John." He stretched out on the sand like a beached whale and began paraphrasing from one of Hugh's books. "The whole flippin' flap started over the world's first beauty contest and the prize was a pippin. John, do you know how to say 'pippin' in Turkish?"

"No, may I say 'apple'?"

"T'aint the same."

"'Sour apple'? 'Bitter apple'?"

"Much wuss!" [much worse]

Hugh said, "Mehmet, it was a golden apple."

"Ah now, Hugh, you done spoiled the whole cotton-pickin' story."

"Tom, really!" said Hugh. "Let me tell Mehmet the story."

Tom put his paw over Hugh's mouth and continued. "Well, there was this big fancy weddin' on Mount Ida—see that mountain over yonder, Mehmet?—and everybody was invited to the shivaree,[32] real high-class people like gods and goddesses, 'ceptin' one—the goddess of Discord, name of Eris—a real crazy. So she crashed the party and tossed a golden pippin onto the weddin' table, shoutin', 'For the slickest chick in the whole wide world!' Well, naturally there was a big ruckus and all them society ladies started clawin' one another tryin' to get at that pippin. John, do you know how to translate 'ruckus' into Turkish?"

"Tom, will you *please* go on and leave the translation of your abominable Southern expressions to me?"

"Language of the gods," said Tom dreamily. "Well, the three most important ladies at the shindig—Aphrodite, Hera, and Athena—they started tearin' one another's hair out till finally their pappy, Zeus, had to step in and separate them cats. He appointed a shepherd named Paris to be the Trojan Bert Parks."[33]

"Oh Jesus!" groaned Hugh.

"Now, Paris weren't no ordinary hired hand, neither. Nosiree! He was, *in fact*, the son of Priam, King of Troy! But when the little tyke was born, one of the local fortune-tellers done told ol' man Priam that Paris would be the downfall and destruction of Troy. So the little tot was thrown to the wolves on the slopes of Mount Ida. But an old shepherd happened along and rescued Paris, and he grew up to be a handsome bastard like me."

Hugh rolled his eyes to heaven and started spitting pomegranate seeds. I translated only "handsome" and Mehmet patted Tom on the back.

"Thank ye, Mehmet. Well, all three of them ladies stripped bare nekkid and tried to seduce that lad. All three of 'em succeeded." Tom heaved a sigh and went on. "Now Athena, she promised Paris wisdom, and Hera offered him power, and Aphrodite—she was the goddess of Love—she gave him the address of a livin' screamin' doll named Helen, care of her husband Menelaus, King of Sparta, Mycenae,

---

32. A mock serenade sung by a group of people to celebrate a marriage.
33. Bert Parks was the TV host of the Miss America pageant from 1955–79.

Greece, no zip code."

Hugh flopped over on the sand, face down, and held his ears.

"So Paris gives the pippin to Aphrodite and he hies hisself off to Mycenae where Helen takes a real shine to the sharp young lad, and they hightails it back to Troy. Big Daddy (that's Priam) and Big Mama (that's Hecuba), they say, 'Welcome, honey, welcome to our clan. You is now Helen of Troy.' Even Hector popped an eyeball at his baby brother's new wife, and he vowed to defend her to the death. How 'm I doin', Hugh? What'sa matter, you got a stomach ache?"

Tom took a swig of white lightning and continued.

"Well, after that, all hell broke loose. Menelaus got all his Greek buddies together—Agamemnon, Ulysses, Achilles, Patroclus, and two Ajaxes—and sailed off to whip the daylights out of them Trojan bastards. That was some war! Sometimes the Greeks was winnin', and sometimes the Trojans—back and forth for 10 years. Even Achilles, the best soldier in the whole world, got discouraged and started sulkin' in his tent. His best buddy, Patroclus, got disgusted with him, so one day he put on Achilles's armor and rushed out and got hisself slewn. 'Cause you see, Hector thought he was Achilles, so he slew 'im. Well, that *really* got Achilles's bile boilin', 'cause he had a real thing for Patroclus, so Achilles rushes out and slews Hector. Then they calls a truce so they can bury all those bodies. And Priam comes down off the mountain to negotiate with Achilles 'bout returnin' the body of Hector so Priam could give him a real good funeral 'cause he really loved that boy. He offered him gold and silver and all kinds of trinkets, but Achilles said no! And he dragged Hector's body up and down the plains behind his chariot. Well, this made Paris boilin' mad, so he stands up on the ramparts—that's a fancy name for walls—and he lets go with a poisoned arrow. Now, remember, Paris used to be a shepherd, and he was a crack shot with the bow 'n' arrow, and where do you think that arrow went? Right into Achilles's heel. Shall I tell Mehmet how Achilles's mama dunked him into the River Styx to make him invulnerable 'cept for that heel she was hangin' onto him by?"

"No!" said Hugh.

"I thought you wasn't listenin'."

"I ain't."

"Well, after that, things got kinda dull and everything bogged down till wily old Ulysses dreamed up a mighty clever scheme. This is the best part, Mehmet. The Greeks built a great big wooden horse and stashed 10 men inside it. They pushed it up to the gates of Troy, then they folded all their tents and got in their boats and sailed away. The Trojans watched them leavin', so they reckoned they had won the war, by default, so to speak. So they dragged that horse up into the city thinkin' it was mighty neighborly of the Greeks to give them a present for winnin' the war. Then they had a slam-bam-thank-you-ma'am, ring-a-ling-ding of a party that night."

"You have my sympathy, John," said Hugh.

"Singin' and dancin' and carousin'—and the next mornin' they was all stone cold dead drunk. Then, Mehmet, the belly of that horse popped open, and them Greeks plopped out nimble as cats, and opened the gates for their buddies who had sailed back during the night. Then slaughter, slaughter, slaughter! Every man, woman, child, and dog! 'Cept Helen, of course. Then they sailed back to Greece, and that was the end of the most beautiful war in history."

Mehmet applauded, clapped Tom on the back, and told him how beautiful he was.

"Thank you, Mehmet, thank you kindly. Now, will you hand me that bottle? My throat's parched from all that preachin'."

The sun was sinking into the Aegean, so we pulled up our tents and went back to the real world—our motel.

We napped, showered, and dressed for dinner. Tom showed up looking like a Shriner from Hawaii—hibiscus shirt and purple shorts. Hugh looked like a shipwreck victim with sawed-off white pants and a sailor's cap. Mehmet appeared in a blue plaid lamb's wool suit. He looked so handsome, I gasped. It was one of my old suits that I had never worn in Turkey—it was too hot—so I gave it to Mehmet only a week before to pass on to some poor person. He had apparently had it cut down to his own size. Achilles in all his shining armor couldn't have looked more handsome. Tom and Hugh whistled, felt the material, and lavished compliments all over him. Mehmet blushed.

After dinner, Tom started his rounds of the dining room to find a fourth person for bridge. (His lady friend from the night before was nowhere to be seen.) The other people cringed when Tom literally threw down the gauntlet (a deck of playing cards) on their table, challenging them to a game of bridge. The dining hall emptied. Tom was despondent and prophesied that the world was going to the dogs. I persuaded them to play Anatolian bridge—a game that I had invented. It takes only three people and I bid both my hand and the extra hand—and never cheat. They grudgingly agreed. I told Mehmet to arrange the extra hand: "All the *piks* together, the *kors*, the *karos*, the *sineks*."

As we were arranging our hands, Mehmet suddenly declared, "Two hearts!" in perfect English.

We all broke up. I realized that Mehmet had observed many bridge games at my house, and since this was his first opportunity to play, he was going to take advantage of it. I looked at his hand—he had exactly two hearts. We made him dummy for the rest of the evening. He was so proud to appear to be playing bridge with a bunch of sophisticated Americans—he preened every time Turkish guests went by on their way to the bar.

I won, naturally. Actually, it was my alter ego since Hugh kept immaculate accounts of the score. After the game, Tom called for a bottle of *kanyak,* and we started planning our next (and last) morning's objective: to find the tomb of Achilles. It wasn't going to be easy because it wasn't on any map. The only reference to it was: "The barrow of Achilles is on the plains near the sea, N.W. of Troy."

The next morning we took a dirt road which followed the Scamander River to the sea, dividing the Plain of Troy in two. But the Plain of Troy was now farms and orchards, so we had to zig-zag right and left till we finally came to a tumulus which Hugh declared, unequivocally, to be the tomb of Achilles.

Well, we did the oiled and naked bit, and I had the bright idea to drive up to the top of the ridge, where we were promptly incarcerated in the Oldsmobile by the Turkish guards.

The Captain duly arrived two hours later and hopped out of his jeep. He rushed over to our car with the two hyenas charging behind him. The Captain (who was young, trim, and handsome) stuck his head in Mehmet's window and gave us the once-over. He observed the two sleeping beauties in the back seat and me cowering in the front. He decided immediately that we were hardly a threat to the Turkish Republic. Then he turned on the two guards and let go with a flood of Turkish, most of which I understood.

"Why, these are Americans! Can't you see that? Why didn't you tell me they were Americans! Why didn't you tell me they were in a big white American automobile! You led me to believe they were saboteurs! Or Russians! Or terrorists! They look like tourists to me!"

"We are," said Mehmet sweetly.

The Captain started shaking his fist at the guards, backing them into their shack until only their two moronic faces were sticking out of the window. Then the Captain returned to Mehmet and began apologizing.

"Please forgive my men. They were only doing their duty. May I know your good name, my friend?"

"Mehmet."

"Mehmet Bey, please apologize to your American friends for this catastrophe. I would myself, but I don't speak English. My men were overzealous. They're very ignorant, but they do try to do their duty. My, this is a beautiful automobile. What kind is it—a Chevrolet?"

"Oldsmobile," sniffed Mehmet.

"Ah, yes. The American automobiles are so beautiful." He leaned back to take it all in.

And then Mehmet let go! Once he realized we weren't going to be arrested or hanged, he lashed out at the Captain. I had never seen him like this before.

"What do you mean by having a military installation right here in this place? This is one of the most famous spots in history! The Trojan War was fought right down there on those plains. It's all in Homer. The apple made of gold! The kidnapping of the Greek lady Helen. Achilles and his broken heel! The false horse made of wood!"

I looked down and muttered under my breath in English, "Mehmet, will you shut up!"

But Mehmet went on flaming. "Why, my friends here were so happy to find the tomb of Achilles, they ran around it bare! With Pepsi-Cola on their chests, just like Big Alexander. Look! I took a picture of them."

"Oh God!" I cringed.

"You shouldn't have guns and tanks up here, and guards and barbed wire. You should have shish kabob stands and soft drinks and beer. We Turks could make a lot of money off tourists. They like all these old ruins! And they like to have something to eat and drink too! Why, we have a whole trunkful of—"

I threw myself on Mehmet's body, half smothering him, and reached my hand out the window to shake the Captain's hand. He was a little startled because he was fascinated by the picture. In my very best Turkish, I said, "Thank you very much, Captain sir. You are very kind. Please don't look at our faults. I'll just take that picture back, thank you, because we're leaving now, aren't we Mehmet? We won't bother you any more—"

"He wants his picture taken," said Mehmet struggling beneath me.

"Oh yes, of course, you bet. Just a minute till I find my

camera—ah, here it is. Now, Captain, you stand right here in front of the Oldsmobile. Good! Hold it! Ah, that's a great picture. Here, it's yours. You can keep it! Don't touch it for about five minutes. We're just leaving now, aren't we, Mehmet? Peace be with you, Captain, we commend you to God!"

"What was that all about?" asked Hugh as we bounced down the hill.

"Nothing!" I barked. "Mehmet, remind me to cut your tongue out when we get back to Ankara."

Mehmet laughed and patted me on the shoulder.

Tom came to. "Where are we? I thought we were under arrest."

"We've been sprung!"

"Bravo! That calls for a drink!"

"I need one, give me that bottle. Why, it's almost empty!"

"Drink deep, John, there's plenty more where that came from."

Tom opened another Johnnie Walker and we passed the bottle around and around till we all passed out, leaving the driving to Mehmet. The last thing I remembered was Tom singing.

"Never knew I could sing, did you, John?" said Tom, whose vocal range was about two half-notes.

Mehmet shook me when we got to Pamukkale. It was nine o'clock at night. Mehmet had driven seven hours straight from Troy. I decided maybe I wouldn't cut out his tongue after all. I woke up the two booze-hounds in the back seat. Stopping overnight at Pamukkale was my idea and surprise. I had been there many years before—the others never had. It was the site of the ancient city of Hieropolis, built on the side of a mountain, with the remains of a Roman bath, the hot springs still flowing. As the water spilled over the side of the mountain, its high calcium content turned the whole mountain white like cotton candy. That's why the Turks named it "Cotton Castle." They built a motel surrounding the baths so that you could step out your front door and into the pool. They had left the bath as unspoiled as possible, with patches of marble flooring and fluted columns, capitals, and lintels scattered in the pool just where they had fallen after an earthquake in ancient times. The water was crystal-clear and the temperature was a perfect 101°, summer or winter. In the middle of the pool was an outdoor restaurant on an island, dominated by an olive tree strung with colored lights. The island was connected to the motel by rustic bridges.

Our room had two bunk beds. Hugh threw his knapsack on an upper, stripped off his clothes, snaked into his bathing trunks, and ran outside and plunged into the pool. I could hear his shouts of surprise when he discovered it was warm water—and it probably felt good for a groggy head.

Tom was a little discombobulated and kept running around the cabin naked, saying, "Where is my *kostum?* My *kostum?*" It was the Turkish word for bathing suit.

"There it is!" I said, pointing to a red bikini in the midst of a pile of clothes that he had dumped on the floor.

Tom struggled into his "costume" saying, "You know, John, you and I may both be fat, but we have teeny behinds." Then he raced out, shouting like a Trojan warrior.

Mehmet had produced a pair of droopy drawers and modestly turned his back to put them on. "How deep is the water?" he asked.

I, in no hurry, was fixing myself a little nip. "Oh, not deep at all. One meter—one and a half meters at most."

Mehmet left and soon I heard him shouting just like Tom and Hugh—"Ooooh! Aaaah! Eeeeh! Aaaah!"—the universal language of surprise and pleasure in warm springs. Then I froze in horror—I realized that Mehmet was drowning!

He didn't know how to swim, and it flashed through my mind that our cabin was right in front of the *only* deep spot in the pool. I flew out of my clothes, jumped into my bathing suit, and took a flying leap out of the cabin into the pool. I came up underneath Mehmet and lifted him out of the water. He was thrashing wildly. My feet could touch the bottom, so I started walking him toward the center of the pool where I knew it was shallow. But he kept beating on my head, tearing my hair, gouging my eyes—so I surfaced and discovered I was holding Hugh high above the water.

"John, let me go! Mehmet is drowning! I'm trying to save him!"

Furious, I pushed Hugh under the surface and dove underneath Mehmet, who was gulping water for the third time. I surged up and caught his flailing thighs and lifted him as high out of the water as I could, trying to assure him that he wasn't going to drown. I struggled toward the center of the pool and finally plunked him down on a Roman pillar, where he leaned over and effortlessly regurgitated gallons of water from his stomach. I was coughing and gasping for breath like a drowning, unwanted puppy dog.

The owner of the motel, a big fat Turk in a black pin-striped three-piece suit, leaned over the edge of the pool and shouted to me hysterically in English: "You there! What do you mean by drowning in my pool! Don't you know it's deep over there! You crazy drunk Americans! You're trying to give my resort a bad name!"

When I caught my breath, I shouted back to him just as hysterically in Turkish: "Don't talk to *me!* I wasn't the one who was drowning! It was this child! He's a Turk! He can't swim!"

I led Mehmet to the edge of the pool. The owner softened his tone and helped Mehmet out of the pool. He hugged him, wet and all, and offered to call a doctor. Mehmet assured him that he was all right.

We all sobered up, changed our clothes, and went to the restaurant for a late dinner. The owner told us the dinner was on him, if we wouldn't sue, because his insurance rates were going higher with every new American tourist.

We ate in silence—except Mehmet. He talked up a storm and wolfed down everything the owner brought to the table.

"I almost drowned, didn't I? You told me it was shallow. One meter! Must have been five or ten meters! I went way down. I should learn how to swim, I know. Remember that time when I almost drowned in the Kizilirmak River? And that time in Antalya when you tried to teach me how to float? I'm too solid, my body is like a stone. I'd like some more lamb chops and I think I'll have some of that *raki*."

I sat beside him pushing my food around the plate. I poured him a couple of fingers of *raki* and me a tumblerful.

"I drank a lot of water from that pool, didn't I? Will it kill me?"

"Well, I don't think so, but there's a sign on that wall over there listing all the elements in the water you drank."

The sign read, in descending percentages:

> Calcium
> Sodium
> Potassium
> Zinc
> Chlorine
> Iron
> Sulfur
> Magnesium
> Barium

"Hmm," said Mehmet, chomping on a thick green onion, "*that* will clean out my pipes, won't it?"

"Yes, Mehmet, I'm sure it will."

Back in our bunks, I thought about how we had tempted the gods by running oiled and naked around the tomb of Achilles; and how the mad Caracalla poisoned his best friend to have someone to grieve over, like Priam over his son Hector; and how we almost found ourselves grieving over Mehmet. The gods were angry and almost punished us.

"Good night, Mister John," said Mehmet.

"Good night, Hector," I whispered.

My Favorite Ruin

≈

MY FAVORITE ruin is Claros. I discovered it late in the summer of 1960 and carried on an eight-year love affair with it until 1968, when I left Turkey for good—but, I hoped, not forever. A few days before I left, I stood in front of Claros and said, "Someday, when I'm a millionaire, I'm going to put you back together again."

I don't like to think that Claros is my favorite ruin *just* because no one has ever heard of it. It's halfway between Izmir and Ephesus, and even though thousands of tourists flock to Ephesus every year, no one ever stops at Claros. I'm sure they couldn't find it, though it is located only a few miles from the main highway in a narrow, pine-covered valley which runs straight down to the Aegean Sea. The map shows three ancient ruins in the valley—Colophon, Notium, and Claros. I had found Colophon and Notium with no trouble, but Claros eluded me. So, one beautiful Saturday morning in Indian summer (the Turks call it *Pastirma*—"Pastrami summer," the time for salting meats for the winter), I set off on my *motosiklet* determined to find Claros or bust.

By that time my Turkish was good enough to converse with farmers and drink tea with old villagers and badger little beasties to run errands for me. I turned off the main highway and plunged down into the valley. The road was abominable, only wide enough for two oxcarts to pass, and full of ruts, gullies, and other pitfalls for my poor Lambretta scooter. In places, stretches of finely laid cobblestones surfaced—vestiges of the ancient Roman road-builders—but these jarred my teeth loose and my scooter bounced up and down like a rubber horse on a pogo stick. I pitied the poor Roman charioteers with their iron-rimmed wooden wheels.

At the first and only village in the valley, I stopped beside two old men who were sipping tea under a scrawny acacia tree.

"Claros!" I shouted.

"Welcome! Join us for tea."

"No, no, no. I'm looking for Claros. Do you know where it is?"

"We don't speak German."

"I'm speaking Turkish!"

"Oh."

"I'm looking for Claros! An ancient city somewhere around here. Ruins! History! The name is Claros!"

"Ah, yes, Claros. Straight ahead."

The road dipped down precipitously and ended in a dry stream bed. I pushed my scooter along the sandy bottom until I found the continuation of the road on the other side. Three tiny girls came along carrying enormous water pots on their heads. I addressed them very politely and asked for directions to Claros. They backed away from me, terrified, grabbed the pots off their heads, and ran shrieking into the woods.

I began losing heart as I went on because I knew I was getting close to the sea—I could smell it—and once again I would have missed Claros. As I rounded a bend in the road, an old man in rags and a white beard came trudging toward me, leaning heavily on his staff.

"Greetings, father, I'm looking for Claros."

He stared at me with bewildered eyes as if I were a creature from outer space—which to him I probably was. I took off my goggles and screamed in his ear: "Claros! Old city! Ruins! CLAROS!"

He winced like I had punctured an eardrum. Then he slowly turned and pointed back in the direction he had come from. "Turn left at that big olive tree."

"Thank you, father, you are very kind," I said softly. I

offered him a Pall Mall which he extracted from the package daintily with knobby fingers. I offered him a light, but he shook his head and with a twinkle tucked it behind his ear. I could envision him in the village savoring it with his tea and making his cronies jealous.

When I got to the olive tree, there actually was a path about three feet wide, going off to the left. This was the turn-off I had obviously missed on my previous excursion. I drove along the path at about one mph, dragging my feet and looking from side to side. The valley was very narrow, not more than 200 yards wide, and then it sloped up to a high ridge. Perhaps Claros was on top of the hill. Suddenly I spotted a piece of marble beside the path. It was about one-foot square, with carved acanthus leaves on it, like a little capital for a tiny column. I got off my scooter and leaned over it.

"Are *you* Claros?" I asked.

The poor pathetic thing didn't answer, but it wouldn't have surprised me one bit if it had squeaked, "Yes, I'm it."

Searching for ruins in Turkey had its ups and downs, thrills and disappointments, breath-takers and blahs. Sometimes I found an amphitheater, sometimes a potsherd. Just then a man on a horse appeared out of nowhere, coming toward me on the path.

"Is *this* Claros?" I asked, pointing indignantly at the wretched rock.

"No, it's over there," he said, pointing behind him.

"Where?"

"There!!!"

I couldn't see anything but a tobacco field.

"Where???"

"Oh, come on, follow me!" he said disgustedly.

He turned his horse around and led me back to the tobacco field. We started down one side of the field and then turned into the rows. He reined his horse aside to let me pass and said, "There's Claros."

"Where?"

"Allah, Allah! Are you blind? Straight ahead of you!"

I pushed my scooter another few yards and suddenly the ground seemed to open up. There, about 20 feet below the level of the tobacco field, was an enormous excavation about the size of a football field, strewn with a jumbled mass of marble ruins.

"My God, Claros!"

"Now you see," said the man, smiling down at me. He pulled his horse around and started on his way, but not before I pressed half a pack of Pall Malls on him.

Claros! I couldn't believe it. From 100 yards away, you'd never see it. Even from 10 feet away! And what fascinating things to feast your eyes on! The first was a row of 15 pillars that had toppled over in perfect formation like a fallen stack of gigantic poker chips. Every piece of each pillar was there, from the pedestal to the capital. Then I noticed a statue lying on its back in the mud. It was headless, but the body was covered with flowing robes down to its bare feet. And it was colossal! Its big toe was taller than I! Then I saw a life-size statue of a girl leaning at a 45-degree angle, frozen in mid-air, as if she were fainting. She had her hair tied up in a band around her forehead and she was wearing a short tunic with cross-straps over her breasts. I was sure it was Diana, the huntress. But there was mud and water everywhere. Claros looked like a half-drained swimming pool.

I climbed down into the pit and crawled all over the ruins, hopping from pillar to post, snapping pictures of myself (using a self-timer). I even had a picnic with Diana. She probably would have hated my Planter's Peanuts, Tootsie Rolls, and Johnnie Walker, but I was happy as a billy goat.

When I reluctantly climbed out of the pit in the late afternoon, I looked back down and said, "This is mine! Theresa's got her mountain, and Mister John has his Claros."

Pastrami summer ended abruptly and the rains came. All winter long I bored my friends with talk of Claros.

The following May on the first warm Sunday, I hopped on my Italian magic carpet and sped out to "my dig." The dry streambed was now an angry torrent, but I wasn't about to turn back. I took off my shoes and socks, put them in my ditty bag, rolled up my pant legs, and started pushing my scooter down the river and up the bank on the other side. I felt like Noah trying to get a recalcitrant mule onto the ark, but I made it.

As I turned at the old olive tree, I heard what sounded like distant thunder, but more repetitive like the putt-putt-putt of a tired motorboat. When I reached the edge of the tobacco field, there was my Claros in all its gleaming splendor! Even *more* so because the waters had receded down to pure mud and I saw archways under the big-toed statue which suggested underground passageways and more mysteries. However, the noise of the thump-thump-thump was deafening! Suddenly I saw a half-naked bearded creature scrambling over my ruins like a wild monkey on all fours. I slid down into the pit to accost him.

Over the din, he introduced himself as Pierre, a member of a French archeological team that was excavating Claros for me. Pierre drew me away from the powerful sump pumps so we could talk. By dredging up all my high-school French, I learned a lot from Pierre, which encouraged him to dig up his high-school English. (Our long-forgotten foreign-language teachers would have been proud of us that day.)

Claros was not a city, but a temple dedicated to Apollo. Built in the 7th century B.C., it was the site of a famous oracle whose fame far surpassed that of the upstart oracle at nearby Didyma. There were indeed underground passageways which contained the Holy of Holies where the oracle sat and made predictions and prophecies after drinking the sulfurous water which bubbled up from a spring underneath the temple. The robed body with the big toe was part of a statue of Apollo. The Frenchmen were hoping to find the head under the mud in the underground passageways.

Then Pierre showed me some of the new things they had uncovered:

—An elegant marble throne with a lengthy inscription all around the base which was all Greek to Pierre and me

—A blue marble staircase leading up to the entrance to the temple where nine white marble pillars once stood. They were now lying in the mud at right angles to the 15 pillars on the side of the temple

—A series of baths where each person had to wash all over and put on purified clothes before entering the temple

—A rotunda with an altar in the middle where the patrons offered sacrifices after hearing their fortunes.

I was exuberant. But Pierre, ever the realist, said, "But ze water, Monsieur John, it is terrible!"

Every winter the site filled up with water from the rains and rivulets coming down off the mountains, and every spring the Frenchmen had to run their sump pumps before they could continue excavations. The Turkish farmers loved the French for irrigating their tobacco fields.

I ventured to say I thought the Ionians were very stupid to build a temple in the middle of a valley that became a raging river every year.

"Aha!" said Pierre, lighting up like the Eiffel Tower, "zat was before ze *tremblements de terre!* How you say zat in Inglish?"

"Tremblings of the ground? Ah! Earthquakes."

"Yes! Urzquakes!"

Hmm, I thought, that little seismic problem might add another half-million to the archaeological bill.

"My God! Where's Diana?" I shouted, suddenly seeing that she was gone.

"*Quoi? Qui? Qu'est-ce que c'est?*"[34]

I explained.

"Ah, yes! Beeyootiful! We transported her to ze museum in Smyrna." He lowered his voice and looked around. "She was not safe here, Monsieur Jean." He acted like he was protecting my property.

Later that summer I took Tom and Kitty to Claros as my specially invited guests. Kitty was as keyed up as an

---

34. What? Who? What is it?

old-fashioned spring-wound toy. Tom, driving the horrible black Mercedes, was as skeptical as a scoffer going to see an oracle. All the doors flew open when we forded the stream. Kitty was enchanted with my "find" and reached into her soft beige slacks. "Here, John. There's five lira for your Save Claros fund."

I finally had to drag Kitty and her camera out of Claros and down to the sea where we swam and sang silly songs. We toasted the hot dogs and marshmallows that Kitty had brought, though Tom was more interested in the thirst-quencher in my ditty bag. We opened the bottle of Johnnie Walker. I felt right at home.

I later took the Russians to Claros because they were so afraid of being seen by *anyone* (the KGB?). No one saw us because no one was *ever* there—except the local beasties who knew me by name and fetched firewood and sometimes tomatoes, cucumbers, lamb chops, grapes, and apricots.

Even after I was transferred to Ankara, I took every opportunity to return to Claros. In 1964 I had business in Izmir and decided to drive from Ankara in the white Oldsmobile with Mehmet. On the last day, after my work was done, we drove out to Claros. Mehmet was not impressed.

But the French were doing a beautiful job for me. Perhaps all I would have to do would be to pay for the re-erection of the temple, and maybe a cofferdam to protect it from the winter torrents, and an underground drainage system leading to the sea to get rid of all the sulfur water that was still bubbling up after who knows how many thousands of years.

Suddenly, I heard Mehmet shouting, "Mister John! Mister John! Come quick!"

I started scrambling like mad—My God, what had he found?

"Where are you?"

"Here!"

"Where?"

"Down here!"

I found him in the passageway underneath Apollo's body, squatting and peering intently at something. I grabbed a crossbeam and swung down to the lower level like an aging Tarzan, then dropped by Mehmet's side.

"Look, Mister John, look!" he said, pointing, his voice full of wonder.

It was a frog!

"Oh, for Pete's sake!"

"Ah, Mister John, now you scared it away."

In 1966 an old American girlfriend came to visit me. Actually she hadn't come to visit *me,* but a Turkish princess who had been one of our classmates at the Yale Drama School. Anne[35] and Shirin were both actresses in New York, but Shirin spent every summer with her parents in Istanbul. That year she persuaded Anne to visit her beloved Turkey. I was working in Ankara, but Anne had promised we would get together. After a week went by I called Istanbul and learned to my horror that Shirin had been taking Anne to parties every night and speedboat rides on the Bosphorus every day—a mad whirlwind of Turkish high life. She hadn't even seen St. Sophia or Topkapi! I decided to take Anne in hand and show her *my* side of Turkey.

I took a week off work, flew to Istanbul, scooped up Miss Anne (with Shirin's approval), and we flew to Cappadocia where Mehmet met us in the white Oldsmobile full of cold beer. We toured Goreme and the Underground Cities, then went on to the Hittite country, King Midas's Gordium, Pamukkale, and finally to Izmir for Ephesus and Bergama. On her last morning, I suggested Claros. She was exhausted and her plane was leaving for Istanbul at noon, but she agreed.

She got the same thrill I did as we walked through the tobacco field, and suddenly Claros was at our feet. But a watchman was there for the first time. I was a little resent-

---

35. Anne Shropshire, stage and film actress (1917–2013).

ful that he had taken over my domain. He scrambled up out of the ruins and bowed politely to Miss Anne, who looked like she had just stepped out of Bergdorf-Goodman.[36] The watchman was fierce-looking, like a Hun, with a shock of wild black hair and wearing a huge olive-drab Army overcoat (in midsummer!). His yellow eyes blazed as he told Miss Anne of the ancient glories of Claros. I was surprised at his grasp of history, perhaps drilled into his wooly head by the Director of Antiquities. When he saw that I could translate as fast as he could talk, he became absolutely Shakespearean! He acted out the ritual of washing his whole body before entering the temple; he played both the supplicant bowing and the oracle going into a trance before delivering his prophecy; he fought several wars with spears and arrows—getting wounded twice; he sat Miss Anne in the marble throne and paid her homage; he was both the earthquake, shaking like a palsy victim, and the temple, collapsing on the ground in a rumpled heap.

Miss Anne was enchanted with him and applauded more than she ever had in a New York theater. He took his curtain calls gravely, bowing almost to the ground, then grinned maniacally. Two teeth were gold, one was steel, the middle ones missing, and the rest tobacco-stained. I took his picture standing beside Miss Anne. He stared grimly at the camera like a deranged Othello with his Desdemona. When he saw the Polaroid print, he slapped himself on the rump and pranced around in a circle, giggling insanely at the picture.

I was pleased that the Turks thought enough of their unwillingly inherited Greek ruins to have provided a watchman for my beloved Claros, but alas! The French were gone. Their grant had run out at the end of 1966. There were no diesel engines removing water. Nature was once again in inexorable control. By 1967 Miss Anne's throne had disappeared. By 1968 the baths were gone. The sacrificial altar

---

36. Luxury New York department store.

was gone—only the top of the rotunda was visible above the mud. The underground arches were under water. There wasn't even a frog.

I haven't been back to Turkey since 1968[37] and I haven't made a million dollars either. But when I do go back, my first stop will be Claros, and I'll pour a suitcaseful of gold coins at the big toe of the sleeping giant and say, "Come on, Apollo, it's time to get up."

---

37. Tumpane took friends on a three-week tour of Turkey in 1982. Mehmet was their driver.

Appendix
A Letter to Readers

≈

Dear *Scotch and Holy Water* fan,

Many people have asked if I have written any other books. Except for *The Gift of Tenyin,* a one-act play published by The Dramatic Publishing Company, 4150 N. Milwaukee Avenue, Chicago, IL 60641—no.

However, I write every day on my brand-new IBM computer—and I love it. But I'm not very methodical about the order of the stories. Sometimes I write about my childhood, or my army experiences such as getting thrown out of the Confessional Box in Manila, or the time I was attacked by wasps in Sri Lanka. And I'm *still* writing stories about Turkey— they haunt me and won't go away until I get them down on paper. I've just started one about a trip I made to Mount Ararat to look for Noah's ark.

Many people have asked me if I kept a diary while I was in Turkey. No. But when I returned to the States 20 years later, the Polaroid pictures gave me total recall. I had written my parents at least once a week while I was gone, and they saved all the pictures I had sent them. I was glad I had included on the backs of the pictures the dates, names, and historical information which was fresh in my mind at the time, such as "This is where Caesar stood when he said, 'Veni, vidi, vici' after he defeated the king of Pontus in 47 B.C.—on this very same hill 240 miles east of Ankara" or "This is the first known Christian church built in a cave near Antakya (Antioch), just after a visit by St. Peter in 42 A.D. Antioch was the largest city in the world in those days."

I'm also working on my book about Saudi Arabia. I spent six years there, just after I left Turkey. It was a rough assignment, but naturally I plan to write only about the funny things that happened—such as the night I almost drowned swimming down Airport Boulevard after a cloudburst. Or the time my houseboy fried tulip bulbs for his breakfast and told me "those onions were *mush quais* (no good)."

I plan to call the book *Sand and Siddiqqi*. There's an awful lot of sand in Saudi Arabia, and *siddiqqi* is the slang word for homemade moonshine. We couldn't get along without it. Happily, the literal meaning of *siddiqqi* is "my friend." But don't send your money in just yet because I write very slowly— *Scotch and Holy Water* took me four years to write.

In the meantime, keep spreading the good word about the "holy book."

Mister John

Sand and Siddiqi

Chapter 1

≈

NO ONE can survive in Saudi Arabia without *siddiqqi*. I have spoken.
It is Moslem moonshine, but I used to call it Arabian rotgut. It is awful stuff! Tastes bad, smells bad—you really had to get drunk in order to drink it. I am one of those blessed souls who never get a hangover, but *siddiqqi* really addled my brains many times. Weaker souls have given up booze altogether after a couple of bouts with *siddiqqi*.

It wasn't all bad. I never used my bathtub for anything but what Allah designed it for, but many people turned their bathrooms into Jack Daniels distilleries, and some became experts in the art. The Aramco[38] crowd were master distillers. They had the finest copper tubing, beakers, Bunsen burners, petcocks, and petri dishes—equipment which they brought in as "household goods." All the necessary ingredients were readily available on the local market: sugar, potatoes, mangoes, papayas, pomegranates, raisins, figs, dates, sugar beets, barley—even sweet corn at times for making bourbon. In addition, the Al-Khudeiri Supermarket on Pepsi-Cola Road flagrantly sold little vials of essence of juniper berries, carroway, anise, kirsch, and other exotic oils. They had hops for sale, prominently displayed and labeled.

---

38. Saudi Arabian Oil Company (formerly Arabian-American Oil Co.)

The oak chips were for aging bourbon, so you could make Jim Beam or Old Grandad, depending on how long you let the oak chips soak in the bottom of the bottle. One Aramco chap sent his "Royal Arabian Scotch" to London for analysis, and they pronounced it purer than Chivas Regal. The secret was in the number of times you distilled it—three times was "Deluxe," and four times was "By Appointment To."[39]

The Saudi authorities knew that Aramco Village was just one cottage industry after another, but they averted their eyes as long as no one got caught selling it to the local thirsties. Once that happened, the Aramco authorities took over and gave the offending distiller 24 hours to get out of town and out of the country—with or without his wife and children. Still, from time to time I was able to buy some Aramco potables through a friend of a friend of a friend. And *were* they potable! Glug! Glug!

Even my best friend Johnnie Walker was available two or three times a year at $70–$100 a bottle. It was usually smuggled in by truck across the desert from Kuwait, Qatar, or Abu Dhabi. The proud bootlegger would point to the dirty, dusty, sandy bottles as proof of its purity.

But mostly we had to put up with *siddiqqi*, which tasted like essence of creosote. Every night we would come home from work and hold our noses as we took the first drink. After two or three belts, it began to taste like mother's milk.

No Westerner ever got into trouble serving *siddiqqi* in his own home unless one of his Saudi guests got sloshed and cracked up his Volkswagen on the way home. One of my trusted interpreters ran straight into a date palm on Eisenhower Boulevard at eleven o'clock at night but managed to convince the police he was on antibiotics. (Not a lie, since no bug could survive *siddiqqi*.)

The Saudis were very ambivalent about the Islamic injunction against drinking alcohol (an Arabic word). If they came alone to my villa, they would match me elbow bend for

---

39. The Royal Warrant, an endorsement by a member of the British royal family to a product or provider of services that they deem worthy.

elbow bend. But if I had other guests when they arrived, they would ask for a Bepsi (the Arabs don't have a "p" in their alphabet). In the Koran, the first injunction against alcohol simply says: "Don't go to the mosque drunk." I think that's a very respectful attitude. But later it says: "Intoxicants are an abomination—Satan's handiwork. Eschew such, that ye may prosper." Well, that did it. But those Moslems who do drink know that the Koran also says there must be two male witnesses to accuse anyone of sin.

But as a shaky Catholic, I survived and prospered six years in Saudi Arabia. I attribute it solely to *siddiqqi*. Ironically and happily, *siddiqqi* means "my friend" in Arabic.

Dear John,
You Send Me Plenty Of

≈

Elvis postcards,
Nuts Creek News,
Plants of yew and Morning Glories,
Ahmed's letters,
Nuts and candy,
But what I want are your new stories.

Thoughts on gardens,
Thoughts on forests,
Always meant to help restore me,
Thoughts on "Wooz,"
Thoughts on booze,
I long instead for *Book Two Stories*.

Notes from fans,
Notes to fans,
No, they're never boring,
Trips to dentists,
Medical exams,
And yet I hope for stories.

Lives of playwrights,
Lives of actors,
Sometimes pretty hoary,
Broadway kingpins,
Lives of writers!
I want to see *your* stories!

Notes on flora,
Notes on fauna,
Place names in Californey,
Notes on diets,
Notes on sex!
I wish it could be stories.

Billy Ernst info,
Titles on photos,
Pruning roses (very gory).
Father Walsh readings,
Shropshire screenings,
I keep wanting your short stories.

I'm not alone
In this I know
All your fans implore ye,
"Please set aside
Tidbits for now
And write a new short story."

If you want my praise
And wild applause
And rides to heights of glory,
You'll sit right down now,
Don't worry 'bout how,
And start upon a story.

Love,
Mary Jean [Lachowicz, John's
"Beloved Baby Sister"][40]

---

40. Keith Lachowicz writes that John loved Mary Jean's poem and that he "took it to heart...for a time." Perhaps it was the impetus for "The Baby Bottle" (facing page), one of John's last anecdotes about Turkey.

The Baby Bottle

≈

"Mr. John, may I ask you a question?"
"Yes, of course." Anyone can ask a question. Whether I give them an answer or the answer they want to hear is an entirely different matter. But I could tell by the way the *kapiji* whispered in my ear that he wanted a favor. The janitor looked around to make sure that no one was listening or watching.
"Would you buy me a baby bottle from the PX?"
"Oh my God!"
"Please, Mister John, you Americans have such wonderful baby bottles—they're called Pyrex—and they don't break when the baby throws them on the ground. You know me and my wife live in the basement—we have only one room—I think you've seen our humble abode—the floor is concrete and my wife can't nurse the baby—her paps have dried up—and the baby keeps throwing the bottle on the floor, and it breaks. My wife is very old—maybe 40—I have twelve other children, but they've all gone—this one was a surprise, so *please*, Mister John, Pyrex, PX?"
He had put his arm around my neck and was practically kissing my ear, fumigating me with rafts of garlic breath. I squirmed out of his embrace and muttered, *"Bakalim, bakalim."* (We'll see, we'll see.)
I fretted for days over his request. To most Americans overseas, the PX card was their most valuable possession. It enabled them to buy Campbell's soup and Hormel's Spam and pork and beans at ridiculously low prices. And on the

back of the card was a strict injunction that it was forbidden to sell or *give* any PX product to any unauthorized person— e.g., my *kapiji*.

I remembered the time I had given my driver Mehmet 100 lira ($10) to buy a bottle of Johnnie Walker on the local market as a gift for a Turkish friend who had invited me to dinner at his house to meet his wife and beasties. Mehmet came back with a bottle that was clearly marked "For Sale by the U.S. Military Services Only."

"Where did you get this?"

"Just down the street, at the *bakal* (grocery store)."

"How much did you pay for this?"

"90 lira."

I blew. "This costs $3 at the PX. It's black market booze! I could have bought a bottle of Johnnie Walker at the PX myself, but I told you I was going to visit a Turkish friend tonight, so I wanted a bottle which had already passed through Turkish customs. You take this back and get a bottle which says "Imported" and the amount is in liters, not ounces!!!"

Mehmet writhed. I felt for him because I knew it was shameful for a Turk to return something—it meant he made a bad bargain. But on the subject of buying $3 PX booze from a Turkish con artist for $9—well, that was the living, screaming end! Mehmet exchanged it at the same shop for a bottle which had come directly from Scotland. He was happy, I was happy, and my Turkish friend to whom I brought it was happy and insisted we open it and drain it. We did.

But a baby bottle!

A few days later, about ten o'clock in the morning, I had occasion to be in the vicinity of the PX. I thought, Ah!—a good opportunity to buy the baby bottle without being observed. I dashed into the building, streaked up the stairs, and said to the bored cashier, "Baby things?"

"Aisle 28. Next to the window."

I ran over to the window, my eyes flashing wildly to spot the Pyrex. I grabbed one with a blue nipple not knowing whether the *kapiji's* baby was a boy or girl. Then Elmira said, behind my back, "Ho! Ho! Ho! John! What are you doing here in this baby section of the PX?"

"Ah—er—oh—hmmm, hello, Elmira!"

She was my bridge partner of two weeks and knew nothing about my private life except that I was a bachelor.

"Oh, I—er—my sister just had a baby, and I was looking for a present."

"You silly boy!" she said, taking the bottle out of my hand and returning it to the shelf, "A bottle is not an appropriate gift from an adoring uncle."

"Well, I'm not sure I'm an adoring uncle, I've never seen the beastie."

"Never mind. Now you come over here and I'll help you select something really nice! Oh, look at this! Isn't it adorable? A baby's bunting! Isn't that the dearest thing you've ever seen in your life? You see, you tuck the baby in here and pull the hood up over its head. Isn't that sweet? Look at this gorgeous stitching around all the edges, and it's only $27.50. Why, in the States, that would cost you double! Aren't you lucky to be overseas here where we have the PX? There now, take this and have the girl wrap it up."

"Couldn't I take the bottle too?"

"Don't be silly!"

Elmira handed the exquisite little poncho to the bored Turkish girl at the cash register. Elmira leaned over to the girl and said confidentially, "It's for him. You charge him. I'm too old to have babies."

"Toowenty sewen vivty," said the girl, punching the machine with one hand and holding out her other for the green stuff. I ripped out my wallet and slapped two twenties into her palm.

Elmira, satisfied, mercifully took her leave. "Don't forget we have duplicate bridge on Monday night, John. We were second last week, but next week we'll be first if it kills me!" (Or me, I thought.)

I watched her depart, then ran back to the baby section, grabbed a bottle, and brought it to the checkout counter before the girl could figure out my change from the two twenties. She handed me my money and I bounded down the stairs with my plain brown paper bag.

That evening I gave the bottle (and the bunting—what the hell) to the *kapiji*. He slobbered kisses all over my neck trying to reach my cheeks.

The baby died a month later.

One evening after work as I was entering the glass elevator, the *kapiji* caught me in a vise-like grip on my arm as I was about to punch the 7-button. He was a mountain of tears—a small mountain—but they were real tears falling on my shoes. I was uneasy. I wanted to console him, but I have always been embarrassed and speechless when it comes to death. I dredged up a Turkish expression I had learned—*"Bashiniz sagolsun!"* It's a very difficult expression to translate because it sounds so cold and heartless: "Long live your head." But it probably means, "May your tribe go on forever and ever."

He thanked me and thanked me, but wouldn't release me. I felt I had to say something more, so I tried, *"Allah buyuktur"* (God is great.) I had learned the expression by osmosis and didn't really know how to use it. But I had learned that whenever I refused a request or a favor that was unreasonable or outrageous, the person would say, with a sigh, "God is great," and go away with absolutely no ill-feelings.

My expression seemed to calm him considerably, and he relaxed his grip on me—my arm was turning blue. "Thank you, Mister John, for the bottle and the bag. We are keeping them as a remembrance of *Gül*. That was the baby's name. Do you know what *Gül* means, Mister John?

"Yes, of course, it means 'Rose.'"

"My wife said the baby died because someone put the evil eye on her, but I think it's because roses can't grow in concrete. Don't you, Mister John?"

About the Author

≈

JOHN D. TUMPANE was born in Worcester, Massachusetts in 1922. He graduated from Yale in 1943 and spent three years in the Pacific as a First Lieutenant in the Field Artillery. After receiving an MFA from the Yale School of Drama in 1949, he taught Speech and Drama for two years at Loras College, Dubuque, Iowa, and for five years at the University of Notre Dame. During the summers, he directed plays and musicals for community theaters in Portland, Vancouver, Hollywood, and Corning.

He then spent 20 years overseas working as a civilian contractor providing logistical support to U.S. Air Force bases in France, Greece, Turkey, Saudi Arabia, and Iran.

While in Saudi Arabia, he wrote two weekly columns for the *Northrop News*, one on the origin of English words from the Arabic, and the other on gardening (successfully!) in Saudi Arabia.

He is also the author of *The Gift of Tenyin*, a Japanese treatment of the Nativity story, and he wrote the lyrics for *The Complaining Angel*, a musical comedy by Natalie E. White.

In 1976 Mr. Tumpane returned to the United States and settled in Walnut Creek, California, a suburb of San Francisco. Mr. Tumpane taught Speech at Diablo Valley College and wrote articles and essays for regional newspapers in the United States.

John Tumpane died in 1997.

John at the University of Notre Dame, 1953

About the Author / 397

Starting work at The Tumpane Company, 1958

At his favorite ruin, Claros, July 1961

On a car trip near Mt. Ararat, September 1966

About the Author / 399

With a friend at Claros, July 1961